D1085128

Gavin Douglas

GAVIN DOUGLAS

A CRITICAL STUDY

PRISCILLA BAWCUTT

EDINBURGH
UNIVERSITY
PRESS

✳

© Priscilla Bawcutt 1976
Edinburgh University Press
22 George Square, Edinburgh

With the financial support of the
Scottish Arts Council

ISBN 0 85224 295 6

Printed in Great Britain by
W & J Mackay Ltd, Chatham

FOR NIGEL

*

Preface

My object in writing this book was to look searchingly at Gavin Douglas's writings, and to re-examine the accepted critical ideas about him. I have laid particular stress upon the way in which Douglas's methods of translation and his response to Virgil were influenced by the classical scholarship of his age; and upon the strength and diversity of the poetic traditions which he inherited. Although I could not deal with every aspect of his work, I have investigated subjects that seemed neglected, such as his debt to the traditions of alliterative poetry, or questions which puzzled me when I first read Douglas and to which I could then find no satisfactory answers. I have tried, above all, to present a balanced picture of Douglas, and to show the complex context in which he wrote; such an approach by no means diminishes and often illuminates his poetry.

I am greatly indebted to the Leverhulme Trust for a grant towards the expense of preparing this book. I have learnt much from earlier critics and scholars, particularly C.S.Lewis, whose writings first kindled my interest in Douglas; and John Small and David F.C.Coldwell, whose editions of Douglas have been continuously useful. I am extremely grateful to Mr John Norton-Smith, who has helped me in many ways, quite apart from reading the whole of my typescript; also to Dr John Durkan, and to the late Professor R.G.Austin, who read several chapters and made valuable criticisms. I owe most of all to the advice and encouragement of my husband; to him

Quhat so it be, this buke I dedicait.

✳

Contents

✳

Texts and Abbreviations

I have used Douglas's own term, *Eneados*, for his translation of the *Aeneid*; the term 'Prologues' includes not only the Prologues to the separate books of the *Eneados* but the various short pieces of writing (such as the Directioun) that follow it. Quotations are from *Virgil's Aeneid Translated into Scottish Verse by Gavin Douglas*, ed. David F.C.Coldwell, 4 vols., STS, 1957–64. References to the *Eneados* are given in the form 'i.v.2' (book i, chapter v, line 2); 'i.v.2n' directs the reader to Douglas's own prose commentary or 'Comment' on the poem. References to Coldwell's Introduction are by volume and page. Quotations from the *Palice of Honour* are from the Edinburgh text of that poem; square brackets indicate that a reading has been adopted from the London text. Both are printed in *The Shorter Poems of Gavin Douglas*, ed. Priscilla Bawcutt, STS, 1967. References to Small are to *The Poetical Works of Gavin Douglas*, ed. J.Small, 4 vols., Edinburgh 1874. When quoting from Douglas's letters, I give page-references to Small; the originals have been checked, however, and some misreadings corrected. As my modern text of Virgil I have used *P. Vergili Maronis Opera*, ed. R.A.B. Mynors, Oxford Classical Texts, Oxford 1969; 2nd rev. edn., 1972. Quotations from Servius are taken from the edition by G.Thilo and H.Hagen: *Servii Grammatici qui feruntur in Vergilii Carmina Commentarii*, 3 vols., Leipzig 1881–7; I have also consulted the incomplete Harvard edition of Servius. References to Ascensius are to Jodocus Badius Ascensius, whose edition of Virgil was well known to Douglas. Modern scholars call him variously Ascensius, Badius, and Josse Bade, but I prefer the form of his name used by Douglas and Coldwell. Unless otherwise indicated, quotations from Ascensius are taken from his first edition of the *Aeneid* (part two of his complete Virgil): *Aeneis Vergiliana cum Seruii Honorati Grammatici huberrimis commentariis . . . cumque familiarissima Iodoci Badii Ascensii elucidatione atque ordinis contextu . . .* (Paris 1501). For Chaucer, Dunbar, Henryson, and Lindsay, I have used the following editions: *The Works of Geoffrey Chaucer*, ed. F.N.Robinson, 2nd edn., 1957; *The Poems of William Dunbar*, ed. W.Mackay Mackenzie, 1932; 2nd rev. edn., 1960; *Poems and Fables of Robert Henryson*, ed. H.Harvey Wood, Edinburgh 1933; *The Works of sir David Lindsay*, ed. D.Hamer,

4 vols., STS, 1931–6. No place of publication is given for books published in London. To avoid ambiguity, all dates are given new-style.

Other Abbreviations

D.O.S.T. *A Dictionary of the Older Scottish Tongue from the Twelfth Century to the End of the Seventeenth,* ed. sir W. Craigie and A. J. Aitken, Chicago and London 1931–.

EETS Publication of the Early English Text Society.

O.E.D. *The Oxford English Dictionary* (a corrected re-issue of *A New English Dictionary on Historical Principles*) Oxford 1961.

SHS Publication of the Scottish History Society.

SRS Publication of the Scottish Record Society.

STS Publication of the Scottish Text Society.

[1]

Gavin Douglas's Life

No other early Scottish poet has a career so well documented as that
of Gavin Douglas. We know very little about the lives of most
medieval poets. We know next to nothing of Robert Henryson, and
only a little more about William Dunbar and his connection with the
court of James IV (1488–1513). Yet we have precise and factual
information about Douglas and his family, and about some of the
major events in his career. There is no need to conjecture about what
circles he moved in. We know of his contacts not only with minor
Scottish clerics and his own servants, such as Matthew Geddes and
Alexander Turnbull, but with men internationally renowned, such as
Polydore Vergil and cardinal Wolsey. Douglas was acquainted with
some of the most distinguished Scotsmen of his day: the theologian,
John Major; John Adamson, provincial of the Scottish Dominicans;
Patrick Panter, secretary to James IV; and Robert Cockburn, bishop
of Ross. We know something of Douglas's genuine friends—such
as Henry, lord Sinclair, or Polydore Vergil; and we may read his
remarks on those whom he regarded as enemies: Andrew Forman is
'yon euyll myndyt Byschop of Murray';[1] the duke of Albany is
'capitalle and dedelie inimye to me and all my hous';[2] and, in a
moment of despair towards the end of his life, his nephew is 'yon
young wytles fwyll'.[3] Likewise we hear the comments of others upon
Douglas: in January 1515 the effusive testimonial from Henry
VIII[4] is counterbalanced by a shrewd report to the English Privy
Council that Douglas is 'quick in calling for his own advancement'.[5]
To the biographer of more recent poets the materials for Douglas's
life may seem scanty, but we probably know more about him than
about any earlier poet writing in English, Chaucer excepted; and
though the documentation of Chaucer's life is more copious, it contains nothing as intimate as Douglas's last painful letter to Wolsey.

Why has so much evidence survived? Not principally because
Douglas was a poet—though his contemporary reputation was high
—but because he was the son of one earl of Angus and uncle of
another; because he became a bishop; because he was involved in
litigation, and participated for a time in the administration of Scotland. Not all the sources of information are of equal value. The most
picturesque are the mid-sixteenth-century historians, such as Robert

I

Lindesay of Pitscottie or the anonymous author of *A Diurnal of Remarkable Occurrents*. These contain vivid anecdotes and phrases — 'all the court was rewlit be the erlis of Angus, Mr Gawin Dowglas, and the Drummondis, but nocht weill';[6] but their chronology and other details are often inaccurate, and they must be treated with caution. The most reliable sources are legal documents and public records: charters and the protocol books of public notaries; the *Acta* of the Arts Faculty of St Andrews University; the Treasurer's Accounts and the Acts of the Lords of Council. Such evidence is sometimes dry and tantalizingly brief; sometimes, however, as with Douglas's trial in July 1515 before the Lords of Council, it is detailed and exceedingly dramatic. Especially valuable are the letters to and from Douglas that have been preserved, chiefly in the British Museum and the Public Record Office.

Coldwell asserts that Douglas's 'biography contributes nothing to the understanding of his poetry'.[7] It is true that his poetry is not deeply personal or autobiographical in the sense in which Wordsworth's *Prelude* is; nor does he create poems from everyday incidents as does Dunbar. It is true also that Douglas's extant poetry belongs to the first period of his life, which is less fully documented than the period after 1513, from which no poem of his is known to survive. Nonetheless, a study of his life has more than a purely intrinsic interest. It is arguable that his biography throws light on some features of his poetry, such as the legal comedy of the *Palice of Honour* (see chapter 3). It is incontrovertible that an understanding of his poetry cannot be achieved without an awareness of his cultural background. I think also that Douglas's poetry is more personal than may at first appear. There is a close kinship between the poet-dreamer of the *Palice of Honour* and the poet-scholar of the Prologues. To some extent this poetic *persona* was shaped by literary convention: the humorous characterization of the poet in the *Palice of Honour* owes much to Chaucer's dream poems. Yet there seems a genuine resemblance between Douglas's self-portrait in his poetry and what we know of his real-life personality, as it emerges from letters and other documents. The poet who was prepared to dispute with Venus and to 'flyte' with Caxton has much in common with the litigious churchman who engaged in repeated controversy with Forman and Albany and other public figures. John Major and Polydore Vergil paint a similar picture of Douglas, as a man who enjoyed debate and was always ready for a dispute, in life as in literature.

Gavin Douglas belonged to a powerful and influential family. His father was the fifth earl of Angus; his mother was Elizabeth, daughter of lord Boyd, one time Chamberlain of Scotland, who was disgraced and fell from power in 1469. Historians have stressed the importance of family bonds at this period of Scottish history. Not only among the clans of the Highlands and the 'surnames' or kinship groups of the Borders but in the Lowlands also there is overwhelming 'evidence of the cohesion of families and of bearers of the same name'.[8] Membership of the Douglas family, with its ambiguous reputation for extremes of patriotism and treachery, could not be ignored by other Scotsmen; it was certainly very much present in Douglas's own mind. He reminded lord Dacre

> our houssys are of the auld allyat and mekyll tendyr acquentans and kyndnes hes beyn betwyx tham of lang tym as approvyt weyll be my grandfather at the sege of Nawart.[9]

That this was no empty feeling for 'house' and kin is vividly demonstrated by Douglas's life. The best known illustration is the way in which his career after Flodden was intertwined with the fluctuating fortunes of his nephew, Archibald. But other evidence, chiefly legal, makes it clear how close were the bonds of family even before 1513. He regularly acted for his family in legal matters: as witness to charters for his father; as 'procurator' for his elder brother, George, master of Angus, and for his sister-in-law, Elizabeth Auchinleck. Later he supported another brother, Archibald Douglas of Kilspindie, in a dispute over the office of Provost of Edinburgh. In many of these transactions the chief motive was to promote the interests of the Douglas family—to defend or acquire land and possessions. Sometimes, however, we see him in the role of peacemaker or arbiter, and in 1520 he acted as tutor and 'governour' to Elizabeth Auchinleck's son.

Douglas was a child during a particularly troubled period of Scottish history. The later years of the reign of James III (1460–88) were marked by continual dissension and the sporadic revolts of over-powerful nobles. Douglas's own father, Archibald 'Bell the Cat', was twice implicated in rebellion. He played a prominent part in the hanging of James III's favourites at Lauder Bridge (1482), and was involved in the revolt that culminated in the murder of the king. Unfortunately, we know very little about these early, formative years of Douglas's life. The date of his birth is not certain, but it probably occurred not later than 1475. The first definite dates in his life are found in the university records of St Andrews, which establish that he matriculated in 1490,[10] and completed his master's degree in 1494.[11] The usual age for matriculation was fifteen, and according to the statutes of the university a master should have attained his twentieth year.[12] This suggests that Douglas was born in 1475, and such a date tallies well with his own words to the Lords of Council in July 1515 that he was 'ane man of xl yeris of age or tharby'.[13] Some lines, written in 1513, suggest that Douglas then thought of himself as only thirty five:

> Sen fer byworn is all my childis age,
> And of my days neir passyt the half dait
> That natur suld me grantyn, weil I wait.
>   (Conclusio, 18–20; IV. p. 187)

Both Douglas's references betray a vagueness and uncertainty about his exact age that were characteristic of the period. The contemporary king of France, Louis XII, seems to have found it impossible to ascertain the year in which he was born.[14]

There is a strong probability that Douglas was born in Tantallon Castle in East Lothian, one of the chief seats of the earls of Angus in the fifteenth century. John Major twice implies that Tantallon was Douglas's birthplace, and points out how short is the distance between it and his own birthplace, Gleghornie (a hamlet near Haddington).[15] Douglas was friendly not only with Major but with a number of other prominent churchmen who were born in East Lothian, such as David Cranston, Major's pupil, and Robert Cockburn. If Douglas spent his childhood at Tantallon, he might have attended Haddington grammar school, at which Major and later John Knox were pupils. But nothing definite is known about his schooling. He might have gone to a school attached to a monastery or cathedral, or he might well (like the sons of James IV) have had a private tutor.

More is known about Douglas's university education. He went to St Andrews, the oldest of the Scottish universities, founded at the beginning of the fifteenth century, with a constitution and a curriculum closely modelled on those of Paris. Douglas successfully completed the Arts course. His name heads the list of *Determinantes* (1493) and of *Licentiati* (1494).[16] Such a position was often a sign of merit and high attainment, but preference was sometimes given to those who, like Douglas, were of noble birth.[17] Since his name is listed in *collegio* not in *pedagogio* Douglas must have belonged to the college of St Salvator, founded in 1450 by bishop James Kennedy. Although Douglas is said to have been 'a man of notable learning in theology and the canons',[18] there is no evidence that he had higher degrees in either theology or law. A knowledge of law seems to have been more valuable than a knowledge of theology to those who sought advancement in the church,[19] and Douglas's career shows his familiarity with many aspects of legal practice and terminology. It may well be that he studied without actually completing the degree. Many Scots went abroad to study law at Orléans or Louvain, but there was a small Faculty of Law at St Andrews, and Douglas could have acquired his legal knowledge there or by attending cases in the courts.[20]

The possibility that Douglas may have studied at Paris will be discussed in chapter 2. Most of the evidence as to Douglas's whereabouts in the late 1490s shows him as being in Edinburgh. On 11 April 1495, for instance, he was in the King's Chamber at Holyrood Abbey, where he witnessed a document concerning the resignation of lands to the king.[21] With him, as co-witnesses, were John Ireland, author of the *Meroure of Wysdome*, and Walter Chepman, notary public. Douglas presumably had as yet no benefice, since he was styled simply as son of the earl of Angus.

It is not surprising that Douglas sought a career in the church, since he was a younger son. Yet his ecclesiastical titles rouse expectations in a modern reader which are not fulfilled. We hear far less of good works and pastoral duties than of his involvement in litigation and steady search for promotion. We are thus left with an impression of an ambitious and extremely self-interested man.

Douglas must be seen in the context of his time, a time when the Scottish church was characterized by extreme worldliness, by nepotism and non-residence, and by bitter strife over church appointments. Contemporary critics, such as sir David Lindsay, laid particular stress on the ignorance and immorality of the clergy. Douglas can hardly be charged with the former; as to the latter, it has been asserted that he fathered illegitimate children. Many priests certainly had concubines, but in Douglas's case there exists no proof more substantial than the report of David Hume of Godscroft, written a century after Douglas's death, that he had a natural daughter.[22] In Douglas's will there are references to a certain David Douglas as 'chaplain' and an Alexander Douglas as canon of Dunkeld.[23] These men may have owed their offices to Douglas's patronage. In Scotland at that time it was not considered blameworthy but positively meritorious for an abbot or bishop to reward his kinsmen in this way[24]—this is not surprising in an age of papal nepotists such as Sixtus IV or Alexander VI. The non-residence of the Scottish clergy was linked with pluralism. Both were the result of a system in which educated churchmen were often public servants, and bishops and abbots acted as diplomats or served in the King's Councils; a system in which 'ecclesiastical benefices came to be regarded as sources of income, divorced from spiritual office, to be appropriated by the crown, or granted as marks of favour, as pension for past service, as expense accounts for civil servants and even as scholarships'.[25]

In late medieval Scotland two evils were particularly prevalent: 'appropriation', or the granting of the revenues of a parish church to the abbey or priory to which it had been assigned, with the consequent neglect of parishes;[26] and the *in commendam* system by which many great abbeys, together with their revenues, were held in trust by 'commendators', often lay members of the nobility, who delegated to others the spiritual work of the benefices.[27] Disputes over elections to benefices were a commonplace. There was strife between the papacy and the crown over church appointments throughout Europe in the fifteenth century. Scottish kings were increasingly concerned over the papal powers of 'reservation' and 'provision', by which election to the greater benefices (bishoprics and the richer abbacies) was reserved not to the chapter nor to the king but to the pope alone. This constituted both a threat to the authority of the crown (kings wished to appoint men they could trust to high position) and a drain on the resources of the kingdom (Scottish clerics were 'purchasing' benefices at the papal curia). In the fifteenth century the Scottish parliaments passed a succession of acts against 'barratry', or the illegal purchase of benefices at Rome, and in 1487 Innocent VIII granted an indult to James III, allowing the king to recommend his candidates for a vacant see, and a period of eight months to put his recommendations to the pope. In 1493 parliament declared that anyone who sued for a benefice at Rome within this period without the king's permission would be declared a rebel and banished.[28]

It is against this background that we must set Douglas's career as a churchman. We must also remember that much of the surviving evidence is juridical; legal records tend to preserve the less savoury details, and present only half the picture of a man and his character. Many of his contemporaries in the Scottish church—Andrew Forman, James Beaton, Patrick Panter—were no less ambitious and pre-occupied with worldly advancement than Douglas; he alone has left posterity a substantial reminder of his scholarly and literary interests.

The first ecclesiastical office that Douglas's name is connected with is the deanery of Dunkeld. He was styled 'dene of Dunkeldene' as early as 28 January 1497, when he acted as a witness, in Edinburgh, to an indenture between his father and lord Kennedy.[29] Later in 1497, on 28 October, Douglas made a complaint before the Lords of Council that master George Hepburn had impetrated the 'denery' at Rome

> incontrar our soverane Lordis inhibicione made be his patent letters under his prive sele that nane of his legis suld pas nor

send to the court of Rome for the purchesing of the sade
denery without his speciale licence . . . nevertheles the sade
Master Georg has of temerarite . . . be his procuratouris pur-
chest the sade denery . . . and has made the sade Master Gawan
to be summond . . . to the Court of Rome, and tendis thairthrow
to vex him in his sade benefice.[30]

James IV seems to have shown particular interest in this case since he
was present at the hearing in person, which was rare, and Douglas
received the royal judgment in his favour. Nonetheless, Hepburn
was still litigating before the Council in June and July 1498.[31] Hepburn's persistence seems to have won him the office, and he was still
in possession twenty years later.[32] Hepburn had studied at St
Andrews a few years earlier than Douglas, and was dean of the Arts
Faculty in 1494.[33] He seems to have been intermittently in contact
with Douglas all his life. Their names are associated—as representing
the different Douglas and Hepburn interests—in a marriage contract
of 1509 and another legal document of 1512.[34] Once Douglas became
bishop of Dunkeld in 1516 he presumably had even closer dealings
with Hepburn, whose virtuous conduct as dean is glowingly described by Alexander Myln.[35]

At about the same time Douglas seems to have been involved in a
dispute concerning his right to the teinds of Monymusk in Aberdeen-
shire. An entry in the Register of the Privy Seal (assigned to September 1497) records that a letter had been sent to the sheriffs in that part

> to command in the kingis naim the Lord Forbes, Duncan
> Forbes, and Duncanis wife, to haf na intromitting with the
> teyndis of Monymusk pertenyng to M. Gawane of Douglas; and
> to charge the parrochineris to obey the said M. Gawane in the
> paying to him and his factouris of the sammyn teindis acording
> to the ordinaris letterz.[36]

There is a further sign of royal favour to Douglas in the presentation
to him on 6 May 1498 of the parsonage of Glenholm 'quhen it sal
happin to vak be resignatioun of Schir Alexander Symson, now pos-
sessour thairof'.[37] In 1501 this church was annexed to the Chapel
Royal at Stirling. It is doubtful whether it definitely came into
Douglas's possession, since the presentation was provisional only,
and no other document definitely assigns it to Douglas.[38] The Cambridge manuscript of the *Eneados* refers to another of Douglas's
benefices, styling him 'person of Lyntoun in Louthiane'.[39] Linton,
a small village in East Lothian, is not far from Tantallon and about
five miles from Dunbar. The church of Linton was appropriated to
the collegiate church of Dunbar in 1342; rectors of Linton (also
known, somewhat confusingly, as Hauch and in modern times as

Prestonkirk) were thus canons of Dunbar.[40] Douglas's possession of this benefice is confirmed by Myln, who calls him 'rector of Hauch',[41] and by a letter in the name of James v, which speaks of Douglas as holding the 'canonry and prebend of Hauch in the collegiate church of Dunbar'.[42] It is not known when Douglas obtained this prebend, which was a valuable one,[43] and which had been held in the 1490s by John Ireland. Presumably he did not acquire it until after February 1504, when George Hepburn seems to have been in possession.[44] Patronage of Linton had passed to the crown in 1434–5, but it seems that in Douglas's time the prebend was no longer in the king's gift. The letter of James v, already mentioned, calls the earl of Bothwell the lay patron. Its bestowal upon Douglas possibly had some connection with the marriage of his nephew, Archibald, to the earl of Bothwell's sister in June 1509.[45]

Douglas's first important benefice was the provostry of St Giles', Edinburgh. This was a rich and well-endowed collegiate church, in the patronage of the king. The exact date of Douglas's appointment is uncertain, but he was in possession by 11 March 1503, when sir John Ireland of Perth was paid nine shillings 'for writing of the citationis and lettrez on Maister Gawin Douglas, provest of Sanct Gelis kirk'.[46] Very little is known about Douglas's activities as provost. Possibly the chief results were to bring him a house in Edinburgh—which stood just to the west of the church—and a substantially larger income. During Douglas's administration St Giles' was much enlarged. To the south of the nave several new side-chapels were added, such as the chapel containing an altar dedicated to St John the Evangelist, founded *c.* 1513 by Walter Chepman, and the new Holy Blood chapel, founded about the same time by sir John White.[47] These extensions may have owed something to the zeal of Douglas, as well as to the piety of his parishioners. One event in which Douglas may well have participated, in view of his office, was the ceremonial welcome of Henry vii's daughter, Margaret, to Edinburgh in August 1503. Sir John Young, Somerset Herald, has left a detailed account of the festivities that accompanied the marriage of James and Margaret. He records that after they entered the town there 'came in Processyon the College of the Perysche of Seint Gilles, rychly revested, with the Arme of that Seint; the wiche was presented to the Kynge for to kysse . . .'.[48] R. L. Mackie states that Douglas himself presented to the king this grisly relic, which bore a diamond ring on one finger;[49] but it should be noted that in this account Douglas is not mentioned by name, although it seems unlikely that if in Edinburgh he would be missing from so important a ceremony.

Two other incidents are recorded concerning St Giles', in which Douglas was definitely involved. On 15 February 1511 master David Lauder, vicar of Earlston, renounced his prebend called the 'bedelry', because master Gavin Douglas, the provost, had not been consulted.[50] From the same source we learn that on 27 February 1511 the provost and prebendaries of St Giles' were reproved for failing to celebrate the mass of the Holy Blood. They bound themselves to celebrate this mass regularly throughout the year, and to pay fines for any breach; if they happened to omit it completely the prebendaries were to pay one merk to the common good of the confraternity of the Holy Blood.[51] The recent discovery of the Fetternear Banner has provided other evidence linking Douglas with this particular devotion to the Holy Blood, which was popular in the eastern towns of late medieval Scotland. The Fetternear Banner bears Douglas's coat of arms beneath a bishop's mitre, and was clearly begun after he became bishop of Dunkeld (1516). In a valuable study of the banner Mgr David McRoberts has argued that it was left unfinished because of Douglas's exile, and suggests also that it was intended for the use of the Edinburgh confraternity of the Holy Blood.[52] Douglas ceased to be provost of St Giles', however, shortly after becoming bishop.[53] He may have still retained a connection with the Edinburgh confraternity, but the evidence that the banner was for use in Edinburgh does not seem indisputable.

Apart from these incidents, we know little of Douglas's activities as a churchman before Flodden. Between 1503 and 1513 we have more evidence for his involvement in secular affairs. He was present at meetings of the Lords of Council in February and March 1505, and again in 1509.[54] He was one of those appointed 'to assist and counsel' the rector of St Andrews University in 1512 and 1513.[55] He witnessed charters for his father at Edinburgh on 4 December 1509; 7 February 1510; and 6 March 1512.[56] There is evidence of other activities on behalf of various members of the Douglas family. On 11 October 1503 he acted as a procurator for his brother George, master of Angus, in a dispute concerning lands in Jedworth Forest.[57] On 20 October 1509 he witnessed a notarial instrument for his brother George,[58] and again on 12 October 1510 he witnessed an instrument of sasine for his father.[59] On 26 June 1509 the indentures of marriage were completed between Archibald Douglas and Margaret Hepburn, sister of the earl of Bothwell: in the event of any debates or quarrels arising, the parties to the contract agreed to 'stand at the correction and counsel of'—among others—'Mr Gavin Douglas, provost of St Giles Kirk'.[60] On 26 November 1512 he was one of the procurators for Elizabeth Auchinleck (wife of his brother,

William) in her disputed claim to the lands of Glenbervy.[61] According to Small,[62] in September 1512 Douglas was a member of the great assise or jury at the trial of William Douglas of Drumlanrig for the alleged murder of Robert Crichton of Kirkpatrick. (William Douglas was acquitted on the grounds that Crichton was a rebel and outlaw.) The names of the earl of Angus and Henry, lord Sinclair, appear on the *magna assisa*, but not that of Gavin Douglas; indeed at this time the clergy were 'excused, and probably debarred, from sitting in judgment in criminal causes'.[63] Douglas's name can be found in another list of lords and prelates, who on the day of the trial (30 September) passed an act that forbade the slaying of outlaws except when resisting capture; all rebels were to be handed over to the royal officers to be dealt with only by the proper judges. Douglas seems here to have participated in a piece of constructive legislation, attempting to restore the rule of law to Scotland.

On 30 September 1513 Douglas was made a free burgess of Edinburgh.[64] This should probably be interpreted not as a compliment to him as a poet but as a sign of the power of his family in the city. The chief interest of this and other scattered fragments of evidence is that they show Douglas's increasing importance as a public figure, his recognized probity, and his continuing involvement in family affairs. Furthermore, they demonstrate the reality that lies behind Douglas's own references to the 'gret occupatioun', 'byssynes', and 'grave materis and gret solicitud' that interrupted his work on the *Eneados* (Tyme, space and dait; IV, p. 194). During these latter years of James IV's reign Douglas must have done much of his reading; towards their end he composed his translation of the *Aeneid*. From a literary point of view they were the most important and fertile years of his life.

Douglas completed the *Eneados* on 22 July 1513; on 9 September 1513 James IV died and his army was routed at the battle of Flodden. He was succeeded by James V, a child of eighteen months. Flodden was a disaster for Scotland; for Douglas it was a turning-point in his career. Politics, which seem previously to have competed for his attention with poetry, now became his chief interest. One reason lies in the increasing intimacy between the Douglases and the Scottish crown. Two of Douglas's elder brothers died at Flodden; their father, the fifth earl died some months later. He was succeeded as sixth earl of Angus by his grandson, Gavin's nephew, who rapidly became prominent in the troubled affairs of Scotland and less than a year after James's death married his widow, Margaret Tudor. From then to his death Douglas's fortunes were closely linked with those of his nephew.

Douglas was appointed one of the Lords of Council on 19 September 1513.[65] At Perth on 22 October 1513 he was one of those 'ordanit to remane daily with the quenys graice to gif hir consell in all materis concerning the wele of the realme'.[66] The queen's marriage on 6 August 1514 to a nobleman as powerful as Angus precipitated a political crisis. She was held to have forfeited the regency by her re-marriage, and the duke of Albany, son of the exiled brother of James III, who had lived in France for most of his life, was summoned to be governor. It is evident that by 26 August 1514 there was a split between the queen's party—led by Angus and Gavin Douglas—and the rest of the Lords of Council. The chancellor, James Beaton, who was opposed to the queen, was temporarily deprived of the Great Seal. This was delivered to the keeping of Gavin Dunbar, Clerk of Register and archdeacon of St Andrews; the keys of the Seal were handed over to Douglas.[67] At Dunfermline on 18 September 1514 Douglas appeared as the queen's representative with instructions 'to except aganis the lordis of consale being suspect to us . . .'.[68] The Lords repeatedly requested that the Great Seal and its keys should be returned to James Beaton.[69] That Douglas had pretensions to the high office of chancellor may be gathered from his signature *Gawinus cancellarius* on the 'memoriale' that was written on the queen's behalf, attempting to justify her actions to John Adamson (14 November 1514).[70]

At this period Margaret was under strong pressure from her brother, Henry VIII, to flee to England with her children. Two letters to Douglas from Adam Williamson, a Scottish envoy in London, in January 1515, disclose some of the inducements that were laid before Douglas to persuade the queen to this course:

> Remembyr my Lord that the Quene has put hyr and hyr chyldryn in your handis; yff yee folow the consell and avysse off hyr brother the Kyng yee canott doo amysse, as I haue vryttyn afore, your blood is maid for euer.[71]

Douglas's replies make it clear that although he was not averse to Henry's help with his 'promocion', he was opposed to the scheme suggested by Williamson.[72] Despite his English sympathies he could perhaps see the folly of allowing the infant James V to leave Scotland and enter the keeping of an English king.

Many important churchmen died at Flodden, among them James's illegitimate son, Alexander Stewart, who was archbishop of St Andrews and also held the abbacies of Arbroath and Dunfermline. Douglas was undoubtedly ambitious—this emerges both from his own words and those of his enemies—and at a time when many rich benefices were vacant he used his connection with the queen to his own advantage. He seems first to have sought the rich abbey of Arbroath. On behalf of James v Margaret wrote several letters in the course of 1514 to pope Leo x, urging Douglas's appointment. In the last of these she lavished praise on Douglas as 'second to none in letters and in personal character', and spoke of him as already in effective charge of the abbey:

> he is *economus* [i.e. administrator of revenues] of the abbey; and his household will not endure a separation unless a more powerful person lay hands on the place . . . the man deserves not merely the monastery but the primacy itself.[73]

Throughout this year the minutes of the Lords of Council regularly refer to Douglas as 'elect' or 'postulate' of Arbroath. On 20 November 1514, however, Leo x granted Arbroath *in commendam* to James Stewart, earl of Moray; on 26 November and again on 8 December papal orders were sent to Douglas to surrender the abbey within six days.[74]

The highest see in the kingdom, the archbishopric of St Andrews, was first offered to William Elphinstone, bishop of Aberdeen. Today it seems fitting that the great founder of King's College, Aberdeen, should be honoured in this way. Douglas, however, did not see it in this light. On 25 February 1514 'Gavyn, elect of Arbroath, askit ane note that he dissassentit tharto at my lord of Abirdene suld persew the said archbischoprik'.[75] After Elphinstone died, the queen offered St Andrews to Douglas and on 23 November 1514 wrote to her brother asking him to support Douglas's cause at Rome.[76] On 28 January 1515 Henry wrote to the pope, praising Douglas lavishly —though not from firsthand acquaintance—for his 'extraordinary learning conjoined with prudence, modesty, probity and a great zeal for the public good'.[77] Unfortunately for Douglas there were more powerful contestants for the primacy: John Hepburn, prior of St Andrews, who had been elected by his own canons; cardinal Cibo, the pope's nephew, who was provided to the see in the first instance; and Andrew Forman, bishop of Moray and archbishop of Bourges, who had much influence at both the French and papal courts. After a complicated juggling with benefices, Andrew Forman was granted the archbishopric together with the abbey of Dunfermline.[78]

Douglas was thus doubly disappointed. In January 1515, however, another rich benefice fell vacant with the death of George Brown, bishop of Dunkeld. Douglas's letters leave us no doubts either as to his ambition or his resentment towards Forman. On 18 January he wrote to Adam Williamson in London:

> the Byschop of Dunkelden is decessyt this Monunday . . . and becaus yon euyll myndyt Byschop of Murray trublys all our

promociones, and has sped Sanct Andris to hymself . . . the Quenys Grace, my self and frendis thinkis nedful I be promouit to that Seyt quhilk now is vacand and but pley, and an rycht gud Byschopry of rent and the thryd Seyt of the realm.[79]

The queen, with the consent of certain Lords of Council, presented Douglas to the bishopric on 20 January 1515.[80] Meanwhile she was writing letters on his behalf both to the pope and to Henry VIII.[81] In an apostolic letter (18 February 1515) Leo X consented to the appointment, but made it conditional upon Forman's admission to the archbishopric.[82] Douglas, like other churchmen, had a procurator at Rome, whose chief task was to assist Douglas's cause. In a letter referring to Douglas's proclamation as bishop of Dunkeld '*consistorialiter,* on Friday forow Whitsunday, viz. xxv. mensis Maij' he voiced his suspicions that the pope's breves had been purchased by Forman, and reveals the part that money played in Douglas's own transactions: 'had nocht bene the respect of that money, we suld nocht haue gotten our entent in Dunkeld'.[83]

It might now seem that Douglas had achieved his purpose, yet he did not take possession of his see for another year, and first had to experience trial, imprisonment, and armed conflict. In May 1515 the new Governor, Albany, landed in Scotland from France, and his presence strengthened those lords who thought the Douglases were becoming too powerful. In July letters sent to Douglas fell into the hands of Albany, and on 6 July 1515 Douglas was summoned before the Lords of Council and charged with breaking the laws concerning the purchase of benefices at Rome. He made a spirited and not wholly truthful defence, but was found guilty.[84] R.K. Hannay considers that the decision was unjust, since the queen had favoured the promotion. He suggests that one reason for Albany's desire to exclude Douglas may have been financial; the temporalities of a see fell to the crown during a vacancy.[85] Indeed, in October 1515, the Lords of Council allowed Albany to uplift the spirituality as well as the temporality of Dunkeld and other vacant bishoprics.[86]

Douglas was not banished but imprisoned in various strongholds, including 'the wyndy and richt vnplesand castell and royk of Edinburgh', and the castle of St Andrews, where he was committed to the charge of John Hepburn, his former rival.[87] Douglas's fortunes were now at their nadir, but he still had friends both at Rome and in the English court. On 4 November 1515 Turnbull wrote to Angus, urging him to 'Remembir apon my *Lord*', assuring him of his own endeavours for Douglas and of the pope's indignation at 'the scharp and gret extremite don to my Lord of Dunkeldin'.[88] The pope himself wrote a severe letter protesting against Douglas's imprisonment, and threatening Albany with *acriores censuras et penas*.[89] Queen Margaret, who in August 1515 had handed over her sons to Albany and fled to England, protested similarly at the treatment of Douglas. In a list of her grievances against Albany she describes how she had interceded both for Douglas and lord Drummond:

> whereupon I come doune to the Holyrodehouse to sollicit and lauboure to the said Duke, sore weping for the saide Lord Drommonde and Postulate, being my counseillouris, but grace gat I none.[90]

Douglas was freed sometime before 30 July 1516, when the 'Elect of Dunkeld' appeared at a meeting of the Lords of Council.[91] On 16 September 1516 he was officially admitted to the temporalities of the see of Dunkeld.[92]

Yet Douglas had one more obstacle to overcome before he was effectively bishop of Dunkeld. This was the claim of Andrew Stewart, brother of John, earl of Atholl, that he was the rightful bishop, having been elected by the chapter of Dunkeld. According to Myln, Stewart was canonically ineligible (not being in major orders), but fear of his powerful brother prompted the election.[93] Douglas had taken steps to get Stewart removed—in 1515 Turnbull reported that a 'monitour penale' had been despatched against him[94]—but when Douglas arrived at Dunkeld after his consecration he found that Stewart's retainers were in possession. Myln, who may have been an eyewitness, tells the story vividly:

> The servitors of the postulate held the palace and the steeple, refusing to surrender in his absence on the ground that they were guarding them in name of the governor; and so the bishop went to the dean's [i.e. George Hepburn's] residence, where he was most honourably lodged. Next day the postulate's men by their shooting prevented him from passing to the church, and he was compelled to celebrate and hear divine service where he was. He summoned the canons, and received their cordial obedience. . . . At dinner, which followed, he consulted the nobles and churchmen with him as to the plan of action. . . . In the midst of the discussion, lo and behold a messenger appeared to say that Andrew, the postulate had taken up arms and was coming next day to defend the palace against the bishop. Then shooting began from the steeple and the episcopal palace, and the nobles who were with the bishop disposed themselves for his defence.[95]

The precise date of this incident is uncertain. Possibly it occurred in September, since it is mentioned in a letter of Albany's to the pope, dated 28 September 1516. Albany stated that a settlement had been reached with Andrew Stewart over Dunkeld, and that Douglas was now 'reconciled with us and admitted to the possession of that church'.[96]

Myln tersely reports that although burdened with debt Douglas now devoted himself to good works, one of which was to complete the bridge over the Tay, begun by his predecessor.[97] Unfortunately, Myln's narrative stops at this point, and lacks the detail which enlivens his account of bishop George Brown. (Myln was a canon and official of Dunkeld, and had known Brown closely for several years.) Some idea of the nature of Douglas's duties and the problems of his diocese may be derived, however, from Myln's account of Brown. We hear of his making provision for preaching in 'Irish'.[98] Dunkeld lies in the Highlands, and there must have been many speakers of Gaelic in the area. We hear of his litigation in defence of church property, and the repulsion of an armed attack on him.[99] Dunkeld was notorious as a place where criminals and outlaws congregated, and in the fifteenth century the bishop had been granted the right to arrest all thieves and rebels at the horn. Queen Margaret was well aware of this when in urging Douglas's preferment she wrote: 'Dunkeld . . . requires a strong man to curb an unruly people'.[100] We hear, too, of Brown's attention to the decoration of his church—his provision of copes, a tabernacle for the altar, and 'a brazen figure of Moyses holding a desk in his arms'.[101] The *Rentale Dunkeldense* itself supplies a few hints as to some of Douglas's everyday duties at Dunkeld: the remission of the teinds of Arleweicht to John Ros 'for service to the late bishop'; or 'the purchase of 4 gallons of ale presented to my Lord the present bishop, officiating at the anniversary of the late bishop'.[102]

It would be a mistake to think that Douglas's life was calm and uneventful once he obtained the bishopric. His quarrel with Andrew Forman seems to have taken a new form: a refusal to render obedience to him as archbishop and legate. The *St Andrew Formulare* gives valuable if undated evidence on this controversy.[103] A commission from Forman to his commissary speaks of Douglas's *manifestam et notoriam contumaciam*.[104] A later letter directs that the servant of 'G.D.' should be excommunicated, and vividly describes an incident which occurred when Forman sent messengers to Dunkeld with *litteras nostras aggravatorias et citatorias*. They were met at the gateway by 'sons of iniquity and limbs of the devil', carrying swords and halbards and other weapons. These servants of Douglas drove Forman's messengers away, and threatened to throw them in the river Tay.[105] Douglas seems to have yielded finally, possibly at the pressure of a papal brief.[106] This incident can perhaps be dated by an entry at 19 June 1518 in the Acts of the Lords of Council: Forman reported that he had 'be vertu of our haly fader the papis brevis denuncit Gawyn bischop of Dunkeld'.[107] A notarial instrument records that Douglas appeared in the monastery of Dunfermline, and at the high altar took the oath of obedience to archbishop Forman.[108] Presumably after this Forman and Douglas were reconciled: a commission in the *Formulare* shows Forman delegating certain duties in the province to Douglas—the power to confer minor orders, to administer confirmation, and to bless vestments, altars and church utensils.[109]

1516–18 was perhaps the high point of Douglas's public career. Instead of composing flattering dedications for his own work (such as that which ends the *Palice of Honour*), he was now in a position to have books dedicated to him. Myln's 'Lives' (completed at the end of 1516 or beginning of 1517[110]) was dedicated to bishop Douglas and the canons of Dunkeld. At about the same time (December 1516) John Major re-dedicated his Commentary on the Fourth Book of Sentences to Gavin Douglas and Robert Cockburn; it had first been addressed in 1509 to Alexander Stewart. Instead of requesting favours Douglas was presumably able to dispense them himself. Certainly his agents thought so; in June 1515 Adam Williamson wrote

> I besek yow be gud Lord to my sister and to hir husband Ninzeane Inglis. I luk for a Prebend of Dunkeld. I spek by tyme, for a dum man gettis seldum land, and I am youris quhether ye will or nocht.[111]

Almost simultaneously, Alexander Turnbull was writing, more humbly, to the same effect:

> Item, as for my simplenes, your Lordschip may remember and reward as your Lordschip thinkis tyme and caus . . . I waite that I serf na Italiane; I traist sickirlie that I serve ane noble, discret, and kind Lord, the quhilk was neuir unkind to nane that deseruit kindnes or reward.[112]

We do not know how Douglas responded to these appeals, but it was probably around this time that Matthew Geddes received the parsonage of Tibbermore, since it was a mensal church of the bishops of Dunkeld. Geddes was Douglas's secretary, 'scribe or writar' of the Cambridge manuscript of the *Eneados*. He accompanied Douglas into exile, and was one of the executors of his will.[113] The various presentations to Dunkeld benefices recorded in the Register of the Privy Seal in the years 1518–20 do not necessarily reveal Douglas's personal patronage; he was simply participating in the ecclesiastical machinery for conferring such benefices.[114]

We may wonder how much time Douglas spent in the beautiful but remote Dunkeld, and how much in the Edinburgh palace owned by bishops of Dunkeld. The Treasurer's Accounts, sparse and vaguely dated though the records are, suggest that Douglas was still involved in public affairs. Various entries refer to the sending of messengers to him by Albany. At some time in 1517 Robert Hart was sent to the bishop of Dunkeld by the Lord Governor 'for his haisting to Edinburgh'. In 1518 a fee was paid to 'Andro Bonar quhilkis raid with lettres of our soverane Lord for the bischop of Dunkeld, erle of Angus and lord Drummond'.[115] The Acts of the Lords of Council confirm the impression that by 1517 Douglas had returned to political activity. On 2 June 1517 a list was drawn up of those lords who were 'to sitt with my lord chancellar apon the session for administration of justice in all partiis'. Douglas was abroad in this month, but on 6 October 'Dunkeld' was one of the names added to this list.[116] On 3 October 1517 'my lord of Dunkeld' was one of those chosen to sit on the Secret Council.[117] I can find no evidence in the Exchequer Rolls, however, to confirm W. Stanford Reid's statement that Dunkeld was acting as one of the Lords Auditors of the Exchequer in July 1517.[118]

By the spring of 1517 Douglas was sufficiently in favour with Albany to be sent on a diplomatic mission to France, together with Patrick Panter, royal secretary and abbot of Cambuskenneth, and Robert Cockburn. Three sets of instructions to the ambassadors are extant, and reveal the growing Scottish distrust of Francis I's intentions.[119] The chief object of the embassy was to renew the old alliances between France and Scotland, and to arrange a marriage between James V and one of the daughters of Francis. The Treaty of Rouen, concluded by Albany on 26 August 1517, provided for a marriage of this kind. The date when Douglas left Scotland can be determined approximately by the safe-conduct issued to him on 3 May—'ane speciale Protectioun and Saufgard maid with consent of the governour to Gawane, Bischop of Dunkeld'.[120] His return to Scotland can be dated by his letter to Wolsey, requesting a safe-conduct through England (Abbeville, 27 June 1517),[121] and the granting of this on 16 August.[122]

In the last few years of Douglas's life it seems that new alignments occurred. Douglas's interests were still closely involved with those of his own family, particularly those of his nephew and his brother, Archibald Douglas of Kilspindie. But the apparent rapprochement with Albany does not seem to have lasted long, and the friendship of queen Margaret turned, after her break with Angus, to disfavour and positive enmity. Margaret returned to Scotland in the summer of

1517 shortly after Albany left for France. Margaret by now was growing increasingly hostile to Angus. He had not accompanied her on her flight to London; he is said to have taken a mistress;[123] and he had appropriated to his own use the revenues from her properties, establishing himself in her house of Newark in Ettrick Forest. Although temporarily reconciled to her husband, in a letter to Henry Margaret was talking of divorce.[124] Margaret repeatedly requested the Lords of Council to take action to produce her revenues, and it seems likely that it was her financial difficulties which most embittered her feelings towards Angus. In this quarrel with her husband it is clear whose side Douglas took. On 23 February 1519 he announced in the name of Angus that Newark had been delivered, as the Lords of Council requested.[125] On 28 February 1519 he acted as 'forspekar' for Angus in the legal dispute between him and Margaret, and quoted chapter and verse from the *Regiam Majestatem* to show that, since Angus was the queen's husband,

> he is lord of hir persoun, doury, and all uthir gudis pertenyng to hir hienes, and maye dispone tharupoun at his plesour, according to all lawis, and in speciall the lawis of this realme here be me schewin and producit . . . quhairfor in his name here I protest that nothir in this nor na uthir actioun hir grace be herd in jugement but his consent and leif, and in his name opponis me tharto. . . .[126]

In view of this it is not surprising that Margaret grew hostile to Douglas, and indeed accused him of being partly responsible for Angus's harshness to her.[127] Neither is it surprising that she sought new allies, and—it was said—intrigued for the return of Albany.[128]

During Albany's absence in France (from 1517–21) the condition of Scotland had grown steadily more faction-ridden and anarchic. A commission of regency had been given to the archbishops of St Andrews and Glasgow, and the earls of Angus, Huntly, Arran, and Argyll. James Hamilton, first earl of Arran, was Lieutenant-general and apparently had the support of the other regents—apart from Angus, who was suspected of stirring up trouble on the Borders. On 6 December 1518 he was ordered not to remain there 'for dreid of intercommonyng with brokin men'.[129] At the end of 1519 the supporters of Angus held Edinburgh and refused to let Arran enter. One focus for conflict between the Douglases and the Hamiltons was the office of provost of Edinburgh, which in the years 1517–19 was held alternately by Archibald Douglas of Kilspindie and the earl of Arran.[130] On 27 October 1519 the Lords of Council noted the strife between Arran and 'certane personis of the town of Edinburgh'; they ordained that Archibald Douglas leave the office of

provost, and requested the town to choose Arran in his place.[131]
Gavin Douglas was doubly involved in this affair: he was both a
Lord of Council and brother to Archibald. On 26 November 1519
he 'askit instrumentis that he refusit allutirlie to tak ony part with
his brodir Archibald in ony brokin or unjust actioune, and becaus he
knew that he had ane just actioun to the provestry of Edinburgh he
wald help and defend him tharin at his utir power'.[132] On 16 December Gavin and other supporters of the Douglases refused to
attend a meeting of the Lords of Council in Stirling.[133] The city of
Edinburgh seems to have supported Archibald Douglas in this
dispute, but Albany intervened. On 21 February 1520 Archibald was
charged to cede his office, and it was declared that no one of the name
of Douglas or Hamilton should be eligible as provost until the
Governor's homecoming.[134]

The feud persisted, however, and came to a head on 30 April 1520,
when a pitched battle occurred between the Douglases and the
Hamiltons in the High Street of Edinburgh. Buchanan and Pitscottie agree in representing Gavin Douglas as a peace-maker and
mediator,[135] but the picturesque conversation between him and
James Beaton, archbishop of Glasgow, is found only in Pitscottie:

> Mr Gawin Douglas passit betuix to sie gif he could finde goode
> wayis betuix the tuo pairties, and in speciall he passit to bischope
> James Bettone quhair he was in the Blak freiris kirk for the
> tyme. . . . Bot bischope James Bettone ansuerit him againe
> witht ane aith, schapin on his breist . . . 'me lord, be my con-
> science I knaw not the matter', bot quhen Mr Gawin had hard
> the bischopis purgatioun and how he chappit on his breist and
> persaiffit the plaittis of his jake clattering, thocht all was bot
> vaine that he had spoken and ansuerit and said into him 'I
> persaue, me lord, ȝour conscience be not goode for I heir thame
> clatter'.[136]

According to Buchanan, Gavin Douglas took no part in the fighting,
'being a priest, and infirm on account of his age' (he was then about
forty-five), and 'to reprove, by his conduct, the unseasonable,
bustling interference' of Beaton.[137] The Hamiltons were defeated,
and many escaped by a ford through the North Loch. Some took
shelter in the Blackfriars, and again Pitscottie describes an incident
for which unfortunately he is the only authority:

> Bischope James Bettone flede to the Freiris, and thair was taine
> out behind the hie allter and his rokit revin off him, and [he]
> had bene slaine had [it] nocht bene [that] Mr Gawin Douglas
> requistit effectuslie ffor him saying it was sin to put hand in ane
> consecrat bischope.[138]

On 5 November of this same year Douglas was involved in more peaceful business, when Elizabeth Auchinleck, the widow of his brother William, became a Dominican nun in the convent of the Sciennes. A contract was made between Elizabeth and Douglas, in which she secured her son in all her lands, subject to yearly payments to the convent and herself; furthermore, Douglas undertook to be tutor and governor of her son, on condition that 'the said reuerend fader sall nocht caus nor counsall the said Archibald Douglas to mary with na party indurand the tyme that he salbe his tutour without the avis and consent of . . . his modir'. [139]

Albany's return to Scotland in November 1521 was by no means welcome to the Douglases. [140] Margaret greeted him with friendship, but Angus fled to the Borders and formed a league with lords Home and Somerville. In December Gavin Douglas was sent to London, carrying a letter from Angus commending his 'derrest uncle' to Wolsey, [141] and another document to be shown to Henry. This made detailed accusations against Albany: he aspired to the Scottish crown; he did not take fitting care of the young king; and he was too familiar with Margaret—'the Quene, be evil and seinister consale, is mekill inclynyt to the plesour of the Duke in al maner of thingis, and ar neuer syndry bot euery day togidder. . . '. [142] Douglas arrived in London on Christmas Eve, and complained of being 'sumpart accrasyt by the way', [143] which is not surprising since he seems to have spent ten days on the journey.

It is not easy to summarize briefly the complicated events of the next few months. There was a flurry of political activity—many plots and counter-plots—in which Douglas seems to have been deeply involved. On 12 December Albany wrote to Henry and complained that in Gavin Douglas he harboured a rebel. [144] According to lord Dacre, Albany also endeavoured to get Douglas summoned to Rome so as to remove his influence from the English court. [145] Margaret, who was now bitterly hostile, wrote to Henry on 6 January 1522:

> I pray his Grace . . . that he help not the said Dunkeld, considdering the grit evill that he hes don to this Realm be his evill counsall, for he has bene the caus of all the dissention and trobill of this Realme . . . and sen I helpit to get hyme the benefice of Dunkeld I sall help hyme to want the samyn. [146]

On 21 February 1522 a decreet was issued by the Lords of Council, stating that Douglas was guilty of high treason, had entered England against the orders of the Governor, and stayed there even after the declaration of war by England; they ordered the sequestration of his Dunkeld estates. [147] If we can judge from the letters that he wrote to Wolsey between December 1521 and January 1522, Douglas counter-attacked vigorously. He criticized not only Albany but Albany's secretary, 'Maister Galteor', and a certain John Duncanson, who had just arrived in the English court:

> he fenyeis hym famyliar wyth me, quharby perauentur I sall knaw sum pert mayr of his mynd, albeyt I knaw ellis the fynes of the man and nayn mayr dowbill in our realm. [148]

Douglas's last surviving letter is a moving one, written from the Inn of Carlyle on 31 January 1522, shortly after news had reached him of Angus's submission to Albany. Douglas clearly felt isolated and betrayed by his own party:

> I am and haif bene so dolorus and full of vehement ennoye that I dar nocht auentor cum in your presence, quhilk causis me thus wryte to your nobill Grace, beseking the samyn of youre grete goodnes to haif compacience of me desolatt and wofull wycht; albeyt I grant I haif deseruyt punycioun, and am vnder the Kingis mercy and youris, not for ony falt or demeritt of my avne, but by raisoun of thair ontreuth that causit me labour for the wele of thair Prince, and thair securite, quhilk now has wrocht thair avne confusioun and perpetuall schayme; . . . [I] in goode fayth am forthir dissauit in this mater then ony vtheris, by raisoun quharof I am so full of sorowe and displesour that I am wery of my avne lyfe. . . . [149]

We are thus left with a pathetic impression of Douglas in the last months of his life: in exile, writing letters of entreaty to Wolsey, filled with bitterness towards his former friends. Small suggests that he may have been reduced to poverty, [150] as his will mentions the pledging of his silver plate. This impression is perhaps false. Although the will mentions debts, it is also full of references to the rents and dues connected with his bishopric. It does not suggest a man either destitute or wholly friendless. The will was made *apud hospitium domini Dacris* in the parish of St Clement's—Douglas was presumably lying ill there—and it abounds in references to Douglas's chaplains and servants, to whom he makes small bequests of money, clothing, and horses and mules *meis servitoribus non habentibus equos*. [151] Polydore Vergil's account of his meeting Douglas 'for recreation' and learned discussion also brightens an otherwise sombre picture (see chapter 2).

Douglas's last recorded activities by no means suggest a man whose spirit has been crushed. He was still hoping for higher preferment. Andrew Forman had died in 1521, and it is clear than Douglas took steps to obtain the archbishopric now vacant. On 14 March Dacre praised Douglas, requesting Wolsey to be 'good and gracius' to him and

to write in his fauor to the Popis Holines for the Archbusshop-
rike of Saint Androwes, seing that is bruted in Scotland that
he is postulate therof, and if it could be purchased it shuld mak
mervellous grete Brek [i.e. dissension] in Scotland. [152]

It is not known whether Wolsey responded to the bait in the last
sentence. In Scotland, Albany and Beaton, his nominee for St
Andrews, clearly feared that Douglas was still powerful and influential. The same proclamation that declared Douglas a traitor also
stated that letters were to be sent to the pope to prevent Douglas's
promotion to St Andrews and Dunfermline. On 8 April 1522 Beaton
(whose motive is evident) also wrote to Christian 11 of Denmark,
seeking his intervention against Douglas who was said to be aiming
at promotion through the Emperor and Henry v111, and asked him
to write to his orators at Rome and 'impede the ambitious schemes
of a proscribed exile'. [153]

Whatever Douglas's schemes, they were frustrated by his death—
apparently from the plague—in September 1522. He asked that his
body should be buried in the Hospital Church of the Savoy, and the
brass tablet which marked the place of interment still survives:
Gavanus Dowglas, natione Scotus, Dunkellensis praesul, patria sua exul.
James Beaton, his rival, was appointed to the archbishopric on 10
October 1522. If Douglas had lived, the whirligig of fortune might
well have raised him high again with the return to power of the
Douglases in June 1526.

The Cultural Background

Sir Walter Scott's idealistic portrait of Douglas is set against a
bleak background:

> Yet show'd his meek and thoughtful eye
> But little pride of prelacy;
> More pleased that in a barbarous age
> He gave rude Scotland Virgil's page,
> Than that beneath his rule he held
> The bishopric of fair Dunkeld.
>
> (*Marmion,* VI.xi.20–25)

Douglas was not as divorced from his age as this might suggest.
Modern scholars have striven to dispel the notion that early sixteenth-
century Scotland was uniformly 'rude' and 'barbarous'.[1] At the end of
the fifteenth century Scotland was still impoverished by comparison
with Burgundy and the rich city states of Italy, but there are many
signs of increasing prosperity in the building of larger houses, the
foundation of collegiate churches, and the growth of trade. Scotland
may have been geographically remote from the rest of Europe, but
she was not isolated, whether economically, politically, or culturally.
There is abundant evidence for commercial dealings with northern
Europe, more particularly with France and the countries that
fringed the North Sea and the Baltic. Politically, James IV involved
Scotland in far more than the traditional friendship with France and
hostility to England; the part that he played in the rivalries between
the Papal States, France, Spain and England led directly to the disas-
trous campaign at Flodden. Culturally, Scotland was by no means a
backwater. Scotsmen travelled frequently abroad. They made
pilgrimages to St James of Galicia, St John of Amiens, and St
Thomas of Canterbury.[2] Some, combining piety with scholarship,
went even further afield: on 12 February 1508 Mr James Watson,
parson of Ellem, had licence 'to pas to Sanct Andres grafe besyde
Napillis, and thairefter to remane in Italie at his study for the space of
vi zeris tocum'.[3] Scottish clerics, such as Andrew Forman or Robert
Cockburn, went on diplomatic missions; other churchmen went to
Rome, sometimes summoned on ecclesiastical charges, sometimes
seeking preferment from the papal curia. Scottish students attended
universities all over Europe, although fewer travelled abroad after

the foundation of universities at St Andrews, Glasgow and Aberdeen. There were Scottish teachers at the universities of Cologne, Louvain, Paris and Orléans:[4] William Elphinstone, for instance, was first a student and then professor of Civil Law at Orléans before 1484;[5] John Ireland taught at the Sorbonne and was rector of Paris university in 1469.[6]

Douglas was a member of this international, Latin-speaking world. At his trial in 1515 he said that he had 'passit his tyme in Scotland, Ingland, France and Rome'.[7] He went abroad on at least one diplomatic mission; and we hear of his being summoned to Rome or issued with safe-conducts to pass into England. We know that he had various dealings with foreigners, including Silvester de Giglis, the Italian bishop of Worcester, and the Friscobaldi, Florentine bankers with a branch at Bruges.[8] Douglas's letters show, if fleetingly, a lively and up-to-date awareness of the world overseas. His letter to Adam Williamson (21 January 1515) discusses the rumour that Louis XII was dead.[9] It seems that Douglas took an interest in the proceedings of the Lateran Council (1512–17), since Turnbull reported that he had sent him 'copijs of the *Constitutiounis in decima sessione Concilij Lateranensis*'.[10]

Foreigners came also to Scotland, sometimes for brief visits, sometimes to stay for many years. We hear of diplomatic visitors, such as Pedro de Ayala, and of Italian clerics who acquired Scottish benefices: John Damian, the 'freir of Tungland' made notorious by Dunbar; or the learned Piedmontese, Giovanni Ferreri, who taught at the monastery of Kinloss. In May 1506 a Frenchman, John Carpenter, was teaching at St Andrews; according to the *St Andrews Formulare* he read in *arte poetica seu oratoria*.[11] During the reign of James IV the Treasurer's Accounts record many payments to Italian minstrels or Flemish painters. Two distinguished fifteenth-century Flemish painters fulfilled commissions for Scottish patrons: Hugo van der Goes, who painted the so-called Trinity Altar-piece, now in the National Gallery of Scotland; and Quentin Metsys, who executed a commemorative medal for William Scheves, archbishop of St Andrews.[12]

Scotland indeed owed much to this commerce with the Continent, particularly with Flanders and France: in art, in everyday life, and in the higher levels of education. Scotland exported chiefly raw materials, such as hides and wool, but it imported not only luxuries, such as spices, jewels and wine, but even such necessities as timber, iron and salt. More significantly, it imported books. The rapidity with which printing was introduced to a country in fifteenth-century Europe seems a pointer not only to its learning but to its technical sophistication. Scotland undoubtedly made a late start in printing. It was not till 1507 that Walter Chepman and Andrew Myllar had licence to establish a 'prent', and not until the second half of the sixteenth century does there seem to have been a substantial output of books from Scottish presses. The early history of printing in Scotland, however, is very difficult to trace, since so many books must have been destroyed either by English raiders or the Reformers.

Nevertheless a keen desire for books existed among many Scots at this time, as we know from John Durkan and Anthony Ross's valuable study, *Early Scottish Libraries*.[13] It was satisfied partly by the traditional method of copying books by hand, partly by importing printed books from the main northern European centres: Antwerp, Strasbourg, and Paris. Vernacular poems still circulated chiefly in manuscript—the Chepman and Myllar prints are a rare exception—and Douglas clearly envisaged that the *Eneados* would be copied by 'writaris' rather than printed:

> Зhe writaris all, and gentill redaris eyk,
> Offendis nocht my volum, I beseik,
> Bot redis leill, and tak gud tent in tyme.
> Зhe nother maggill nor mysmetyr my ryme.
> (*Tyme, space, and dait,* 21–4; IV. p.194)

Two at least of his copyists were known to Douglas: Matthew Geddes, and Thomas Bellenden, one of the scribes of the Lambeth manuscript.[14] There is no evidence that any of Douglas's poems were printed in his own lifetime. Many Scottish scholars had their own books printed abroad, especially in Paris.[15] Jodocus Badius Ascensius, the Flemish humanist-printer, published the works of several Scottish authors at his press in Paris during the early decades of the sixteenth century: Robert Galbraith's *Quadrupertitum in Oppositiones,* 1516; Hector Boece's *Vitae,* 1522, and *Scotorum Historiae,* 1527; John Vaus's *Rudimenta Puerorum in Artem Grammaticam,* 1522; and many of John Major's works, including his *Historia Majoris Britanniae,* 1521.[16] One reason for this was that such authors wrote in Latin, and for the most part lived and taught in Paris; their books were designed not solely for a Scottish audience but for an international one. Another reason was that large, experienced printers established a reputation for excellence. John Vaus taught at Aberdeen, but he made a special journey to Paris to get his book published. His prefatory letters to Ascensius complain of the difficulty of learning and teaching in Scotland: *ob librorum praesertim paenuriam, et scribentium dictata nostra negligentiam ac imperitiam.*[17]

It would be difficult to over-emphasize the importance of Paris to educated Scotsmen during the fifteenth and early sixteenth centuries. Its university was the model on which the early Scottish universities had been formed; a centre to which the most distinguished and ambitious Scottish scholars flocked; and a channel for the transmission not only of scholasticism, for which Paris had long been famed, but also of the tenets and values of the humanists. It was a place where could be met famous French scholars, such as Guillaume Fichet, Robert Gaguin and Jacques Lefèvre, and also Flemish, Dutch and Italian writers—Philippus Beroaldus, Girolamo Balbi, Fausto Andrelini, and above all, Erasmus.

Douglas was a graduate of St Andrews. The chief emphasis of the arts course there, as at Paris, lay on logic and philosophy, particularly on the works of Aristotle and his commentators. 'The first year was to be devoted to the Summulae (elementary Logic). In the second year the students were to begin to take down the Logic of Aristotle in their own hand; in the third year they were to proceed in the same fashion to Physics and Natural Philosophy; and in the fourth year they had to write out at least the first seven books of Metaphysics'.[18] The nominalist school of philosophy was dominant. Teaching was in Latin, and was conducted by dictation of the set books and their subsequent discussion; examining consisted of a series of public disputations. This formal curriculum, with its stress on logic, left few obvious traces in Douglas's poetry. The list of 'wyse and lerned men' in the *Palice of Honour* (249–62) includes Aristotle and two of his great commentators, Porphyry and Averroes, but such lip-service is conventional enough. The digression on sound in the same poem (364–81) may owe something to university discussions of the *Physica*.[19] The most interesting recollection of Douglas's experience at university occurs in Prologue I of the *Eneados*, where he discusses the difficulty of translating class-names or universals, such as *animal* or *homo*. He is clearly thinking not of the language of Virgil but the medieval Latin of the schoolmen:

> For thar be Latyn wordis mony ane
> That in our leyd ganand translatioun has nane
> Less than we mynys thar sentens and grauyte
> And ʒit scant weill exponyt. Quha trewys nocht me,
> Lat thame interpit 'animal' and 'homo'
> With many hundreth other termys mo
> Quhilkis in our langage suythly as I weyn
> Few men can tell me cleirly quhat thai meyn.
> Betweyn 'genus', 'sexus' and 'species'
> Diuersyte in our leid to seik I ces.
> For 'obiectum' or 'subiectum' alsswa
> He war expert couth fynd me termys twa,

Quhilkis ar als ryfe amangis clerkis in scuyll
As evir fowlis plungit in laik or puyll.
Logicianys knawys heirin myne entent,
Vndir quhais boundis lurkis mony strange went.
    (363–78)[20]

There is an ambivalence in Douglas's tone: respect for the fine distinctions possible in Latin; yet unmistakable flippancy towards the logicians of the schools. There is no sign here of Skelton's 'sturdy and lifelong devotion to *dialectica*'.[21]

Whether Douglas studied abroad has been much debated. Thomas Warton refers to 'undoubted proof'[22] that he finished his education at the university of Paris, but Coldwell speaks more cautiously of its 'strong probability'.[23] There is no evidence in the university records so far printed by modern scholars that Douglas was formally enrolled as a student at Paris.[24] Yet the Paris records for this period are incomplete. Douglas included France in the list of places where he had 'passit his tyme', and in 1516 John Major wrote that he had enjoyed Douglas's friendship both at home and in Paris—*contubernio tam domi quam Parisiis*.[25] There was a thriving colony of Scottish students and teachers at Paris in the 1490s and early 1500s, particularly at the austere college of Montaigu.[26] Among them were Hector Boece, later principal of King's College, Aberdeen, Patrick Panter, George Dundas, George Hepburn,[27] Ninian Hume and David Cranston. Some of these men are known to have associated with Douglas; with the most distinguished of them all, John Major, he seems to have had a genuine friendship, though he was never in any sense a member of his 'school'. Major (1467–1550) was a scholar and theologian, with a European reputation, who taught in Paris for many years, although he maintained his links with Scotland, becoming principal of Glasgow university in 1518 and provost of St Salvator's, St Andrews, in 1533.[28] He was only a few years older than Douglas, and may possibly have known him in childhood. In December 1509 the Treasurership of the Chapel Royal, Stirling, was offered to Major. The presentation pertained to the king, but the concluding phrase in the Register of the Privy Seal, *gratis M. Gawino Dowglace,* implies that he was excused the usual fee to the Keeper of the Signet as a concession to his friendship with Douglas.[29]

That Douglas desired Major to return home from Paris about this time 'to cultivate the vineyard of the lord' is implicit in a remark attributed to him in the *Dialogus inter duos famatos viros magistrum Gauuinum Douglaiseum . . . et magistrum Dauidem Crenstonem,* prefixed to Major's Commentary on the first book of Peter Lombard's Sentences (29 April 1510):

27

velim ut relictis scholicis exercitiis natale solum repetat: atque illic vineam dominicam colat: et concionando semina euangelica: vnde optimos fructus animae fidelium demetant late longeque dispergat.[30]

This *Dialogus* is an imaginary conversation between Gavin Douglas and David Cranston on the subjects they consider fitting to be treated by a theologian—*de materia theologo tractanda*. It is an interesting composition, and throws light on Douglas's attitude to some of the controversies that pre-occupied the churchmen of his time. Although the wording may well be Major's, the contrasted roles of the two speakers and the opinions they express seem to have a basis in real life. Cranston's role is to defend Major and the values of scholasticism. He was in fact a favourite pupil of Major's in Paris—in the *History* Major tells how French students teased him about the Scottish 'habit of using oaten bread'[31]—and wrote commentaries and philosophical treatises of his own.[32] I take the speeches attributed to Douglas similarly to represent views that he genuinely held. The *Dialogus* may well be the literary counterpart to arguments and debates in which Douglas had participated fairly recently. If he spent some time in Paris, it seems to me likely that it was not in the 1490s but in the years shortly before this *Dialogus* appeared. It is interesting that there seems to be no allusion to Douglas in the Scottish records between 1505 and 1509.

Douglas is portrayed as a critic of scholastic philosophy. He attacks the undue prominence of Aristotle, and quotes approvingly Aeneas Sylvius's disparaging remark about him. He complains that the theologians of his time quote Aristotle more often than the doctors of the church, and he criticizes the emptiness, sterility and obscurity of modern theology:

> videre enim nequeo quantum theologię conducat tot friuolas positiones de relationibus intensione formę an sint ponenda puncta in continuo: et de cęteris id genus prodigaliter pertractare. siquidem aditum ad theologiam haec non ministrant: sed obfuscant et obtenebrant.[33]

Views similar to Douglas's had been expressed by Jacques Lefèvre and Erasmus. Lefèvre proclaimed:

> Suppositiones, ampliationes, restrictiones, appellationes, exponibilia, insolubilia, obligationes, et proinde hec a philosophia rejecta putentur.[34]

In a letter to Thomas Grey (1497) Erasmus ridiculed the 'pseudo-theologians' of Paris, and in his *Antibarbari* poured scorn on both the form and the content of late medieval thought.[35] It is revealing how often in the *Dialogus* Douglas quotes from Lorenzo Valla, who in his *Dialecticæ Disputationes* had attacked the ignorance of medieval philosophers and lamented the baneful influence of logic upon theology. To quote from Valla was to proclaim where one's loyalties lay. Cranston's exasperated reply shows the different response that he evoked from the schoolmen:

Ad dicta Laurentii respondere inopportunum est. nulli hominis generi (vt nosti) vir ille pepercit: et in eius dialecticę (potius in deliramentis philosophiae) plura errata inseruit quam maculę in pardo reperiantur.[36]

In the *Dialogus* Douglas aligns himself with those humanists who had attacked scholastic theology and advocated a return to the Biblical and patristic sources of Christianity. This attitude seems compatible with the views expressed in those parts of Douglas's poetry that discuss problems of belief and conduct. Douglas is strikingly lacking in references to scholastic thinkers. John Ireland studs his *Meroure of Wysdome* with such names as Pierre d'Ailly, Robert Holcot, Bradwardine, Scotus and Aquinas, but for Douglas the great authorities, much cited in Prologue XI, are St Augustine, and the Bible, above all St Paul.[37] Yet in Prologues IV, X and XI Douglas expresses views that would have been acceptable to most Christians of the time. He adopts the phrasing of the Nicene creed to refer to the mysteries of the Trinity (x Prol 41–5). His lines about the Redemption

Thocht thou large stremys sched apon the rude,

A drop had bene sufficient of thy blude

A thousand warldis to haue redemyt, I grant.

(x Prol 131–3)

find a close parallel in Ireland's 'a drop of his precius blud had bene sufficient and excedand for þe redempcioune of all the waurld . . .'.[38] Douglas's remarks about man's salvation do not reveal a new or distinctive concern with divine grace, let alone, as Kurt Wittig suggests, anticipate Presbyterian teaching.[39] Douglas speaks of the need for both faith and 'gude warkis' (*Palice of Honour*, 1393–4), and of grace and merit (XI Prol 151 ff.). He seems in these passages to express the traditional Catholic view that man must co-operate with divine grace in the act of salvation. Clearly, insufficient evidence survives to speak with any exactitude of Douglas's theological position, but what there is suggests that although responsive to new ideas he was fundamentally orthodox.

There is no evidence that Douglas ever met Lefèvre or Erasmus, or had definitely read any of their writings, as did other Scots of his time. David Laux (or Lowis) of Edinburgh was a pupil of Lefèvre's, and read the proofs of some of his works for him, including the

Introduction to Logic, which appeared in 1496.[40] Many Scots were contemporaries of Erasmus at Montaigu in the 1490s. To one of them, Hector Boece, Erasmus dedicated a volume of poems in January 1496.[41] Erasmus taught Alexander Stewart in Italy for a while, and wrote a fine eulogy of him after his death.[42] Although proof is lacking of direct contact between Douglas and such northern humanists, it is clear that their ideas were freely circulating by word of mouth, by letter, and by formal treatise. If we can accept the testimony of the *Dialogus*, some of their ideas were not only available to Douglas but congenial to him.

Douglas may have disagreed with some of Major's views, yet the tone of the *Dialogus* is friendly—both speakers refer to *noster Major*. Two other friendships, with Robert Cockburn and Polydore Vergil, are interesting because they illustrate the range of Douglas's contacts and some of the opportunities that he had for literary discussion. Most of Cockburn's life was spent in diplomacy, first as James IV's envoy to Louis XII of France, then after Flodden at the court of Francis I. He seems to have utilized the many contacts that his travel must have afforded him, and became the friend and correspondent of Symphorien Champier, humanist, moralist and physician to the duke of Lorraine. Cockburn stayed at Champier's house in Lyons, and figured in his *Duellum Epistolare*, which defended French culture against Italian accusations of barbarism.[43]

Douglas's friendship with Polydore Vergil, the Italian author of the *Historia Anglica*, who had been resident in England since 1502, is even more interesting. They seem only to have met in London in the last year of Douglas's life. They may have become acquainted through their common link with Wolsey, but Vergil implies that they were drawn together by their interest in Scottish history. (As early as 1509 Vergil had written to James IV, asking for information about the kings of Scotland.[44]) He says of Douglas

> when he understoode that I was purposed to write this historie he camme to commune with me; in forthe with wee fell into friendshippe, and after he vehementlie requiered mee that in relation of the Scottishe affaires I showlde in no wise follow the president of an historie of a certaine contriman of his, promisinge within few dayse to send me of those matters not to be contemned, which in deade hee perfourmed.[45]

Douglas the controversialist is apparent once more. The unnamed 'contriman of his' was Major, whose *History of Great Britain* had been published recently in Paris (April 1521). Major had shown great scepticism about the legendary early founding of Scotland by Gathelus, an Athenian prince, and his Egyptian wife, Scota—'I count it a fable'.[46] Douglas, however, handed to Vergil a summary of the old legends, much as he might have read them in Fordun's *Scotichronicon*. Vergil clearly shared Major's scepticism, and reports—perhaps with a tinge of wishful thinking—that he succeeded in modifying Douglas's views. Polydore Vergil had the detachment of a foreigner. Douglas perhaps had the poet's love of fable and the patriot's rather uncritical attachment to the early legendary history of his country. One interesting aspect of this episode is the check it administers to over-simplified judgments. Major, the schoolman, is here aligned with Vergil, often regarded as the type of the new, rational historian. Douglas, who in the *Dialogus* might appear a critic of late medieval thought, is here as 'credulous and uncritical'[47] in his historical views as Hector Boece.

It is clear that Douglas had more in common with the humanists than an antipathy to certain aspects of scholasticism. He shared with men such as Erasmus not only an admiration for Lorenzo Valla but a belief in the high importance of the classics, and a particular interest in ancient history, poetry, and rhetoric, often at this time called *bonae literae*. He shared the desire of Ascensius and Sebastian Brant and other scholar-printers to make such works available to as wide an audience as possible. In his stress on following the actual 'text' of Virgil he seems to have experienced something of the need to return *ad fontes* that led to the beginnings of textual criticism in classical studies, and inspired the new critical editions of the Bible in Greek and Hebrew.

We cannot say definitely where Douglas acquired these values. Mrs Dunlop has suggested that the 'extraordinary' or special lectures outside the curriculum increased in importance at St Andrews about this time, and that new teachers, such as William Lowrie (who owned a manuscript of Cicero's *De Oratore*), James Watson, and John Carpenter (see above, pp. 23–4) may have 'exposed men like Gavin Douglas and William Dunbar to classical and humanistic influences'.[48] Although we do not know who were Douglas's teachers, we know something about the books he read and admired. In the transmission of ideas books are no less important than personal contacts. This is particularly true of a poet like Douglas, whose poetry abounds in allusions to other writers and echoes of their works, who says much of his literary likes and dislikes, and who sometimes gives precise and accurate references:

> I refer to Iohn Bocas in the Genealogy of gentille Goddis, onto the nynt buyk thereof, and first c. of the sammyn.
> (1.i.82n)

To Douglas books were almost like living creatures. He 'spittit for dispyte' to see the *Aeneid* travestied (1 Prol 150), and he sometimes speaks of his own work with the indulgence one might use of a child—'Affectioun sa far my rayson blindis' (IX Prol 81). Nothing from Douglas's own library survives, unfortunately, yet several books owned by his acquaintances or near-contemporaries are extant. They afford precious if fragmentary evidence that Douglas 'did not mature in a cultural vacuum'.[49] His knowledge of some Italian authors and his interest in the Latin classics were shared—no doubt, with varying degrees of familiarity—by other Scottish churchmen. Alongside the massive legal works—Panormitanus on the Decretals, Bartolus on the Digests—and the writings of scholastic theologians, they possessed Livy, Sallust, Lucan and Horace, Tibullus and Catullus, Martial's Epigrams, Valla's translation of the *Iliad*, Ficino, and Boccaccio's *Genealogy of the Gods*.[50]

Douglas knew something of the first generation of Italian humanists. He mentions Petrarch and Boccaccio in the *Palice of Honour* (903, 915), and Boccaccio's Latin works, particularly the *Genealogy of the Gods*, influenced not only his thinking as a poet but even the subject matter of his poetry. Douglas's special interest in Lorenzo Valla is evident not only in the *Dialogus* but in the *Palice of Honour* (910, 1233) and his approving reference to

> The worthy clerk hecht Lawrens of the Vaill,
> Amang Latynys a gret patron sans faill.
> (1 Prol 127–8)

Although some theologians were disturbed by Valla's critical spirit and the modified Epicureanism of his views,[51] his *Elegantiae Linguae Latinae* was regarded as a textbook of correct Latin style, and was extremely influential. Erasmus summarized it at the age of eighteen; copies of it were possessed by some of Douglas's contemporaries, such as William Elphinstone and James Leslie, 'student of Banff'.[52] Douglas's disparaging reference to 'bastard Latin' (1 Prol 117) suggests that he shared the humanistic contempt for medieval Latin—a contempt that he may have learnt from Valla, who spoke similarly of 'kitchen Latin'.[53] In the *Palice of Honour* Douglas mentions other distinguished Italian humanists. Poggio Bracciolini is remembered today chiefly for his zeal in discovering lost manuscripts of classical authors. Among his contemporaries he was also famed for his polemical writings, particularly his *Invectives* against Filelfo and Valla; it is this latter aspect of Poggio that Douglas chooses to emphasize:

> Poggius stude with mony girne and grone
> On Laurence Valla spittand and cryand fy!
> (*Palice of Honour*, 1232–3)

In the same poem (911–12) Douglas mentions Pomponio Leto, who founded the Roman Academy for the study of Latin antiquities, and edited and commented upon several classical authors, including Virgil.

Another distinguished Italian, whose work Douglas clearly admired, was Cristoforo Landino, a member of the Florentine Academy, closely linked with the court of the Medici, and a commentator on the works of Virgil, Horace and Dante. (Douglas's knowledge of Landino is discussed in chapter 4.) Douglas makes no reference, however, to the most famous Neoplatonists, Marsilio Ficino or Pico della Mirandola. Although he shared some of their interests—such as the allegorical interpretation of ancient myth, and the harmonizing of pagan and Christian doctrines—I can see no obvious trace of their thought in Douglas's poetry. Indeed the attitude to love expressed in Prologue IV is far removed from that of the Neoplatonists. Douglas's 'twa luffis, perfyte and imperfyte' (IV Prol 112) have nothing to do with the twin Venuses of Ficino, but form an orthodox medieval contrast between love and lust.[54] The concept of love expounded in this part of Prologue IV, derives, as a marginal note indicates, from St Augustine. One of the few close contemporaries mentioned by Douglas is Fausto Andrelini (*Palice of Honour*, 910). Andrelini (?1460–1518) was a pupil of Filelfo and Pomponio Leto; in 1488 he came to France and taught at the university of Paris. Whether or not Douglas had met Andrelini personally, he clearly knew of his reputation as a teacher of the classics—he commented on Livy and Suetonius—and as a poet. He was famous chiefly for his erotic verse, *Livia seu Amores*, and for his *Invectives* against Balbi, a Venetian and fellow-teacher at Paris.[55] In view of Douglas's taste for 'flyting', I suspect that it was Andrelini's *Invectives* that he particularly admired.

Many humanists aspired to be proficient in Greek, but it is unlikely that Douglas could read Greek with any ease despite his patron's request that he 'translait Virgill or Homeir' (I Prol 88). It is difficult to believe that Greek was widely known in Scotland at this time; even on the continent Erasmus had difficulty in getting tuition in that language.[56] Douglas perhaps had a smattering of Greek—he knew that there were Greek words in Latin (I Prol 115). He makes no mention of the Greek dramatists nor of any poet apart from Homer. To Douglas Greek literature seems to have meant not imaginative writing but philosophy; and this came to him through the medium of Latin, in translation or through the discussions of other authors. Aristotle's *Ethics*, to which Douglas alludes in XI Prologue 53 ff., was available in several different Latin versions;

there is a possibility also that Douglas knew Oresme's translation of one of these into French.[57] Douglas knew something of the thought of Plato, but both his references are at second hand, the one derived from Landino (1.iii.100n) and the other from Augustine, who 'repreuys the opynion of Plato, that haldis God the sawll of the warld' (1.v.2n).[58]

Among Latin prose writers Douglas seems to have read fairly widely. The evidence as to his reading, however, must be treated with caution. His allusion to 'Plynyus in his Naturall History' (1.iii.85n) clearly derives from a passage in Boccaccio's *Genealogy of the Gods* (VII.7).[59] Many humanists felt a special admiration for the prose style of Cicero, and Douglas's desire for 'fowth of langage' (1 Prol 120) may have been inspired by his reading of 'facund Cicero' (*Palice of Honour*, 261). But there is little evidence that Douglas was a 'Ciceronian', and few signs that he had a close acquaintance with his work. A phrase in the *Palice of Honour* (1294) — 'Till mak the heirars bowsum and attent' — may derive from the discussion of the exordium in *De Inventione*, 1.15.[60] The one work of Cicero's that Douglas alludes to specifically is the *In Catilinam* (*Palice of Honour*, 1772–3); grammarians called this work *Invectivae Orationes*, which perhaps affords a clue to Douglas's interest in it. Douglas had probably read some of the other moralists and rhetoricians that he mentions, such as Seneca and Quintilian, but it is the historians who seem to have interested him most. He had read Sallust and Suetonius, who was not very popular in medieval times.[61] There is a note of admiration in what he says of Caesar's 'Commentareis' (1.v.102n), and still greater enthusiasm in his reference to 'the mast nobill and famus historian and mylky flud of eloquens, gret Tytus Lyuius' (1.v.28n). Much of the Comment and a section of the *Palice of Honour* (1657–92) testify to this interest in Roman history.

There is no doubt that the Latin poets who meant most to Douglas were Ovid and Virgil; their importance to him will be discussed later, particularly in chapters 3 and 4. Another Latin poet whom Douglas seems to have genuinely admired was Lucan, who in the Middle Ages was highly regarded as a historian. It is to this, I think, that Douglas refers when he speaks of 'the trew Lucane' (*Palice of Honour*, 900); elsewhere he calls the *Pharsalia* a 'gret volum' (1.v. 102n), seeming to link Lucan as a historian with Caesar and Suetonius. Douglas may also have been aware of Lucan's medieval reputation as a thinker and philosopher. He quotes approvingly a line from the splendid passage where Cato refuses to consult the Oracle of Jupiter: *Iuppiter est quodcumque vides, quocumque moveris* (*Pharsalia*, IX. 580; see 1.v.2n). Dante had given this same line a Christian interpretation.[62] It is likely that Douglas was impressed by Lucan's rhetorical brilliance—in Quintilian's phrase, *magis oratoribus quam poetis imitandus*—and by his gift for pithy phrases, one of which Douglas echoes in VII Prologue 152: 'Na thing is done quhil ocht remanys ado' (cf. *Pharsalia* II.657). There is perhaps a hint of Douglas's preferences also in the poets to whom he gives special prominence at the court of the Muses in the *Palice of Honour* (895 ff. and 1186 ff.): 'the Satir Poet, Iuuenall' (907, 1229); Statius, whom he sees very much through Chaucer's eyes as chief authority for the story of Thebes (909 and 1583); Horace, who appears traditionally and a little dully as 'the Morall, wise Poet' (913). Douglas chooses more interesting epithets for Martial—'mixt and subtell' (908)— and later jokes about his medieval appellation *Coquus*—'Martiall was Cuik till roist, seith, farce and fry' (1231). An interest in Martial is not, as far as I know, shown by earlier poets writing in English. Douglas mentions Plautus and Terence, speaking in the same breath of Virgil who 'playit the sportis of Daphnis and Corydone' and Terence who 'playit the Comedy of Parmeno, Thrason and wise Gnatone' (1225–8).

We should beware, however, of attaching an over-personal significance to this list of the Muses' followers. There is nothing very individual in the taste that places Homer at the head of the procession, followed by Virgil; or in which alliteration seems sometimes to count for more in the grouping than poetic affinity. The court of the Muses includes not only poets but prose writers and rhetoricians; it mixes twelfth-century poets like Gautier de Châtillon and Alain de Lille (904–5) with classical poets and humanists. In this diversity and absence of rigid categorization into 'medieval' and 'classical', it is probably highly representative of contemporary taste. The presence of a poet's name may not necessarily mean that Douglas had read him. Conversely, the absence of a poet—such as the Scottish poet, Robert Henryson—is no proof that Douglas was unacquainted with his writings. Douglas nowhere mentions Catullus, yet Professor R. G. Austin[63] has plausibly suggested that there is an echo of Catullus's

> quare habe tibi quicquid hoc libelli,
> qualecumque
>   (1.8–9)

in Douglas's self-depreciating dedication of the *Eneados*:

> Quharfor to hys nobilite and estait,
> Quhat so it be, this buke I dedicait.
>   (1 Prol 101–2)

Catullus had been neglected during the Middle Ages, and the

reminiscence of this passionate and individual poet throws an interesting light on the range of Douglas's reading. Nonetheless, if we can judge from the allusions and echoes in his own poetry, Douglas's taste in classical poetry does not seem to have been strikingly wide-ranging or advanced for his time. The poets that Douglas most admired were medieval favourites also. It seems likely that he would have concurred with Chaucer's homage to

> Virgile, Ovide, Omer, Lucan, and Stace.
> (*Troilus and Criseyde*, v.1792)

Although many of the values of the humanists were congenial to Douglas, he himself was not a humanist in the strict sense of the word.[64] He was not a teacher of *studia humanitatis*; he did not edit the classics or write scholarly commentaries on them; he did not translate Greek works into Latin. As far as is known, he did not compose any poem in Latin. In this respect Douglas contrasts with his own contemporary, James Foulis, who in 1510 published at Paris *Calamitose pestis deploratio et alia quedam carmina*.[65] He contrasts still more strikingly with George Buchanan (1506–82), who in his own century had an international reputation and is still regarded as 'the greatest of all Scots Latin poets'.[66] Douglas can perhaps best be described as a 'vernacular humanist'. He wrote not in Latin but in his own native Scots. He wrote not for an international audience of scholars and clerics, but, if his own words can be trusted, for courtly laymen. His two major poems were dedicated not to other churchmen but to James IV and a Scottish nobleman. His main work, the *Eneados*, was an attempt to introduce into the vernacular the riches of a Latin classic. Douglas was clearly familiar with the cosmopolitan world of Latin culture and scholarship. But his own poetry, though modified by this tradition, was rooted in the traditions of Scottish life and literature. So too with his language: he acknowledges the presence of 'Sum bastard Latyn, French or Inglys' word (1 Prol 117), yet proudly claims to speak 'as I lernyt quhen I was page' (1 Prol 112). Although he seems to have known Paris, and the culture that it symbolized, as a poet Douglas essentially belonged to Edinburgh.

At the beginning of the sixteenth century vernacular poetry was far richer and more flourishing in Scotland than in England; Douglas was more fortunate than his English contemporaries, such as Stephen Hawes, William Neville, or John Skelton. (Scottish prose, however, was not so sophisticated as Scottish poetry.) The Bannatyne Manuscript and the Maitland Folio, two great anthologies compiled in the middle of the sixteenth century, have preserved many poems from this period, and make us aware of the variety of styles and genres—religious lyrics, narrative poems, love allegories and fantastic burlesques—as well as the essential conservatism of Scottish literary taste.[67] The English courtly tradition, dominated by Chaucer, was extremely important to Douglas as to earlier Scottish poets. Yet Scottish poetry was not in any sense a 'poor relation' of English. The Scottish tradition had its own distinctive characteristics, while the peculiar weaknesses of much fifteenth-century English verse—metrical and syntactic clumsiness—are not nearly so common among Scottish poets. To understand something of Douglas's position as a poet it is important to be aware of the existence of the 'English' tradition, and also of the achievement of his distinguished close contemporaries, Robert Henryson and William Dunbar. Two other factors in his literary inheritance seem relevant also: the remarkable persistence and vitality of the alliterative tradition in the north; and the popularity of Scottish verse chronicles, such as the *Bruce* or the *Wallace*.

Scottish attitudes to England and English culture at this time were complex. The War of Independence had led to a lasting political hostility and well-founded suspicion of the English crown. But there was a very different attitude to the English language. Barbour and Hary celebrated the heroic deeds of Robert Bruce and William Wallace against the English, but they referred to their own language as 'Inglis' or English. Until the end of the fifteenth century the term 'Scots' normally applied to Gaelic, the Celtic tongue then spoken widely in the northern and western areas of Scotland. The language spoken in the Lowlands was called 'Inglis' with good justification. Historically, it was a northern dialect of English, although in the fifteenth century it was diverging considerably in pronunciation and vocabulary, and to a slighter extent in syntax. Douglas seems to have been among the first to make the distinction that later became widely accepted, using 'Scottis' of his own tongue and 'Inglis' of the language spoken in England (*Eneados* 1 Prol 117–18).[68] Douglas's abandonment of the term 'Inglis' for his own language is not, I think, a sign of hostility towards England—later his political sympathies seem to have been markedly pro-English. But the First Prologue does reveal Douglas's strong sense of Scotland's separate identity, coupled perhaps with a desire for consistency of nomenclature: Caxton, who is 'of Inglis natioun' (1 Prol 138), writes in 'Inglis'; Douglas, a Scot, writes 'in the langage of Scottis natioun' (1 Prol 103).

Scotsmen at the close of the fifteenth century inherited what was, in essentials, the same language as English; in much the same way they inherited the literature written in English. English books, whether in print or manuscript, seem to have circulated freely in Scotland. Other Scots besides Douglas had read works printed by Caxton. Towards the end of 1494 Adam Loutfut, Kintyre Pursuivant, made a copy of Caxton's *Order of Chivalry* (1484),[69] and John Major refers frequently and disparagingly in his *History* to Caxton's edition of the *Brut*, or *Chronicles of England*. The works of Lydgate, Gower and Hoccleve were evidently known in Scotland, even if sometimes in rather a corrupt form. Bad Scottish manuscripts exist of part of Lydgate's *Troy Book*.[70] The contents of the Selden Manuscript (dated between 1488 and 1513), which was owned by lord Henry Sinclair and probably executed for him, reveal something of the literary tastes of Douglas's friend and patron. In addition to the *Kingis Quair* and *Quare of Jealousy*, the manuscript contains *Troilus and Criseyde*, the *Parliament of Fowls*, the *Legend of Good Women* and other courtly poems of Chaucer, together with some English poems wrongly attributed to Chaucer, such as Hoccleve's *Mother of God* and *Letter of Cupid*. John Ireland included a version of the *Mother of God*, similarly misattributed to Chaucer, in his *Meroure*.[71] In 1508 Chepman and Myllar chose to print some English poems for their Scottish readers, namely the romance of *Sir Eglamour* and the *Maying or Disport of Chaucer*, better known today as Lydgate's *Complaint of the Black Knight*. (Copies of the latter are also found in the Selden and Asloan Manuscripts.)

There seems to have been no sense of an undue English ascendancy or resentment at the prestige of English poets, rather pride in a common inheritance, shared equally by both Scots and English. Dunbar praised Gower and Lydgate for adorning '*our* rude langage', and called Chaucer 'in *our* tong ane flour imperiall' (*Goldin Targe*, 254ff.). When poets wished to emphasize this cultural unity, they spoke of the two countries as 'Britain', 'Albion' or 'this Ile'. It is true that at this time and later in the century Scotsmen spoke apologetically about their language, its status and its powers. But when Douglas spoke of 'our tungis penuryte', he was comparing it not with English but with

> fair Latyn
> That knawyn is maste perfite langage fyne.
> (1 Prol 381–2)

This sense of the inferiority of the native language and the perfection of Latin (cf. also 1 Prol 359ff.) was not peculiar to Douglas or indeed to Scotsmen. It was not that 'Scottis' was considered specially 'harsk', 'lewit' or barbarous. Writers in most of the European vernaculars at this time chose similar terms to express what they felt

was the inadequacy of their native languages. Some of Douglas's
English contemporaries spoke of English as being 'rude', 'rural',
'base' and 'vile'.[72] The act of translation forced a writer to become
acutely aware of such questions, and Douglas was one of many
sixteenth-century translators who defined the problem as in part a
need to extend and enrich the vocabulary:

> Lyke as in Latyn beyn Grew termys sum,
> So me behufyt quhilum or than be dum
> Sum bastard Latyn, French or Inglys oys,
> Quhar scant was Scottis — I had nane other choys.
> (1 Prol 115–18)

Of all the English poets it was Chaucer who was esteemed most
highly, by Scottish readers as by English. An interest in him was
widely diffused. The theologian, John Ireland, defends his own use of
prose on the authority of the *Parson's Tale*: 'And quhen chauceire
him self cummys to sad and gret materis, he wsis þis maner of spek-
ing, as jn þe persounis taill, and vtheris.'[73] There are signs of
Chaucer's influence in the *Wallace*, whose author is not customarily
labelled as a 'Scottish Chaucerian'. Yet it was the courtly poets who
defined what it was in Chaucer that was important to them: not his
humour, nor his genius as a story-teller, but his enrichment of the
language of poetry. 'They considered him . . . the father of modern
English poetry, the man who purified, regularized, and clarified
English, and so made it possible for highly civilized and highly
wrought poetry to be written in the vernacular.'[74] Dunbar, like Lydgate and other English writers, praised Chaucer, above all, for his
style and diction:

> Thou beris of makaris the tryumph riall;
> Thy fresche anamalit termes celicall
> This mater coud illumynit have full brycht:
> Was thou noucht of oure Inglisch all the lycht,
> Surmounting eviry tong terrestriall,
> Alls fer as Mayis morow dois mydnycht?
> (*Goldin Targe*, 256–61)

Douglas followed Dunbar in his own formal tribute to Chaucer:

> venerabill Chauser, principall poet but peir,
> Hevynly trumpat, orlege and reguler,
> In eloquens balmy cundyt and dyall,
> Mylky fontane, cleir strand and roys ryall,
> Of fresch endyte, throu Albion iland braid . . .
> (1 Prol 339–43)

It is no accident that these lines recall the eulogy of Virgil at the
opening of Prologue 1. To his successors Chaucer was what Virgil

had been for centuries to Latin poets: a 'flude of eloquens' and 'patroun of poetry' (1 Prol 4 and 5).

Douglas undoubtedly knew many of Chaucer's poems at first hand.[75] He shared the taste of lord Sinclair and many of his contemporaries for Chaucer's courtly, chivalric poems in high style. There is no mention of the 'cherles tales' or trace of their influence on his own poetry, although he clearly knew many of the *Canterbury Tales*. Douglas seems to have most admired *Troilus and Criseyde*, the *Legend of Good Women*, and the *Knight's Tale*; of the shorter poems he admired the *Complaint of Mars*. Yet Douglas's interest in these poems must have been intensified—if not kindled—by his own choice of subject. When he wrote the *Palice of Honour* he recalled and in part imitated two of Chaucer's dream poems, the *House of Fame* and Prologue to the *Legend of Good Women*. When he came to translate the *Aeneid* the poems of Chaucer that Douglas seems to have had most in mind were those that treated specifically Virgilian themes or that dealt more generally with the matter of Troy or the world of antiquity.

Chaucer was important to Douglas in many different ways. He was the acknowledged master of a type of poem still the dominant literary form—the dream allegory. He had popularized several of the complex stanza forms that Douglas himself was to use in his *Palice of Honour* and the Prologues to the *Eneados*. Above all, Chaucer was the source of harmonious cadences, splendid diction, and rich and allusive imagery. Some of Douglas's reminiscences of Chaucer may be interpreted as unconscious echoes of a poet he knew intimately. Most, I think, are conscious enrichments of his style, and would be recognised as such by many, if not all, of his readers. Sometimes Douglas incorporates in his own writing phrases and images almost unaltered, with much the same application as Chaucer's. IV Prologue 21 dismisses lovers scornfully: 'And ȝour trew seruandis sylly goddis apys'. This contains a direct allusion to Pandarus's

> How often hastow maad thi nyce japes,
> And seyd that Loves servantz everichone
> Of nycete ben verray Goddes apes.
> (*Troilus and Criseyde*, 1.911–13)

Here Douglas resembles Lydgate and other fifteenth-century poets who took over Chaucerian phrases and even whole lines as a simple embellishment of their own work. All too often Lydgate damages or dilutes the effect of his original.[76] Douglas, however, re-handles Chaucer's words by putting them in a different context or giving them a jocular or ironic twist. In so doing he makes them his own. Douglas transforms Chaucer's pastoral image of

thise lytel herde-gromes
That kepen bestis in the bromes
   (*House of Fame*, 1225–6)
and places it in a different and bleaker world:
   Puyr lauboraris and bissy husband men
   Went wait and wery draglit in the fen.
   The silly scheip and thar litil hyrd gromys
   Lurkis vndre le of bankis, woddis and bromys.
      (VII Prol 75–8)
He takes Chaucer's line about the Prioress—'And al was conscience
and tendre herte' (General Prol, 1.150)—and humorously re-applies
it to himself:
   As all for consciens and devoit hart,
   Fenȝeand hym Iherom forto contyrfeit.
      (XIII Prol 134–5)
Chaucer was important also to Douglas in ways less easy to define.
The humorous projection of the narrator's personality in the *Palice
of Honour*, the conversational vitality and remarkable range of tone in
many of the Prologues, all seem to me to show the influence of
Chaucer.

Like other Chaucerians, Douglas called Chaucer his 'master'. This
was no empty, conventional phrase but an acknowledgment that he
had learnt from Chaucer, rather as an apprentice might learn from a
master craftsman. Yet Douglas's genuine admiration for Chaucer did
not preclude the right to hold different opinions. He criticized
Chaucer twice, both for claiming 'that he couth follow word by
word Virgill' (I Prol 345) and for misinterpreting the story of Dido
(I Prol 410ff.). Such independence might be regarded as characteristic of Scots at this time. Henryson similarly questioned Chaucer's
authority: 'Quha wait gif all that Chauceir wrait was trew?' (*Testament of Cresseid*, 64). To me it is all of a piece with Douglas's response
to Chaucer. He admired him but did not adopt unthinkingly either
his fine phrases or his attitudes.

Douglas says little of other English poets. He makes no mention
of Hoccleve or Langland; 'Peirs plewman' is named but placed with
Robin Hood and 'Raf Coilȝear' among the folk heroes of anonymous,
secular tales (*Palice of Honour*, 1711–19). Douglas is orthodox in
choosing 'moral' Gower and Lydgate as companions of Chaucer at
the court of the Muses (*Palice of Honour*, 918–21). He speaks of
Gower's *Confessio Amantis* with respect (IV Prol 213), but never
singles out by name any of the many works of Lydgate. Yet Lydgate's courtly allegories, such as the *Complaint of the Black Knight* and
the *Temple of Glass*, and his translations, such as the *Troy Book*,

41

formed an important part of Douglas's literary inheritance. Lydgate also transmitted to later poets Chaucerian themes and phrasing— sometimes it is impossible to disentangle his influence from that of Chaucer. When Douglas writes

> Lo, quhou Venus kan hir seruandis acquyte!
> Lo, quhou hir passionys onbridillis al thar wyt!
>   (IV Prol 85 ff.)

he seems to be recalling Lydgate's

> Lo, her the fyne of lover[e]s seruise.
> Lo, how that Love can his seruantis quyte ...
>   (*Complaint of the Black Knight*, 400 ff.)

Yet the *repetitio* on 'Lo' recalls also Lydgate's source in *Troilus and Criseyde* v.1849–55. There are other resemblances of phrasing and imagery. Douglas, like Lydgate, uses the conduit and the well as symbols of excellence.[77] He uses a phrase very popular with Lydgate when he speaks of the sun coming 'Forto alichtyn and glaid our emyspery' (XII Prol 28).[78] Yet in few cases can Douglas be definitely said to be indebted to Lydgate. To know something of Lydgate assists one's understanding of Douglas, not because he was a distinctive influence upon Douglas but because he illustrates so much that was fashionable in fifteenth-century poetry—themes, genres, phrasing and topoi.

At the court of the Muses Douglas distinguishes the poets 'of this Natioun' from those of England (*Palice of Honour*, 922–4). Yet whereas Dunbar's *Lament for the Makaris* names twenty-one Scottish poets, Douglas here mentions only three. Of these Dunbar alone is well known, the others being Walter Kennedie, with a handful of poems attributed to him, and the mysterious 'Quintine with ane Huttok on his heid'. Yet the shortness of this list does not necessarily indicate that Douglas lacked interest in Scottish poetry. The three names are clearly a selection, designed to balance the English triad. The English list is short also, perhaps to suggest the smallness of the vernacular achievement besides that of the great Latin authors —Chaucer is specifically said to be unrivalled 'in his vulgare' (920).

It seems probable that Douglas knew Dunbar personally. Both lived in Edinburgh, and had links with the court of James IV. Both seem to have composed much of their poetry within the first decade of the sixteenth century. Yet there is little affinity between them as poets, except perhaps for certain similarities between the *Goldin Targe* and the *Palice of Honour*, and I can find no evidence that the older poet, Dunbar, influenced the younger. Indeed Dunbar and Douglas contrast in almost every respect, except in their equal 'fouth' of language. It is difficult to generalize about such a brilliant poet as

Dunbar, who wrote on many subjects in a diversity of styles and metres. (This versatility contrasts with the more homogeneous output of Douglas.) Yet many of Dunbar's most characteristic poems deal with real people and everyday incidents. His poems preserve—like flies in amber—some of his own acquaintances, such as sir Thomas Norny or 'James Dog, kepar of the Quenis Wardrop'. He is sufficiently up-to-date to mention, in a moral poem, *Of The Warldis Instabilitie*, 'the newfund Yle'. Douglas rarely deals in such topicalities. The courtiers of James IV do not enter his poems, with the exception of sir Henry Sinclair, who significantly is 'fader of bukis' (1 Prol 85). Douglas's letters show that he felt as strongly towards some of his contemporaries as did Dunbar, but in his First Prologue it was a writer, Caxton, who was under attack, not Andrew Forman. Dunbar was important, I think, to Douglas, because he showed the rich potentialities of the vernacular: it was possible for a writer in Scots to be almost as eloquent as Chaucer, if not perhaps as Virgil. Dunbar was less a model to be imitated than a brilliant rival with whom to vie.

It is curious that Douglas did not place Henryson in the court of the Muses, since he was a Scottish poet whom Douglas respected and one with whom he had much in common. Douglas referred later to Henryson in a note on the *Eneados*:

> of the ix Musis sum thing in my Palyce of Honour and be Mastir Robert Hendirson in New Orpheus.
>
> (1.i.13n)

This passage on the Muses in *Orpheus and Eurydice* (29–63) contains a mixture of mythology and learned etymologizing which Douglas clearly found congenial; it resembles much that he found in the *Genealogy of the Gods*, and quoted in his Comment. Yet it perhaps indicates a change of taste or education that Douglas's account of the Muses in the *Palice of Honour* (853–79) has a different source from Henryson's. Henryson's lines derive from a thirteenth-century work, Eberhard of Béthune's *Graecismus*;[79] Douglas, however, made a fairly literal translation of a poem, *De Musis*, which was commonly but mistakenly thought to be Virgil's. It is probable that Douglas knew Henryson's *Moral Fables*. He certainly knew the *Testament of Cresseid*, and seems particularly to have admired the splendid planet portraits, to judge by the use that he made of them in his own Prologues. Certain images in his description of winter, such as the 'gret ische schouclis lang as ony speir' (VII Prol 62), recall Henryson's portrait of Saturn (160–61). The apostrophe which opens Prologue III

Hornyt Lady, pail Cynthia, not brycht,
Quhilk from thi broder borrowis al thi lycht . . .

incorporates a detail, small but verbally close, from Henryson's portrait of Diana (258). In Prologue XII Douglas describes the sun god in terms which recall Henryson's account of Phoebus (197–217). Like Henryson Douglas speaks of the sun's steed at dawn, Eous, and applies the same unusual epithet to him—'of cullour soyr'; he stresses the sun's dazzling effect—'For quhais hew mycht nane behald hys face'; and praises him similarly as 'lord of lycht and lamp of day' (XII Prol, 27, 38, and 252). These and other reminiscences,[80] slight as they may seem, tell us something of Douglas's response to Henryson. Intermingled with similar echoes from Chaucer, Ovid and Virgil, and placed in passages of ornate description, they suggest that Douglas saw Henryson not simply as a moralist and homely fabulist but as a vernacular master of the high style.

I have already mentioned the remarkable vitality of the alliterative tradition in late fifteenth- and early sixteenth-century Scotland, when it was moribund if not quite extinct in England. The use of alliterative verse by late medieval poets ultimately derived from the technique employed by Anglo-Saxon poets, yet as far as Scotland is concerned there is an apparent discontinuity and it seems better to talk of a revival rather than a survival of its use. Sir William Craigie noted that evidence of its use by early Scottish poets was lacking, and argued that it was a fashion introduced from England.[81] What seems undoubted is the popularity of alliterative verse in Douglas's time, particularly in combination with an elaborate thirteen-line stanza, and the variety of subjects for which it was employed. It was used by the anonymous writers of comic tales or romances, such as *Rauf Coilȝear* and *Golagros and Gawane*. It was also employed by more courtly poets: Dunbar used the rare unrhymed alliterative line for his *Tretis of the Tua Mariit Wemen and the Wedo*. Douglas was clearly acquainted with the tradition. He mentions *Rauf Coilȝear* in the *Palice of Honour* (1711), and he probably knew one of the best and most original of the alliterative poems, Richard Holland's *Buke of the Howlat* (*c*.1450). Douglas's rebus on his own name—'The DOW ionyt with the GLAS richt in a lyne'[82]—recalls a similar word-play on Douglas and *dow* (i.e. 'dove') in the *Buke of the Howlat* (989–90).[83] It would not be surprising for him to be aware of a poem, 20 of whose 77 stanzas are devoted to praise of the Douglas family:

> That word is so wonder warme, and euer ȝit was,
> It synkis sone in all part
> Of a trewe Scottis hart,
> Reiosand ws inwart
> To heir of Dowglass.
> (386–90)

The best evidence for Douglas's familiarity with the alliterative tradition, however, is his own Eighth Prologue:

Of dreflyng and dremys quhat dow it to endyte?
For, as I lenyt in a ley in Lent this last nycht,
I slaid on a swevynnyng, slummyrrand a lite,
And sone a selcouth seg I saw to my sycht,
Swownand as he swelt wald, sowpyt in syte
(Was nevir wrocht in this warld mair wofull a wycht)
Ramand, 'Resson and rycht is rent by fals ryte,
Frendschip flemyt is in Frans, and faith hes the flycht,
Leys, lurdanry and lust ar our laid starn,
Peax is put owt of play,
Welth and weilfar away,
Luf and lawte baith tway
Lurkis ful darn.'
　　(1–13)

The rhyme pattern here—*ababababcdddc*—is that favoured in other Scottish alliterative poems. There is the same excess of alliteration in the long lines, and occasional deficiency in the short lines of the stanza.[84] Douglas's liking for alliteration is apparent in all his poetry, yet the satirical subject matter and ranting tone of this Prologue suggest that he was aware of a decline in the status of alliterative verse, at least in its stanzaic form. In the sixteenth century it became increasingly specialized, being used chiefly for comic and satiric purposes. Indeed, James VI called it 'tumbling verse', and considered it especially appropriate for 'flyting or invectives'.[85]

There existed another type of Scottish verse, which I think was important to Douglas, although—unlike Dunbar in the *Lament for the Makaris*—he never mentions its chief exponents, John Barbour, Andrew Wyntoun, and 'Blind Hary'. These were verse-historians. Wyntoun's *Original Chronicle* (*c*.1420), despite its title, is the least original; it attempts a history of the world from its *origin*, with a considerable amount of space devoted to Scotland, and is a rather pedestrian work. Barbour's *Bruce* (*c*.1375), which Wyntoun admired, is a far more interesting piece of writing. In its style of story-telling it has much in common with the romances. Yet Barbour's hero was a real man, and many of the events that he described were not far remote from him in time. Barbour voices ideals of patriotism and national freedom, yet gives the impression of searching for the historian's virtues of accuracy and impartiality. Hary's *Actis and Deidis of Schir William Wallace* (*c*.1470), which celebrates the hero of the War of Independence, is a far more partisan work. Burns (who

probably read it in the version of Hamilton of Gilbertfield, 1722)
said that

> it poured a Scotish prejudice in my veins which will boil along
> there till the flood-gates of life shut in eternal rest.[86]

Douglas's interest in the history of his own country is apparent
from Polydore Vergil's anecdote, mentioned earlier in the chapter.
The range of his reading is suggested by his allusions not only to the
recently published *History* of Major but to one of the most famous of
early historians, Bede. There are other small clues to Douglas's
historical awareness, such as his singling out of three particularly
distinguished Scottish kings — 'Gregour, Kenneth, and King Ro-
bart' — in the *Palice of Honour* (2027). We may also note the reference
to 'the Scottis cornikle'[87] in an unsigned Memorial; this is said by
Small to be in Douglas's hand, and is accepted as his by Gordon
Donaldson.[88] Most of the Scottish chronicles, like the *Scotichronicon*
or *Liber Pluscardensis*, were written in Latin, and Douglas may well
have read them in this language. But the vernacular histories of
Barbour and Wyntoun were popular and accessible. The *Wallace* was
the most recent of these poems — Major says it was composed in his
own childhood[89] — and seems to have been in sufficient demand for
it to be one of the first works printed by Scottish printers (*c.* 1509),
although unfortunately only a few fragments of this edition now survive.[90] I think that Douglas almost certainly knew this poem, and
that its heroic subject and style, often strikingly alliterative, made an
impact on him, which is reflected in his translation of the *Aeneid*.

It is an equal over-simplification, whether we represent Douglas as
living in a 'barbarous' or a 'golden' age. Douglas was a member of a
complex and changing society, and in this chapter I have tried to
illustrate the diversity of traditions and influences to which he was
exposed. Inevitably my treatment has been selective: some topics,
such as the significance to him of Virgil, will be treated later in the
book; others, such as the possible influence upon Douglas of Gaelic
and its literature, I am not equipped to explore. I have stressed those
persons, books and currents of thought that seem to have meant
most to Douglas. The evidence suggests that the two most important languages for him were the vernacular (English as well as Scots)
and Latin; that his reading was wide but not uncharacteristic of his
age; and that although devout he was not a profoundly religious
man. What interested Douglas most deeply were ethical problems,
history and legend, and, above all, poetry and the interpretation of
poetic myth.

The Palice of Honour

Douglas's creative period as a poet belongs to the reign of James IV, and the *Palice of Honour* ends with a dedication to the 'Maist gracious Prince, our souerane Iames the Feird' from his 'pure leige vnleird' (2145 ff.). The respectful phrasing and distant, impersonal tone contrast with the far greater warmth of Douglas's references to his other patron:

Fader of bukis, protectour to sciens and lair,
My speciall gud Lord Henry, Lord Sanct Clair.
(1 Prol 85–6)

There is no evidence of any close friendship between Douglas and James, although the two were of much the same age and clearly knew each other. The relationship between the king and Douglas's father had fluctuated considerably. In July 1491 Archibald was besieged by the king's forces on suspicion of intriguing with Henry VII; yet by the end of the year he seems to have been reconciled and on 21 December received from James a velvet gown lined with lambskin.[1] Between 1492 and 1497 he was Chancellor of Scotland. Douglas seems to have enjoyed the favour of the king at this time and later. Some of his benefices were in the crown patronage, including the most lucrative, the provostry of St Giles'. Opinions about James's education have differed widely. The diplomat Pedro de Ayala described him as a well-read man who spoke many languages; against this must be balanced the verdict of George Buchanan: *ingenio quidem acri sed vitio temporis ab literis inculto.*[2] It is equally difficult to assess the degree of James's interest in vernacular poetry. He was the patron of Dunbar, yet Dunbar painted a black picture of his court, filled with flatterers, parasites and charlatans. From the *Treasurer's Accounts* there emerges the impression of an active, sociable man, who took pleasure in hawking, riding, playing cards or chess, listening to 'Heland bardis' and Italian minstrels. If Douglas spent much time in James's company he may perhaps have spoken to him of his own and others' poetry, yet he is even more likely to have played at dice or 'bylis' with the king as did his own father or his rival, Andrew Forman.[3]

There is an uncertainty about the canon of Douglas's writings, which is characteristic of his age. Sir David Lindsay speaks of 'his worthy workis, in nowmer mo than fyue', yet names only one of these—'the trew Translatioun off Virgill' (*Testament of the Papyngo*, 32–4). The longest but least reliable list of Douglas's works is found in John Bale's *Scriptorum Illustrium Majoris Britanniae* . . . *Catalogus, Posterior Pars* (Basle 1559). Bale mentions, in addition to the *Palice of Honour* and the *Eneados*, three other works:

Aureas narrationes, Lib. I
Comoedias aliquot, Lib. I
De rebus Scoticis, Lib. I[4]

The last item derives from some phrases in Poydore Vergil's anecdote about Douglas, of which a translation was quoted earlier (p. 30). It is unlikely that Bale ever saw this work, which seems to have been simply a collection of notes. The existence of the other vaguely titled works is equally doubtful, since Bale supplies no *incipits* with them, as he does with the *Palice of Honour* and *Eneados*. Bale was inclined 'to multiply works as well as authors'.[5] The Maitland Folio does indeed contain two poems attributed to Douglas, but Bale's titles do not describe them adequately. One of them, *King Hart*, is a homiletic allegory with affinities to *Everyman* and other morality plays. It is an interesting poem in its own right, but I think it highly unlikely that Douglas wrote it. The ascription is not in the hand of the transcriber of the poem, and is unsupported by other, independent testimony to Douglas's authorship; stylistically and linguistically, as I have argued elsewhere, the poem is uncharacteristic of Douglas.[6] The other poem, *Conscience*, is a slight piece of work, yet I think there are stronger grounds for accepting the scribal attribution to 'bischop douglas of dunkelden'. It is a well-founded attack on the cupidity of churchmen, that has something in common with Prologue VIII:

For sciens both and faythfull conscience
So corruptit ar with this warldis gude
That falset ioukis in everie clerkis hude.
(19–21)

Although short, the poem contains unusual words and idioms characteristic of Douglas (such as *ioukis* and *wes adew*),[7] and there are several of his favourite tricks of style—word-play, rhetorical figures, such as *exclamatio* and *repetitio*, and a climactic use of internal rhyme that is found also in the *Palice of Honour* (2116–42, 2166–9).

Douglas mentions neither of these poems, however, although he delights to talk about his work, and takes great care that his claim to certain poems shall not be forgotten. At the end of book XII of the *Eneados* is a rebus 'to knaw the naym of the translatour'. It is he himself who gives us the most precise information about his own writ-

ings and the date of their composition. He says that he finished the
Eneados on 22 July 1513:

> Completyt was thys wark Virgilian
> Apon the fest of Mary Magdelan,
> Fra Crystis byrth, the dait quha lyst to heir,
> A thousand fyve hundreth and thretteyn ʒeir.
>   (Tyme, space and dait, 1–4; IV.p.194)

In the Directioun to this work Douglas also says:

>   now am I fully quyt,
> As twichand Venus, of myn ald promyt
> Quhilk I hir maid weil twelf ʒheris tofor,
> As wytnessith my Palyce of Honour,
> In the quhilk wark, ʒhe reid, on hand I tuke
> Forto translait at hir instance a buke:
> Sa haue I doyn abufe, as ʒe may se . . .
>   (119–25)

If these dates are correct—and there seems no reason to doubt them
—Douglas finished the *Palice of Honour* in 1501, or possibly a little
earlier. No manuscript of the poem is extant, and the two printed
editions—London (*c.*1553) and Edinburgh (1579)[8]—are too late
to be helpful on this point. Douglas's dedication to the king was
partly a plea for patronage from one 'quhais micht may humbill thing
auance' (2160). It has been plausibly suggested that there was a connection between this dedication and Douglas's appointment to St
Giles' sometime before March 1503.[9] Douglas implies elsewhere that
the *Palice of Honour* was his second work, preceded by a mysterious
juvenile work no longer extant:

>   ʒoir ago in myne ondantit ʒouth,
> Onfructuus idlynes fleand, as I couth,
> Of Lundeys Lufe the Remeid dyd translait;
> And syne off hie Honour the Palyce wrait:
>   (Mensioun, 3–6; IV.p.139)

The meaning of 'Lundeys Lufe' has never been satisfactorily explained. Ruddiman's emendation to 'Ovideis Lufe' is palaeo-
graphically not very convincing, yet a reference here to the *Remedium
Amoris* would make good sense, in view of Douglas's liking for
Ovid.[10]

The form of the *Palice of Honour* suggests that it was designed for
a courtly audience, whose literary taste was sophisticated but essentially conservative. The allegorical dream poem owed its popularity
to the twelfth-century *Roman de la Rose,* and at the end of the fifteenth
century was still the dominant poetic form. The dream allegory, like
the novel today, could be put to many and varied uses. It might be

long or short; erotic or religious; a means of paying a courtly compliment or delivering a sermon. Above all, it was a vehicle for psychological exploration and the discussion of ideas. The *Palice of Honour* is a long, ambitious poem; in it Douglas combines the debate of moral and aesthetic issues with the pictorial richness that was traditionally associated with the form. His processions of exemplary figures, with their vivid dress and symbolic attributes, could almost serve as a blue-print for the real life 'padgeanes' that were then so popular in Scotland, as throughout Europe. Douglas might well have witnessed the ceremonial tableaux—of the Annunciation or the Judgment of Paris—that greeted Margaret Tudor on her arrival at Edinburgh in 1503.

Douglas is a learned and allusive poet. In the *Palice of Honour* he refers frequently to poets and other writers (as the preceding chapter has shown), and he delights in allusions to stories from the Bible, classical antiquity, and medieval romance. The very shape of the poem owes much to Douglas's reading, more particularly to his familiarity with the traditions of courtly allegory. The most striking features of its structure are highly conventional, and can be paralleled in many medieval poems: the dream-framework and the shock awakening at the end; the journey in search of a palace of a god or goddess, set upon a high mountain; the description of the *locus amoenus,* and many other smaller topoi or rhetorical features, such as the Complaint to Fortune or the ballad in praise of May. The *Palice of Honour* is part of a long and complex tradition, which includes poems written many centuries earlier in medieval Latin or French, as well as poems, such as the *Kingis Quair,* far closer to it in date and language.[11]

The *Palice of Honour* has affinities with many other poems. But it has no one source and few precise debts, except to Douglas's favourite poets, Chaucer, Ovid, and Virgil, and also to Boccaccio's Latin treatises on classical mythology and ancient geography. Although Douglas mentions the name of Petrarch (903), I am not convinced by R.D.S. Jack's recent argument that the *Trionfi* formed a 'major influence' on the *Palice of Honour*.[12] He suggests similarities between the two works that seem, when examined, to dissolve into commonplaces and sometimes to be non-existent. The description of Venus's followers is one of the most popular themes in medieval poetry, and Douglas's long account (562–98) is no closer to Petrarch's *Trionfo d'Amore* than to other catalogues of lovers in Chaucer, Gower, Lydgate, or many French poets.[13] Moreover, some of the very figures that Douglas's list, according to Jack, 'shares' with Petrarch's (such as Caesar, Livia, Oenone, Andromede, Orpheus and Eurydice)

are not even mentioned by Douglas. Douglas's processions may owe
more to the pictorial tradition of the *Trionfi*; to Petrarch's illustrators
than to Petrarch himself. The elephant, for instance, on which Diana
rides (330) seems incongruous to a modern reader; yet in tapestries
and other representations of the *Trionfi* an elephant commonly
draws one of the triumphal cars, usually that of Fame rather than of
Chastity.[14]

Critics have noticed that the opening of the *Palice of Honour*
resembles that of Dunbar's *Goldin Targe*: both describe a dawn
landscape in similarly jewelled imagery. Yet the tone and structure
of the two poems are quite dissimilar. The *Palice of Honour* might as
profitably be compared with another of Dunbar's dream poems, the
Thrissil and the Rois, in which the dreamer's persona is sketched
humorously, rather as is Douglas's. The *Thrissil and the Rois* was
written to celebrate the marriage of James IV and Margaret, yet
Dunbar includes in it a distinct rebuke to the king. Douglas also
conveys an exhortation to the king in his poem: his account of the
court of Honour (1792–1827) is clearly a picture of the Scottish
royal household, not as it was in reality but as it ought to be. Neither
of these poems can be called the source of the *Palice of Honour*.
(Indeed, since Douglas's poem may well have been composed earlier
than both of Dunbar's, it is arguable that any influence might well
be the other way round.) What they illustrate is the vitality and
flexibility of the poetic genre that Douglas adopted, and its continuing popularity in Scotland.

The subject of Douglas's poem was clearly of interest to contemporary audiences. There was a vogue among the courtly French poets
of his time for works with very similar titles: Jean Molinet's *Trosne
d'Honneur* (1467); Octavien de Saint Gelais's *Sejour d'Honneur* (1490–
95); or *Le Temple d'Honneur et de Vertus,* composed by Jean Lemaire
de Belges as a lament for the death of Pierre II of Bourbon (1503).
Lemaire described another elaborate palace of Honour in *La Con-
corde des Deux Langages* (1511). A close contemporary of Douglas's,
Alexander Barclay, inserted into his Fourth Eclogue a description of
the 'Tovvre of vertue and honour into the which the noble Haward
[admiral sir Edward Howard, who died in 1513] contended to enter
by worthy actes of chiualry'.[15] Several of these works are consola-
tory or panegyrical, as is a Spanish poem, Juan del Encino's *Triunfo
de la Fama y Glorias de Castilla.* At its climax the poet is taken to the
Temple of Fame: sculptured in the different halls are first the great
deeds of antiquity, then the glories of Spain, and finally the achieve-
ments of Ferdinand and Isabella.[16] Poems like these indicate both the
far-flung European character of the poetic tradition in which Douglas

was writing, and the topicality of his subject. Honour may have been a talking-point, because of the word's very ambiguity: 'it wavered before men's eyes with the same dazzle as (in later ages) "Nature" or "Wit" or "Democracy".'[17]

Critics seem agreed on the central theme of the *Palice of Honour*.[18] What is honour? How is it to be achieved? The varied processions that pass before the poet represent some of the different paths by which men have sought to obtain honour: wisdom; asceticism; love; poetry, or imaginative literature. When the poet is granted a glimpse of the inmost court of Honour, he learns that true honour must be distinguished from worldly glory, and that the surest path to it is that of virtue. Yet the poem's meaning is richer than this analysis suggests, its structure more varied and more complex than a mere sequence of processions. Perhaps because of this critics have disagreed over the interpretation of some parts of the poem, and have sometimes denied it any over-all significance: 'the poem as a whole illustrates the furthest point yet reached in the liberation of fantasy from its allegorical justification'.[19] Although there are indeed puzzles and ambiguities in the poem, its structure seems to me reasonably coherent. Douglas is at times over-anxious to impress on us the inner *significatio* of events, interspersing the text with signposts such as these:

Wait ȝe, quod I, quhat signifeis ȝone rout?
(238)
                    I knew the signe
Was Acteon...
(320–1)
I vnderstude be signes persauabill
That was Cupyd...
(481–2)

Like so many dream-allegories, the *Palice of Honour* is concerned with a poet's education. Like Dante or Langland, the poet is learning —partly from his own experiences, partly from such bizarre instructors as Achitophel and Calliope's nymph. Although one critic has termed the dreamer not 'very educable',[20] by the end of the poem he —and by implication the reader—has acquired new insights (or shed some at least of his ignorance) about love, poetry and honour. That the dreamer is not as he was when the poem opened is indicated clearly enough by his revulsion towards the garden he first described as a 'paradice':

Out of my swoun I walknit quhair I lay
In the Garding quhair I first doun fell.
About I blent, for richt cleir was the day,

Bot all this lustie plesance was away.
Me thocht that fair Herbrie maist like to Hell.
    (2090–4)
The poem begins traditionally with the poet walking at dawn in
this beautiful garden:
    The fragrant flouris blomand in thair seis
    Ouirspred the leuis of natures Tapestreis;
    Abone the quhilk with heuinly Harmoneis
    The birdis sat on twystis and on greis,
    Melodiously makand thair kyndlie gleis,
    Quhais schill noitis fordinned all the skyis.
        (19–24)
He falls into a trance, and the scene changes to a monstrous wilder-
ness:
    This laithlie flude rumland as thonder routit,
    In quhome the fisch зelland as eluis schoutit.
    Thair зelpis wilde my heiring all fordeifit.
    Thay grym monsturis my spreitis abhorrit and doutit.
    Not throu the soyl bot muskane treis sproutit,
    Combust, barrant, vnblomit and vnleifit,
    Auld rottin runtis quhairen na sap was leifit.
        (145–51)
The two scenes are effectively contrasted: the green and fertile
garden is replaced by a barren wasteland; glittering 'beriall stremis'
by a 'hyddeous flude'; melodious birds by yelling fish. The poet who
earlier had been 'full of all delice' is now 'not but caus . . . abaisit'
(163). The dreamer is clearly in a world ruled by the caprice of
Fortune, and a formal Complaint to Fortune follows logically,
emphasizing the contrasts with its stock antitheses (165–92). As so
often in allegorical poems, landscape mirrors the inner state of the
dreamer. Love was traditionally represented as a paradoxical state,
being (like Fortune) 'now hait, now cald', 'now seik, now haill'.
The juxtaposed scenes suggest that the dreamer is passing through
an experience similar to that of love's 'joly wo'. The dreamer does
not represent himself unequivocally as a lover, but he dallies with the
notion. He rises to do his 'obseruance' in May (6), and pledges
himself to be a servant of Nature and Venus—he is their 'man' (93,
97); Venus later in the poem calls him a renegade to her service
(954).
    Three processions now pass before the dreamer, led respectively
by Minerva, Diana and Venus. The processions are carefully contrasted. Minerva, clad in imperial purple is carried in a golden
chariot, drawn by four white horses. The description harks back to

the Roman triumphal procession. Diana in a simple woodland dress rides upon an elephant, here symbolizing chastity. There are other contrasts, sometimes ironic, as that between the scantiness of Diana's following and the multitudinousness of Venus's. It is striking how different are the dreamer's reactions to these processions. Minerva and Diana excite in him chiefly curiosity and fear. By contrast, the court of Venus rouses powerful if conflicting emotions: he desires a glimpse long before it arrives, he lavishes hyperboles on its beauty and splendour, yet he then sings a 'ballat' highly critical of Venus. Minerva and Diana neither welcome him nor do him harm, but he becomes for a while disastrously involved with Venus.

This part of the poem is increasingly dominated by Venus. On the story-level, the poet is put on trial for his 'blasphemy', is found guilty, and awaits a fearful punishment. Only the arrival of the Muses and the intercession of Calliope save him. It is debatable how far this has a personal or autobiographical application to Douglas himself. The dreamer's predicament serves chiefly as a peg for exploring various ideas about love, such as the close resemblance between love and fortune. Venus's clerk is *Varius*, and Douglas stresses the tensions and contradictions, and above all the mutability of her court:

> I knew that was the Court sa variabill
> Of eirdly lufe quhilk sendill standis stabill.
>   (484–5)

Douglas is concerned also with the relationship between love and poetry, and love and honour. Poets have reviled the state of love— 'blasphemit' it like Douglas himself. Yet it is they also who have sung its praise, and made immortal the names of Helen of Troy and many other followers of Venus. Venus's chief charge against the poet dreamer is that he attempted to 'degraid and do my fame adew' (947). After Calliope has interceded for him, the penance exacted is that he should turn his art to the praise of love: Venus commands Douglas to write a short 'ballat . . . Tuitching my Laude' (995–6).

The trial scene offers a good illustration of what is evident throughout the *Palice of Honour*: Douglas's familiarity with the rich traditions of love poetry. Ovid had represented Love as both law-giver and judge:

> quidquid Amor iussit, non est contemnere tutum;
>   regnat et in dominos ius habet ille deos.
>   (*Heroides,* IV. 11–12)

Many medieval poets portrayed Venus as a stern and vengeful judge, and there was a vogue among French courtly poets for describing love trials, which reached its peak in the fifteenth century, notably in the *Arrêts d'Amor*, attributed to Martial d'Auvergne. Douglas may have recalled how Cresseid was charged with blasphemy against Venus and Cupid in Henryson's *Testament of Cresseid*. It is a dream poem of Chaucer's, however, to which Douglas is here most clearly indebted. In the Prologue to the *Legend of Good Women* the poet had a vision of the god of Love, attended by a large retinue; like Douglas he was accused of a crime against Love—in Chaucer's case, with heresy; he too had an advocate, Alceste, and in atonement was instructed to 'spek wel of love' (Prologue, G, 481). Douglas employs themes and motifs very similar to Chaucer's, but his tone and style are quite distinctive. In the *Palice of Honour* the dreamer is a 'clerk', and this introduces a potentially comic discrepancy between 'spirituall' and 'seculair' which does not exist in Chaucer's poem.

Despite these literary antecedents, it is the trial scene which links the *Palice of Honour* most closely not only with Douglas's Scotland but with Douglas's own career. Douglas's humorous employment of the procedures of the Scottish law courts reminds us how prone to litigation were the churchmen of his time, and how Douglas himself throughout his life was ever ready to participate in legal controversy, both as principal or 'forspekar'. In the poem he uses stock legal phrasing to reject the jurisdiction of Venus:

> Inclynand law, quod I with peteous face:
> 'I me defend, Madame, pleis it ʒour grace.'
> 'Say on', quod scho; than said I thus but mair:
> 'Madame, ʒe may not sit in to this cace,
> For Ladyis may be Iudges in na place.
> And mairatouir I am na seculair.
> A spirituall man—thocht I be void of lair—
> Clepit I am, and aucht my liues space
> To be remit till my Iudge ordinair.

> I ʒow beseik, Madame, with bissie cure
> Till giue ane gratious Interlocuture
> On thir exceptiounis now proponit lait.' (691–702)

For Douglas's contemporaries there must have been a special piquancy in hearing the poet who had recently litigated with George Hepburn before the Lords of Council now bandying legal terms and precedents with Venus. For posterity the scene has a further irony in that several years later Douglas's fictional defence and its rejection were to be paralleled in real life. In July 1515, when Douglas was charged with purchasing the bishopric of Dunkeld in Rome 'contrare the statutis of the realme',

the said postulat allegit that he was and is ane spirituale man,

and tharfor my lord governour and lordis of consell ar na jugis
to him in the said mater . . . the lordis forsaid all in ane voce be
sentence interlocutour decretis and deliveris that nochtwith-
standing the said exceptiouns my lord governour and lordis of
consell ar jugis competent.[21]

Each part of the *Palice of Honour* has different emphases. If Venus
and her court over-shadow the other processions in book I, it is the
Muses that dominate book II. Their court includes writers of all
kinds as well as poets, but it is the poets in whom Douglas is most
interested. This book is chiefly concerned with poetry, and what it
means to Douglas. It forms the true centre of the poem, despite the
final, climactic position reserved for Honour.

What then does Douglas say about poetry? One thing that
emerges is the joy that poetry brings. As the Muses approach, he
experiences not the fear that Diana or Venus provoked but an in-
explicable lightening of his spirits:

> All haill my dreid I tho forȝet in hy
> And all my wo, bot ȝit I wist not quhy.
> (781–2)

He repeatedly associates with the Muses 'mirth', 'merines', and
'singing, lauching, merines and play' (1252). This is indeed the
gayest and most light-hearted section of the poem. Douglas also
reveals something of his own ambitions as a poet. Of all the processions that pass before him, that of the Muses is the one that means
most to him; it is as a poet, if at all, that he will make his own claim
to lasting honour. It is the Muse of heroic poetry who intercedes for
him with Venus, and to whom he swears allegiance (1065–7). Since
Calliope admits him into her company, his fellowship with other
poets is made clear—but not as an equal. It is humorously implied
that he is a beginner, a novice, who has much to learn about poetry.
He is allowed to accompany the Muses to Hippocrene, but—in a
subdued echo of a famous line from Persius—he 'micht not taist a
drew' (1143). Favoured by the Muses, Douglas's imagination takes
flight. His marvellous journey is partly a tribute to the Muses and
their power to open up to the mind realms of new experience; but it
seems designed also as an initiation or apprenticeship. Douglas is
learning what it means to be a poet.

The dreamer does not at first recognize who the Muses are, but
they are identified by Venus and her company:

> 'Ȝone is,' quod thay, 'the Court Rethoricall
> [Of polit termys, sang poeticall,]
> And constant ground of famous storeis sweit.
> Ȝone is the facound well Celestiall,

Ʒone is the Fontane and Originall
Quhairfra the well of Helicon dois fleit.
Ʒone ar the folk that comfortis euerie spreit
Be fine delite and dite Angelicall,
Causand gros leid of maist gudness gleit.

Ʒone is the Court of plesand steidfastnes,
Ʒone is the Court of constant merines,
Ʒone is the Court of Ioyous discipline,
Quhilk causis folk thair purpois to expres
In ornate wise, prouokand with glaidnes
All gentill hartis to thair lair Incline.
Euerie famous Poeit men may deuine
Is in ʒone rout . . .'   (835–51)

Douglas here expresses the traditional view of the poet's office: to
teach and to delight. There is a hint of paradox in the phrase 'Ioyous
discipline', which recalls the Horatian synthesis of the *dulce* and the
utile. Poets undoubtedly give pleasure—'the folk that comfortis
euerie spreit'; but they also instruct—'prouokand . . . All gentill
hartis to thair lair Incline'. A modern reader may be surprised by the
juxtaposition of 'rethoricall' and 'poeticall' both here and in earlier
lines (819–20). Yet Douglas's contemporaries would have found
the near equation of rhetoric and poetry congenial. It was of poets
that Henryson was speaking when he referred to 'thair polite termes
of sweit Rhetore' (*Fables*, 3), and Dunbar praised Chaucer as the rose
not of poets but of 'rethoris' (*Goldin Targe*, 253). Most medieval
writers underwent a training in rhetoric, and during the fifteenth
century there was a heightened interest in *elocutio,* the branch of
rhetoric concerned with style and diction. Both in this poem and in
what he says of Virgil it is evident that Douglas shared the admiration of his time for choice diction—'polit termys'—and skilfully
patterned language—'castis quent, Rethorik colouris fine' (819).
These very stanzas illustrate his fondness for one particular 'colour',
repetitio, the repetition of the same word or phrase at the beginning
of consecutive clauses.[22] The term 'eloquence' was traditionally used
of such a rhetorically brilliant and polished style. Hoccleve com-
mended Chaucer as the 'flour of eloquence' (*Regement of Princes,*
1962), and similar phrases were applied to Chaucer by many writers,
including Douglas.[23] Although Douglas denies such 'eloquence' to
his own *Palice of Honour* (2161), the mock-modesty should not be
taken too literally.

This section of the poem pays a double tribute to poets: they are
both the recipients and the givers of fame. If heroic deeds are to be

remembered, they must be recorded. Fame is thus dependent on chroniclers, writers of all kinds, but above all poets. For Douglas, as later for Spenser,

> who so will with vertuus deeds assay
> To mount to heauen, on Pegasus must ride,
> And with sweet Poets verse be glorifide.
> (*The Ruins of Time*, 425–7)

The ultimate source of such honour lies with the Muses, particularly Calliope:

> For scho of Nobill fatis hes the steir
> To write thair worschip, victorie and prowes,
> In kinglie stile, quhilk dois thair fame Incres
> (875–7)

Douglas stresses that poets are story-tellers, the source of 'historyis greit' (797), and the 'ground of famous storeis sweit' (837). The commemorative function of poetry is implicit even in phrases that one is inclined at first to regard as line-fillers: 'as Statius dois tell' (1583) or 'as Poetis can define' (1613). Douglas's lines on Catiline's attempt to enter the palace of Honour illustrate the converse of this: an eloquent writer has the power to strip someone of his good fame:

> Lucius Catiline saw I thair expres
> In at ane windo preis till haue entres,
> Bot suddanelie Tullius come with ane buik
> And straik him doun quhill all his chaftis quoik.
> (1770–3)

In the *House of Fame* Chaucer describes how the great poets 'bore up' the fame of Troy, Thebes, or 'pius Aeneas'. There are many other parallels of theme and structure between Douglas's poem and Chaucer's.[24] Yet it is characteristic of Douglas, when echoing a Chaucerian motif or phrase, to give it a fresh application and sometimes modify it profoundly. Chaucer called Ovid Venus's clerk—

> That hath ysowen wonder wide
> The grete god of Loves name.
> (*House of Fame*, 1488–9)

But to Douglas, Ovid was the poet of heroes as well as of lovers, and in the *Palice of Honour* he appears as 'Clerk of Register' to Calliope (1187). It might seem more fitting for Virgil to be so associated with the Muse of heroic poetry. Yet although Virgil is mentioned respectfully in the poem, it is Ovid, after Chaucer, who is the most important influence upon the *Palice of Honour*. Douglas calls Ovid the 'father poet' (899), refers to him as an authority—'as men in Ouide reidis' (1199 and 1847)—and mentions several of his poems, including the *Heroides,* the *Metamorphoses,* and the 'craft of lufe' (1220). In his role of 'Clerk of Register' Ovid has to answer the question, 'quha war maist worthie of thair handis' (1188). It was Ovid who had made memorable many of the heroes whose names fill the *Palice of Honour.* His poetry was a treasure house of heroic story and myth, and this was his primary importance to Douglas as to many other poets. But Ovid was also a master of style, 'digest and eloquent' (1190), and as such was to be imitated as well as admired. Douglas seems to have been particularly impressed by book 11 of the *Metamorphoses.* Ovid's description of the palace of the sun lies behind several of the more striking passages in the *Palice of Honour,* such as the elaborate gate,

> The warkmanschip exceding monyfold
> The precious mater, thocht it was fynest gold.
> (1862–3)[25]

There are other signs of Ovid's influence upon the *Palice of Honour.* Words like 'translatit' (324), 'transformit' (316), or 'transfiguratioun' (774) are pointers to Douglas's own preoccupation with metamorphosis. We hear not only of the transformations effected upon Actaeon and Io by wrathful pagan goddesses, but of the Biblical changes of Lot's wife and Nebuchednessar. Later we are told of the marvels of 'nigromancie', which read like a grotesque parody of Ovid:

> Of ane Nutemug thay maid a Monk in hy,
> Ane Paroche Kirk of ane penny py.
> (1725–6)

Douglas even has a Scottish metamorphosis of his own to counter those of Ovid—the barnacle goose:

> Als out of growand treis thair saw I breid
> Foullis that hingand be thair nebbis grew.
> (2075–6)

More subtly Ovidian is Douglas's fear as to how Venus may punish him:

> ʒit of my deith I set not half ane fle.
> For greit effeir me thocht na pane to die.
> Bot sair I dred me for sum vther Iaip,
> That Venus suld throw hir subtillitie
> In till sum bysnyng beist transfigurat me
> As in a Beir, a Bair, ane Oule, ane Aip.
> I traistit sa for till haue bene mischaip
> That oft I wald my hand behald to se
> Gif it alterit, and oft my visage graip.
> (736–44)

In the third part of the poem the poet reaches the dwelling of Honour, 'the finall end of our trauaill' (1248). The increasing seriousness of Douglas's subject is heralded by his invocation of the Muses (1288–96), traditionally called upon by a poet about to tackle new and demanding material.[26] Douglas also heightens the reader's expectations by exclaiming

> The hart may not think nor mannis toung say,
> The Eir nocht heir nor ʒit the Eye se may,
> It may not be Imaginit with men
> The heuinlie blis, the perfite Ioy to ken
> Quhilk now I saw; the hundreth part all day
> I micht not schaw thocht I had toungis ten.
>   (1255–60)

This is a skilful example of the 'inexpressibility' topos—Douglas uses similar devices throughout the poem to suggest the high value of what he is describing.[27] But these lines take on greater solemnity from their echoes of St Paul (Corinthians 2.9) and possibly of Virgil (*Aeneid* VI.625). There are hints that the poet is about to view honour *sub specie aeternitatis,* and leave far below 'this brukill eird, sa litill till allow' (1348). The dreamer's role is increasingly passive. At one point his hair is seized, and he is carried

> till the hillis heid anone,
> As Abacuk was brocht in Babylone.
>   (1340–1)

The image is humorous, yet the allusion to an Old Testament Prophet leads us to see the poet not as an idle dreamer but as a seer, one favoured with revelations not granted to all men. He is privileged, even if unworthy. He does not always understand the implications of what he sees—'stupifak' (1460) and 'halflingis in ane Farie' (1872). Nonetheless he must observe and record: 'Quhat now thow seis, luik efterwart thow write' (1464). The dreamer often reverts to the fearful, uneasy mood in which his dream began; yet now he has a guide and instructor, like Chaucer or Dante in similar predicaments.

Honour's dwelling is remote and difficult of access; like so many allegorical palaces or temples it is set upon a high mountain. (Yet the lasting marble of which this is made contrasts with the mountain of ice on which Chaucer's more ephemeral House of Fame was set.) 'Pleneist with plesance like to paradice' (1413), it can be reached only after crossing a horrifying abyss. Its transcendence of earthly rules and values is suggested by the realm in which it is placed:

> I saw ane plane of peirles pulchritude
> Quhairin aboundit alkin thingis gude . . .

> Still in the sessoun all things remanit thair
> Perpetuallie but outher noy or sair.
> Ay rypit war baith herbis, frute and flouris.
>   (1414ff.)

The topography is here rather complicated. Besides the fantastically beautiful palace there is an outer ward containing a 'garth' (1466) in which Venus has her court. The Muses dwell on the outskirts of the palace, in what is termed both garden (1960) and island (2104). Honour himself is enthroned in the inmost hall of the 'riche castell' (1766 and 1918 ff.). Douglas is apparently attempting to distinguish between different kinds of honour. It is perhaps significant that when the dreamer visits the court of Venus, he has to turn his back on the 'principall place' (1450) of Honour (1462). Again, although he converses jocularly with Venus, he is permitted but a brief glimpse of Honour:

> Schute was the dure; in at a boir I blent,
> Quhair I beheld the glaidest represent
> That euer in eirth I, wretchit Catiue, kend.
> Breiflie this proces to conclude and end,
> Methocht the flure was all of Amatist,
> Bot quhairof war the wallis I not wist.
>
> . . . .
>
> Enthronit sat ane God Omnipotent,
> On quhais glorious visage as I blent,
> In extasie be his brichnes atanis
> He smote me doun and brissit all my banis.
>   (1903 ff.)

The interpretation of this scene is perhaps not self-evident. It seems to me that Douglas's imagery—such as the glance through a 'boir', or chink, and the jewelled hall that he sees—derives partly from St John's vision of the New Jerusalem (Revelation, 21), partly from traditional ideas about contemplation associated with the writings of St Gregory:

> it is a struggle wherein the mind disengages itself from the things of this world and fixes its attention wholly on spiritual things, and thereby raises itself above itself, and by dint of a great effort mounts up to a momentary perception of the 'unencompassed Light', as through a chink; and then, exhausted by the effort and blinded by the vision of the Light it sinks back wearied to its normal state.[28]

Douglas is not a mystic, but by using such imagery he seems almost to equate Honour with God himself. Later he expresses a highly medieval rejection of all forms of earthly glory in favour of the true honour that survives death and transcends the understanding of the world (1972–89).

Yet there is an ambiguity in Douglas's conception of Honour, which is emphasized by the different readings at line 1921: the Edinburgh edition has 'ane God Omnipotent'; the London edition has 'a god armypotent'. The former reading makes sense, yet the London edition often has the better if more difficult reading, and the martial epithet 'armypotent' may be what Douglas intended. Douglas's Honour seems at times to have more affinity with Mars than with the Christian God. There are several signs that he is celebrating a special form of honour, which a later writer, Gervase Markham, was to praise as 'the food of euery great spirit, and the very god which creates in high minds Heroicall actions'.[29] Honour's court contains chiefly heroic warriors and patriots, some of whom might find it difficult to get into the Christian heaven:

> The strangest Sampsoun is into ʒone hald,
> The forcie puissant Hercules sa bald,
> The feirs Achill and all the Nobillis nyne,
> Scipio Affricane, Pompeius the ald . . .
>   (2017 ff.)

Earlier Douglas described Honour's followers as 'maist vailʒeand folk and verteous in thair liues':

> For thay with speir, with swords and with kniues
> In Iust battell war fundin maist of mane.
>   (1964 ff.)

Douglas affirms that virtue alone is the path to true honour (1999–2015). Classical writers had stressed the close connection of virtue and honour—*honos sit praemium virtutis*[30]—and by the sixteenth century the idea had achieved the status of a proverb.[31] Yet Latin *virtus* must often be translated as 'valour, courage'; Valerius Maximus tells how the consul Marcellus dedicated twin temples to Honour and Valour (*Honori et Virtuti*).[32] (This anecdote may be the ultimate source of Douglas's poem and other poems deifying Honour.) In English the word *virtue* possessed a wide range of meaning, and sometimes had the sense 'courage' as well as 'moral excellence'. Douglas dedicated his poem to a king noted for his love of tournaments and other military sports; and he prayed that James might be granted the 'palme of victorie' and 'Renoun of Cheualrie' (2143–7). It seems appropriate for one who follows the Muse of heroic poetry to voice such a heroic conception of honour; and it ties in logically with those earlier sections of the poem that record the 'gestis' of heroes, often in great detail.

Nonetheless there would seem to be, at this stage of the *Palice of*

Honour, unresolved contradictions in Douglas's thought. His conception of Honour is more secular and this-worldly than perhaps he would admit, and not fully reconcilable with the explicitly Christian doctrines — of sin and redemption, for instance — that he also expounds. (In Prologue XI Douglas distinguishes 'moral vertuus hardyment' (25), which has eternal rewards, from 'warldly' courage and 'hie renown of Martis cheualry' (1).) Artistically, too, the third book seems to me the least satisfactory section of the poem. There is an imbalance between the passivity of the dreamer and the excessively magisterial and didactic nymph. The book is also overweighted by the long, rather pedestrian account of the sights to be seen in Venus's Mirror (1476–731). By contrast, the list of those who dwell in Honour's Court (2017–28) is brief and something of an anti-climax.

Douglas is much preoccupied with style in the *Palice of Honour*. There are many references to his own 'craft' (128), and that of other poets. Elsewhere Douglas argues that in choosing his words a writer must take into account both 'Hys mater, and quhamto it entitillit is'. One's style

> Suld conform to that manis dignitye
> Quhamto our wark we direct and endyte.
> (IX Prol 28, 34–5)[33]

Douglas 'directed' the *Palice of Honour* to a king, and in it professed allegiance to the Muse associated with the 'Kinglie style . . . Cleipit in Latin heroicus' (877–8). It is not surprising that he himself attempted his 'purpois to expres in ornate wise' (846–7), and thus to achieve the kind of eloquence that he most admired. In this poem Douglas describes examples of the highly wrought 'warkmanschip' of painters and sculptors; he sought to create in words a similar effect of artifice and rich profusion.

The Prologue and first two books are written in a nine-line stanza, which rhymes *aabaabbab*:

> The Dasy and the Maryguld vnlappit,
> Quhilks all the nicht lay with thair leuis happit
> Thame to reserue fra rewmes pungitiue.
> The vmbrate treis that Tytan about wappit
> War portrait and on the eirth yschappit
> Be goldin bemis viuificatiue,
> Quhais amene heit is maist restoratiue.
> The Gres hoppers amangis the vergers gnappit,
> And Beis wrocht materiall for thair Hyue.
> (37–45)

This intricate stanza is particularly associated with poems written in the high style, such as the Complaint in Chaucer's *Anelida and Arcite* or Dunbar's *Goldin Targe*. The rhyme pattern is difficult and demanding, and Douglas is clearly attempting to show off his metrical dexterity in using it for a long poem. In the last book he adopts a slightly different rhyme scheme (*aabaabbcc*), which had been used by Chaucer in the *Complaint of Mars*. At other points in the poem he inserts songs or 'ballatis', and concludes with a song to Honour (2116–42), which makes ingenious but not wholly successful use of cumulative internal rhyme.

The stanza quoted above illustrates other features of the ornate style, such as the mythological allusion (here comparatively trite), grammatical archaism—'yschappit'[34]—and the verbal patterning that we see in 'goldin bemis viuificatiue'. The poem abounds in instances of *interrogatio, circuitio, exclamatio,* and other 'colours' of rhetoric. The very disclaimer of 'craft' towards the opening of the poem (127–35) is in itself highly rhetorical: a *captatio benevolentiae,* designed to win the sympathy of Douglas's audience and make them 'bowsum and attent'. The vogue epithet 'amene' reveals another feature of the style—its tendency towards the abstract and the ideal. Throughout much of the poem Douglas seeks to idealize the world he depicts, by the use of eulogistic adjectives like 'dulce', 'lusty', and 'heuinly'. He frequently employs the figure of *superlatio,* asserting that a person or thing is peerless, or the 'maist gudliest and richest that micht be' (1168). He is particularly fond of the special kind of comparison that has been called the 'outdoing' topos:[35]

> And as the Ceder surmountis the Rammall
> In perfite hicht, sa of that Court a glance
> Exceidis far all eirdlie vane plesance.
> (1879–81)

Words like 'pungitiue', 'vmbrate', and 'viuificatiue' illustrate Douglas's fondness for learned, polysyllabic words, often of Latin origin. This is a persistent feature of his style, even in the *Eneados* and the Prologues, and seems to have had a variety of causes. Douglas had a personal predilection for learned neologisms, yet his familiarity with Latin as a second tongue may have led him to transfer such words into Scots, almost unconsciously; and when he came to translate the *Aeneid,* his vocabulary was clearly influenced by the vocabulary not only of Virgil but of his Latin commentators. In the *Palice of Honour,* however, stylistic motives seem uppermost. It was then fashionable for poets with any pretension to high style to avoid the language of everyday, and select 'exquisite termis quhilkis ar nocht daly usit'.[36] Even against this background the *Palice of Honour* is remarkable for the sheer abundance of words like 'virgultis' or 'diatesseriall'; phrases like *ad lyram* or *in periculo mortis*; and whole lines like

> Maist nutritiue till all thingis vegetant
> (48)

Douglas may have been attracted not only by the learned associations of such words but by their sonority. The exigencies of his rhyme scheme certainly account for the presence of some of them— 'dulcorait' (808), for instance, instead of the synonymous but more commonplace 'dulce'.

Such Latinate words cluster particularly thickly in the Prologue and descriptive passages. C. S. Lewis seems to me misleading, however, when he says: 'You rendered beauty by aureation; for terror (as for bawdy and invective) you became "boisteous" and native'.[37] Lewis quotes the rhyme words in the description of the 'laithlie flude' (145–53)—'routit', 'schoutit', etc.,—as evidence for the 'native' quality of the passage. Yet we might well have been equally impressed by its Latinate character, if he had quoted the stanza immediately before:

> My rauist spreit in that desert terribill
> Approchit neir that vglie flude horribill,
> Like till Cochyte the riuer Infernall,
> With vile water quhilk maid a hiddious trubil,
> Rinnand ouirheid, blude reid, and Impossibill
> That it had bene a riuer naturall;
> With brayis bair, raif rochis like to fall,
> Quhairon na gers nor herbis wer visibill
> Bot [skauppis] brint with blastis boriall.
> (136–44)

Douglas's technique here is much the same as in the description of the beautiful garden; there are classical allusions, rhetorical patterning (as in 'vglie flude horribill'), and a similar tendency to generalize, only with dyslogistic adjectives, such as 'hiddeous', 'terribill' or 'abhominabill'. There is indeed an admixture of vernacular words —'skauppis' or 'runtis'—and it is they which make the passage vivid and down to earth. But it is possible to exaggerate their numbers; nor are such homely words completely absent from the Prologue.[38] It seems to me that there exists no simple correlation between Douglas's choice of subject and his choice of a certain stratum of the vocabulary. A high proportion of learned Latinisms was characteristic of the high style; but this style was not confined solely to the description of pleasant or beautiful scenes. Douglas's desert is a more powerful piece of writing than his garden; but both are exercises in the same style.

It must be emphasized that Douglas could also write in a simpler style. He can be terse and often monosyllabic in narrative passages and dialogue:

> Tho saw I Venus on hir lip did bite,
> And all the Court in haist thair horsis renʒeit.
>
> (639–40)

> 'thou subtell smy, God wait,
> Quhat, wenis thou to degraid my hie estait,
> Me to decline as Iudge, curst creature?
> It beis not sa, the game gais vther gait.'
>
> (705–8)

But passages like these are comparatively rare. *Descriptio* is Douglas's most characteristic activity in the *Palice of Honour*, and his descriptive style—like that of most medieval poets—is essentially full and leisurely. Douglas was clearly aware of the stress that rhetorical handbooks laid on the technique of amplification. His liking for the utmost fullness of expression is evident in the smaller features of style, such as his preference for the figure of *repetitio*, his frequent coupling of nearly synonymous words—'destanie and sort', or 'mercie and pietie'—and his piling up of numerous small details:

> Pinnakillis, Fyellis, Turnpekkis mony one,
> Gilt birneist torris, quhilk like to Phebus schone,
> Skarsment, reprise, Corbell and Battelingis . . .
>
> (1432 ff.)

It is these catalogues that best illustrate Douglas's desire to be as all-inclusive as possible, to cram his poem with 'Euerie famous Poeit men may deuine' (850) or

> euerie famous douchtie deid
> That men in storie may se or Chronikill reid.
>
> (1693–4)

Yet Douglas's catalogues are not as random or 'pell-mell'[39] as sometimes appears. If we examine the long list of Venus's followers attentively, we may note how Douglas hints at the extraordinary diversity of love: solitary figures are contrasted with pairs or even trios of lovers; famous classical names like Helen and Dido are paralleled by Scriptural names, such as Bethseba, and heroes and heroines of romance; faithful lovers are matched with unfaithful, happy with unhappy, 'kind' with 'abhominabill'. In the poem as a whole, as I have already noted, one list or procession is often contrasted significantly with another. Denton Fox regards the catalogue as 'the basic structural device' of the *Palice of Honour*.[40]

The *Palice of Honour* has other qualities, which may be more congenial to the modern reader than allegory and rhetoric. The poem is humorous, and often witty. Douglas fires several shafts at the inconstancy or unchastity of women—there is indeed a trace of antifeminism in the poem. But his humour is chiefly self-directed. The poet-dreamer is placed in one comic predicament after another: hiding in the 'muskane aikin stok' (300), or trembling with fear at the imagined 'stichling' of a mouse (308). He portrays himself as both timorous and obtuse. A series of abusive names and images is applied to him—'schrew', 'veillane', and 'scheip'; last indignity of all, he is accused of having 'ane wyifes hart' (1937). Such slight but continuous self-mockery recalls Chaucer's humorous presentation of the dreamer in the *Parliament of Fowls* and the *House of Fame*. Douglas's narrator is not as sympathetic or credible as Chaucer's, yet he is distinctive: erudite and a little pedantic, brusque and argumentative. The poem is striking also for the wild, fantastic quality of Douglas's imagination. He takes advantage of the dream-form. The poem is full of the bizarre events and abrupt changes of scene or mood that are not uncommon in dreams; Lewis speaks aptly of 'figures hithering and thithering as the narrative proceeds'.[41] The dream often becomes a nightmare, and communicates a strong sense of fear. In the trial scene Douglas holds a distorting mirror up to nature, and produces a grotesque reflection of the life of his times. The Ovidian images and allusions reinforce the nightmarish effect, and contribute to the weird sense of instability that the poem produces. On the human level Douglas shows flashes of insight, as when he notes how talking to another can relieve a sense of misery:

Ʒit glaid I was that I with them had spokin.
Had not bene that, certes my hart had brokin . . .
   (310–11)

He is perceptive too about the dreamer's inner paralysis at a moment of crisis:

I micht not pray, forsuith, thocht I had neid.
   (735)

The poem contains many striking images. Some, such as the desert, with its 'skauppis' or bald, round pieces of rock, may spring largely from his own imagination; others, such as the horses, 'schynand for sweit, as thay had bene anoynt' (1239), may have been sparked off by Douglas's reading of other poets.[42]

The *Palice of Honour* seems to me very much a young man's poem. At one point the dreamer is addressed as 'Galland' (1308); the image of an elderly and venerable 'bishop of Dunkeld' is both distracting and inaccurate. There is an element of bravura about the poem, as if Douglas wished to show off newly acquired ideas and techniques. The rhetoric is insistent and obtrusive; in the Prologues to the

Eneados its use is far more varied and subtle. There is an unevenness too about the writing which perhaps betrays the beginner. Douglas's language is often vivid and energetic, yet at other times there are unhappy resemblances to Lydgate both in his syntax, with its long, sprawling sentences and dangling participles, and in the over-abstraction of his vocabulary. Yet there are several anticipations of the Prologues in Douglas's ideas about poets and poetry; a similar readiness to express himself through traditional forms; and many affinities of style.[43] There is a clear continuity between the *Palice of Honour* and Douglas's later poetry.

[4]

Douglas's Virgil

G. Gregory Smith passed a sweeping and possibly still influential judgment on Douglas: 'his Vergil is, for the most part, the Vergil of the dark ages, part prophet, part wizard, master of "illusionis by devillich werkis and coniurationis".'[1] This is perverse and highly misleading. Not only does it quote one line (1 Prol 216) completely out of context; it stresses unduly a tiny element in Douglas's response to Virgil, and gives a simplified and inaccurate picture of his total attitude. Douglas's Virgil might better be described as the Virgil whose Dido moved St Augustine to tears, and who guided Dante through hell. Douglas's Virgil is a writer who was read in schools by young children and was also the focus for much learned commentary and debate; a pagan who nonetheless became an *auctor* to Christians; and a poet who had been read and admired by other poets for over fifteen centuries. What Douglas says of Virgil must be seen against this complex background. He was not perhaps deeply learned, but he had read widely and intelligently. He was indebted to the scholarly pedagogic tradition: he knew the fourth-century commentary of Servius and Macrobius's *Saturnalia*, and had read more recent writers, such as Boccaccio, Cristoforo Landino, and Jodocus Badius Ascensius. He was also aware of the more popular and ill-informed ideas that circulated about Virgil and the *Aeneid*. Douglas's attitude to Virgil cannot be categorized simply; labels such as 'dark ages', 'medieval' or 'Renaissance' do not take us very far towards understanding him. Douglas's response to Virgil was inevitably complex; he saw the pagan Latin poet from the differing standpoints of one who was a Christian, a writer in the vernacular, and, above all, a practising poet.

Virgil the 'wizard', in fact, receives little mention in Douglas. Of the many marvellous and quite unauthentic legends that circulated about Virgil in the medieval period Douglas alludes to one only, that in which Virgil's mistress left him suspended in a basket from her bedroom window:

> Men says thou brydillyt Aristotyll as ane hors,
> And crelyt vp the flour of poetry.
>   (IV Prol 31–2)

Douglas is writing of Love's power over the mightiest and wisest

69

of men, and it was highly traditional to couple Aristotle and Virgil
in this way, along with Solomon, Samson and David. At much the
same time as Douglas was writing there was built the tomb of
Philippe de Commynes (*c*. 1506); this shows Aristotle bridled, Virgil
in a basket, and Amor in a medallion as a child triumphant.[2] Sometimes the theme is given an anti-feminist slant: Aristotle and Virgil
then figure as pagan exemplars of the 'greit mischief be wemen done
to men'.[3] If it still seems astonishing that Douglas could mention
such a story about the poet he venerated, one should note the tact
with which he refers not to Virgil but to the 'flour of poetry'; and
the slight doubt which 'men says' casts on the whole affair. The
author of the *Spectacle of Luf* had a far heavier hand:

> And was nocht vyrgill þe gret poyet and nygramessour sa
> Inchantit with þe luf of a woman þat scho drew him to þe
> middis of a tour in cummyng to hir chalmer quhar scho leit him
> hyng . . .[4]

A poet's use of a legend does not necessarily imply belief in its
authenticity; and if Douglas had rejected the story completely he
would have been far ahead of his time. The Virgilian legends had
never circulated only among the ignorant and the superstitious,[5]
and they persisted long after the medieval period. J.W. Spargo has
shown that some of them 'were perpetuated by the very persons and
often in the very works responsible in large degree for the most
advanced thought of the Renaissance.'[6]

Virgil never ceased to be read throughout the Middle Ages. A tradition of close study and interpretation of his text started in Virgil's
own lifetime, and has continued to the present day. From an early
period we hear of Virgil being used in schools, studied not only for
his own sake but to teach the niceties of Latin grammar.[7] The schools
in Douglas's Scotland inherited this tradition:

> Ane othir proffit of our buke I mark,
> That it salbe reput a neidfull wark
> To thame wald Virgill to childryn expone . . .
> Thank me tharfor, masteris of grammar sculys,
> Quhar ȝe syt techand on ȝour benkis and stulys.
>   (Directioun, 41 ff.)

There is plenty of evidence that other Scots, chiefly churchmen like
Douglas himself, maintained an interest in Virgil beyond the school-
room. Some of the texts that were possessed by his near-contempor-
aries still survive: a fifteenth-century manuscript in Edinburgh
University Library;[8] the *Opera* (Louvain 1476), which belonged to
Thomas Cranston, abbot of Jedburgh in 1484;[9] or the edition

(Milan 1493) that was owned by the Franciscans at Perth.[10] Possession of a book does not guarantee that its owner has read it, and stronger evidence of an informed admiration for Virgil is provided by the many quotations that adorn the text of John Major's *History*,[11] or Patrick Panter's elegant compliment to pope Julius II:

> it is likely that his Holiness may lay claim, named as he is, to the words of Virgil and 'bound his empire by the ocean, and his fame by the stars' (= *Aeneid* I.281).[12]

Alexander Stewart, the pupil of Panter and later of Erasmus, seems to have carried his enthusiasm for Virgil to the point of making a special visit to the Sibyl's cave at Cumae.[13]

Yet there was a long-standing ambivalence in the response of medieval Christians to Virgil. He was greatly admired both as a model of style and a repository of wisdom, but he was nonetheless a 'Gentile', who described the pagan gods and their immoral behaviour, heathen sacrifices, and many other things abhorrent to Christians. The duality is illustrated by St Jerome, who in his own writings quoted Virgil frequently and said of him that he was *poeta eloquentissimus*, and *alter Homerus apud nos*;[14] yet in his Epistle to Eustochium, recounting his famous dream, he asked a question whose rhetoric has echoed down the centuries: *Quid facit cum psalterio Horatius? cum evangeliis Maro? cum apostolo Cicero?*[15] Several centuries later a similar dilemma was expressed crudely but vividly in the story told of Odo of Cluny, to whom Virgil appeared in a dream like a vase, beautiful without but within full of serpents.[16]

Douglas himself directs our attention to such criticisms of Virgil. In the Prologue to book VI he attacks those who found it 'Al ful of leys or ald ydolatryis' (10) and 'Vayn superstitionys aganyst our richt beleve' (22). At the close of Prologue x he himself pours scorn on the pagan gods, calling them 'mawmentis' or idols. Prologue XIII shows that Douglas knew of Jerome's dream; he was also familiar with an equally famous confrontation of the pagans by a Father of the Church—St Augustine's *City of God*. Douglas, however, lived not in the fourth century but at a time, when, as he put it, 'blissit be God, the faith is now mair ferm' (1 Prol 218). Was Virgil's paganism a genuinely living issue for Douglas and his readers? In the thirteenth century Dante apparently felt few scruples about the propriety of reading Virgil.[17] Yet in the fourteenth and fifteenth centuries several Italians (including Boccaccio, Coluccio Salutati, Pierpaolo Vergerio and Maphaeus Vegius) discussed the legitimacy of reading pagan poets,[18] and felt it necessary to defend Virgil against his critics. The writings of some of Douglas's contemporaries in northern Europe suggest that the debate still continued, and that the study of pagan literature had enemies, particularly (it seems) among the religious orders and the theologians of Paris and Louvain.[19] Melanchthon is said to have been disturbed by Virgil's paganism.[20] In the *Adages* Erasmus makes fun of those who impute to the study of Virgil or Lucian 'the vice that comes from youth or weakness of character'.[21] The problem was one that much concerned Erasmus, and formed an important theme of his *Antibarbari*: 'his mission was to open the eyes of his generation, to convince them that the classics, far from being pagan, were a magnificent inheritance to be used in the cause of Christ'.[22] I think that for Douglas, as for many of his contemporaries, the study of Virgil presented not an agonizing dilemma, not an acute crisis of conscience, rather an interesting but not insoluble problem: that of reconciling his admiration of a pagan work with his faith as a Christian.

The defence of a pagan poet such as Virgil was inextricably linked with the defence of poetry itself. The same charges were laid against poets and pagans—both were purveyors of falsehood, *mendacia*:

> Bot trastis weill, quha that ilke saxt buke knew,
> Virgill tharin ane hie philosophour hym schew,
> And vnder the clowdis of dyrk poecy
> Hyd lyis thar mony notabill history—
> For so the poetis be the crafty curys
> In similitudes and vndir quent figuris
> The suythfast materis to hyde and to constreyn;[23]
> All is nocht fals, traste weill, in cace thai feyn.
> (1 Prol 191–8)

There is little novel about Douglas's argument here. In the twelfth century Bernard Silvestris had termed Virgil a *philosophus*, and had distinguished between the outer surface of his poetry and the inner truth that it contained: *et veritatem philosophiae docuit et figmentum poeticum non praetermisit*.[24] John of Salisbury said similarly of Virgil that *sub imagine fabularum totius philosophiae exprimit veritatem*.[25] Other classical poets besides Virgil were subjected to allegorical interpretation. There were many medieval commentaries on the *Metamorphoses*: perhaps the most popular was Pierre Bersuire's *Ovidius Moralizatus*, versions of which were being printed (by Ascensius) and translated (by Caxton) in Douglas's lifetime.[26] The defence of poetry itself in such allegorical terms had become a commonplace. What Henryson said of the beast-fable was relevant to other types of poetry:

> Sa lyis thair ane doctrine wyse aneuch
> And full of fruit, under ane fenyeit Fabill.
> (*Fables*, 17–18)

Douglas could have found ideas so widely diffused in many writers,[27] yet it seems reasonable to suppose that he himself was influenced by the particular work to which he directed his readers:

> Bot quha sa lawchis heirat, or hedis noddis,
> Go reid Bochas in the Genolygy of Goddis;
> Hys twa last bukis sall swage thar fantasy.
> (Directioun, 67–9)

Boccaccio's *Genealogy of the Gods* was a remarkably popular and influential work until well into the sixteenth century. It not only furnished poets with a handbook of mythology, its 'twa last bukis' (xiv and xv) constituted a virtual 'Defence of Poetry'.[28] The notion of poetry as 'veiled truth' permeates the whole work, but is most explicitly stated in xiv.7: poetry impels the soul *velamento fabuloso atque decenti veritatem contegere*; and *mera poesis est, quicquid sub velamento componitur et exponitur exquisite*. The crucial distinction between fiction and falsehood—cf. Douglas's 'All is nocht fals, traste weill, in cace thai feyn'—is discussed at length in xiv.13, entitled *Poetas non esse mendaces*. This chapter might well interest Douglas, since much of the discussion centres on Virgil and concludes *Et sic non mendax fuit Virgilius*.

The interpreters of pagan poets, and of the myths which formed the stuff of their poetry, found different kinds of truth or 'sentence' beneath the literal surface (the *figmentum* or *integumentum*) of their writing. In Douglas one may distinguish three main approaches, all traditional: the euhemeristic, in which the pagan gods were reduced to men of extraordinary abilities, heroes rather than divinities; the allegorical, which found in pagan myth important truths about human nature or the physical universe; and lastly, and not always very precisely demarcated from the former, the approach that perceived in such myth foreshadowings or adumbrations of specifically Christian doctrines.

Euhemerism had pagan origins[29]—Virgil himself represents Faunus, Janus, and Saturn as ancient Italian kings (*Aeneid* vii. 48 and 177 ff.; viii.319 ff.)—but the method was seized upon by the early Christian polemicists as a weapon to make the pagan gods ridiculous. With later medieval writers, however, euhemerism became a means not of attacking but of defending the study of the classics.[30] This is so with Boccaccio, and so too with Douglas, who, as he himself acknowledges, owes several of his interpretations to the *Genealogy of the Gods*. In the Comment to the *Eneados* we read that 'in verite Iuno was bot ane woman' (i.i.82n); that Aeolus was 'an naturall man' who learnt to foretell the direction from which the winds would blow—'for the quhilk rayson, with the rud pepill, was he nammyt kyng or god of wyndis' (i.ii.3n); and that Neptune, 'for

73

that the partis of his heritage lay in Creit by the sey cost, and for he vsit mekill salyng and rowyng, and fand the craft or art therof, therfor is he clepit god of the sey' (1.iii.54n). In Douglas the euhemeristic explanation of a myth is usually combined with an allegorical one, to which he often devotes more space. In this he resembles Boccaccio, and often follows him closely. Thus Aeolus was not only 'an naturall man' but also signified 'raison, set hie in the manis hed, quhilk suld dant, and includ law[31] in the cave or boddum of the stomak, the windis of peruersit appetyte, as lord and syre, set be God almychty therto' (1.ii.12n). So too Boccaccio gives first a historical and rationalizing explanation of Aeolus, and then continues

> Sunt tamen qui velint hac in fictioni Virgilii, Eulum sublimi in arce residentem rationem esse, sedem habentem in cerebro; ventos vero illecebres appetitus in antro humani pectoris tumultuantes.

> (XIII.20)

Douglas clearly felt no sense of incongruity in discovering such extraneous 'sentence' in Virgil or in yoking together such varied 'proprieteis' (1.i.82n) in the gods. Multiple interpretation of a text was long familiar from its use in Scriptural exegesis. In his note to 1.vi.1 the rationalizing explanation that Venus was called the mother of Aeneas because 'he had a fayr lady to his moder, quhilk for hir bewte was clepit Venus' is accompanied by this:

> 3e sall vndirstand that Venus is fen3eit to be modyr to Eneas becaws that Venus was in the ascendent and had domynation in the hevyn and tym of his natyvite ... and thus it is that poetis fen3eis bein full of secreyt ondyrstandyng ondyr a hyd sentens or fygur ... And that Venus metis Eneas in form and lyknes of a maid is to be onderstand that Venus the planete that tym was in the syng of the Virgyn, quhilk betakynnyt luf and fawouris of wemen.

The allegory here is not moral but 'physical' or astrological: the pagan gods are identified with the planets that bear their names. The interest that medieval people felt in astrology is well known; in the poems of Chaucer or Henryson the symbolic use of such planetary deities is often extremely subtle. But it is well to remember that the search for astrological truths in ancient myth was not a peculiarly medieval preoccupation, but originated in antiquity itself.[32] Coldwell attributes the presence of such astrological notes in Douglas to the influence of Cristoforo Landino.[33] Douglas was familiar with some of Landino's writings, but had no need to consult him at this point. He seems to have derived this particular note partly from

Ascensius, partly from a more ancient source to whom Ascensius may well have directed his attention: *Seruius argute docet rem physicam esse, et ex visceribus astrologię fictionem hanc excerptam.*[34] Douglas, eclectic as always, is recalling two passages:

> nam innuit venerem fuisse ęneę in medio horoscopi et dominam coeli in natiuitate eius. Vnde veneris filius existimatus est . . . Quę ergo a poetis finguntur altioris sapientię medullas continent.
>
> (Ascensius on *Aeneid* 1.314)
>
> illud etiam mathematici [i.e. astrologers] dicunt,[35] Venere in Virgine posita misericordem feminam nasci: atque ideo Vergilius fingit in habitu virginis venatricis Venerem occurrisse filio.
>
> (Servius on *Aeneid* 1.223)

The earlier parts of this same note of Servius's clearly contributed to Douglas's other astrological comments: on the 'constylation' between Jupiter and Venus (1.v.2n); and the significance of Mercury (1.v.122n).

The commentary of Servius contains many brief allegorical notes of different kinds,[36] but systematic allegorical interpretation of the *Aeneid*—more particularly of the first six books—seems to have begun with Fulgentius's *De Continentia Virgiliana* (fifth century), and to have continued in the twelfth century with Bernard Silvestris's *Commentum super sex libros Eneidos Virgilii*, and the brief exposition in John of Salisbury's *Polycraticus*. There is no definite evidence that Douglas knew these writers, but he was clearly familiar with the tradition that they jointly bequeathed to the later Middle Ages. The *Aeneid* was an image of human life:

> In all his warkis Virgil doith discrive
> The stait of man, gif thou list vnderstand,
> Baith lif and ded in thir fyrst bukis fyve;
> And now, intil this saxt, we haue on hand,
> Eftir thar deth, in quhat plyte saulis sal stand.
>
> (VI Prol 33–7)

Douglas was sufficiently up-to-date to have read one of the most widely admired and influential of the recent interpreters of Virgil, Cristoforo Landino. His most famous work, the *Quaestiones Camaldulenses*,[37] is a debate as to the merits of the active and the contemplative lives; various members of the Florentine Academy take part, but the principal speaker is Leon Battista Alberti. Books III and IV offer a full-scale Neoplatonic allegorization of the first half of the *Aeneid*. Douglas seems to have read this work attentively, and summarizes briefly but reasonably accurately Landino's interpretation of Aeneas as man searching for his *summum bonum*, of Italy as a figure for the contemplative life and Carthage for the active life, of Aeolus as *ratio inferior* and Neptune as *ratio superior*:

> Cristoferus Landynus, that writis moraly apon Virgill, says thus: Eneas purposis to Italy, his land of promyssion; that is to say, a iust perfyte man entendis to mast soueran bonte and gudnes, quhilk as witnessyth Plato, is situate in contemplation of godly thyngis or dyvyn warkis. His onmeysabill enymy Iuno, that is fenʒeit queyn of realmys, entendis to dryve him from Italle to Cartage; that is, Avesion,[38] or concupissence to ryng or haf warldly honouris, wald draw him fra contemplation to the actyve lyve; quhilk, quhen scho falis by hir self, tretis scho with Eolus, the neddyr part of raison . . . fynally by the fre wyll and raison predomynent, that is ondyrstand by Neptun, the storm is cessit.
>
> (I.iii.100n)

'In the light of Neoplatonism the humanists discovered in mythology something other and much greater than a concealed morality; they discovered religious teaching—the Christian doctrine itself'.[39] Many scholars have made us aware how widespread and how diverse were the attempts made at this time to reconcile the teachings of pagan poets and philosophers with Christianity, attempts pursued not only by the Italian Neoplatonists such as Ficino but also by writers in northern Europe.[40] It is the Flemish Ascensius whom Douglas cites as his authority for saying of Virgil: 'Feil of his wordis bene like the appostilis sawis' (VI Prol 74).[41] A writer such as Ascensius—who in his commentary sometimes cites the opinions of Landino, Filelfo, or Politian[42]—was a channel for transmitting the ideas of Italian scholars to a wider and less learned audience. Yet the 'Christianizing' of Virgil had ancient origins, and few of the arguments put forward by Douglas were distinctively new or humanistic. St Augustine and other fourth-century Christians had adorned their writings with innocuous phrases culled from Virgil and other pagan poets. More significantly, they sometimes re-applied in a Christian sense lines referring to the pagan gods, and occasionally subjected whole passages to a Christian interpretation.[43] Douglas was clearly familiar with some of Augustine's writing:

> Quhou oft rehersis Austyne, cheif of clarkis,
> In his gret volume of the Cite of God,
> Hundreth versis of Virgil, quhilk he markis
> Agane Romanys, til vertu thame to brod!
> (VI Prol 61–4)

Douglas may also have been acquainted with the works of Augustine's less distinguished contemporaries, who were still read and esteemed in the late medieval period. The *Cento* of Proba, for instance, which uses Virgilian lines and half-lines to tell the story of the Creation, actually accompanies the works of Virgil both in a fifteenth-century manuscript[44] and a small edition printed for Ascensius.[45] As so often with Douglas, the opinions that he voiced were congenial to his age yet written within a tradition of great antiquity.

Douglas's discussion of Virgil's relationship with Christianity is mostly to be found in Prologue VI. This is not surprising, since book VI of the *Aeneid* had long provoked mixed reactions. Some medieval readers saw Aeneas's descent to the underworld as mere 'fable'; Caxton omitted it from his *Eneydos*, calling it 'fayned, and not to be byleued'.[46] Others, of whom Dante was the greatest, saw it as 'Virgil's closest approximation to the higher truths of Christianity'.[47] Douglas's stance is careful and circumspect. He repeatedly says that Virgil was a 'gentile' and 'na Cristyn man' (VI Prol 53, 78, 79), and concedes that some of his opinions were erroneous. Nonetheless on many questions that concerned the Christian, such as the season of the Creation,[48] or the life after death, Virgil was 'ane hie theolog sentencyus' (VI Prol 75):

Twichand our faith mony clausis he fand
Quhilk beyn conform, or than collaterall.

Schawis he nocht heir the synnys capital?
Schawis he nocht wikkit folk in endles pane,
And purgatory for synnys venyall,
And vertuus pepil into the plesand plane?
　(VI Prol 39–44)

Douglas asserts not that Virgil was a Christian, but that many of his doctrines are compatible with those of Christianity. So too Landino wrote of Virgil: *qui non christianus omnia tamen christianorum uerissime doctrine simillima proferat*.[49] (In chapter 5 I discuss the charge that Douglas foisted upon book VI the late medieval doctrine of Purgatory, thereby distorting his translation.)

As one illustration of Virgil's harmony with Christian thought Douglas says

Ane movar, ane begynnar puttis he,
Sustenys all thing, and doth in all remane,
And, be our faith, the sammyn thing grant we.
　(VI Prol 126–8)

Douglas seems here to have in mind not only *Aeneid* VI.724 ff. but Georgic IV.221 ff. (*deum namque ire per omnis / terrasque tractusque maris*), and possibly *Eclogue* III.60 (*Ab Ioue principium Musae: Iouis omnia plena*). These passages, which express a partly Stoic conception of God as *anima mundi*, were regularly linked by the Virgilian commentators, and often quoted, separately or together, by patristic writers such as Augustine or Jerome.[50] The early Christians found the lines striking—as did Douglas—because they seemed to presage the doctrine of divine immanence.[51]

Christians who saw Virgil as a prophet, consciously or unconsciously, of Christ among the Gentiles, found the most convincing evidence in his fourth *Eclogue*. Allusions in Prologues v and ix show Douglas's interest in this *Eclogue*, and in Prologue vi.72 he paraphrases the famous lines *iam redit et uirgo . . . iam noua progenies caelo demittitur alto*. Later in the Prologue Douglas interprets the lines in the customary way, the *uirgo* referring to Mary, the *noua progenies* to Christ. Such a Christian interpretation had been put forward as early as the fourth century. Although ridiculed by Jerome, and subjected in Douglas's own time to critical scrutiny, it had been accepted by Augustine, Dante, and many other eminent Christians.[52] Douglas was traditional in this and also in linking the Cumaean Sibyl with Christian prophets (146).[53] Where he seems less orthodox is in his further identification of the Sibyl with Mary:

> Sibilla, till interpret propirly,
> Is clepit a maid of goddis secret preve,
> That hes the spiret divyne of prophecy.
> Quha bettir may Sibilla namyt be
> Than may the gloryus moder and madyn fre,
> Quhilk of hir natur consavit Criste, and buyr
> All haill the mysteris of the Trinite . . .
> (vi Prol 137–143)

This may be Douglas's own personal interpretation, but I suspect that he probably derived it from an as yet unidentified source.

Co-existing with the learned, Latin tradition (which involved contact of some kind with the text of Virgil) was a more widely diffused tradition, accessible to people other than 'clerks', in which the story of Aeneas formed only a small part of the huge, heroic story of Troy. Virgil was but one of many tellers of this tale, and sometimes, like Homer, was considered inferior in authority to 'historians', such as Dictys Cretensis and Dares Phrygius, who were believed to have been actual eye witnesses of events at Troy. The fourth-century *Ephemeris Belli Troiani* (attributed to Dictys) and the fifth- or sixth-century *De Excidio Troiae* (attributed to Dares) were for long highly esteemed. Even more widely read and influential in the later medieval period were Benoit de Saint Maure's diffuse and leisurely *Roman de Troie* (*c.*1165) and Guido delle Colonne's *Historia Destructionis*

Troiae (completed in 1287). Guido's success can be gauged by the fact that at least three Middle English translations of his work were made, the most popular of which was Lydgate's *Troy Book* (1420).[54] (This was printed in 1513, at the request of Henry VIII, when Douglas was finishing his *Eneados*.) From these and other sources the Troy legends were transmitted, often strangely altered, to romance-writers and chroniclers in every language of western Europe. Medieval interest in the Trojans was reflected in the visual arts, more particularly in manuscript illustrations (such as those that accompany the *Roman de Troie*), ivories, and tapestries. There was no decline, rather an upsurge of interest in the later Middle Ages — indeed the fifteenth century witnessed 'the greatest production of tapestries dealing with the Trojan war'.[55] Stories from Troy were represented on tapestries in the Great Chamber of Holyrood at the time of James IV's wedding;[56] and in the palaces of James V were tapestries illustrating both the story of Troy and the story of Aeneas.[57] Scotland was clearly not exempt from the widespread interest in the Trojans. Fragments exist of a fifteenth-century Scottish version of Guido in octosyllabic couplets;[58] Archibald Whitelaw, secretary to James III, possessed an Italian manuscript *Historia de Origine Troianorum*;[59] and a treatise in the Asloan Manuscript summarizes the story of Aeneas, and dates the coming of Brutus to England precisely 1,105 years before the Incarnation.[60]

The perennial appeal of the Troy story perhaps makes it unnecessary to seek an explanation of its enormous medieval popularity. One factor that may have contributed, however, was the common belief that many western European countries had been founded by Trojans. Just as the city of Padua traced its origin to Antenor and Rome to Aeneas, so, on the authority of Geoffrey of Monmouth's *Historia Regum Britanniae* (1135), London or 'Troy Novant' claimed to have been founded by Brutus, one of the descendants of Aeneas. As Britons were descended from Brutus, so Frenchmen were descended from a legendary 'Francus of a ryall fame / That France of 3it has þe name'.[61] In his frequently reprinted *Illustrations de Gaule et Singularitez de Troie*, Douglas's contemporary, Jean Lemaire de Belges, 'distributed the names of the various Trojan heroes, like spoils of war' among Bretons, Flemings, Scandinavians and Spaniards.[62]

The *Aeneid* itself was subjected to numerous re-tellings in verse and prose, in Latin and the different vernaculars. In the twelfth century appeared the anonymous *Roman d'Eneas*, and a German version of this, Heinrich von Veldecke's *Eneide* (*c*.1174–84); to the same century is attributed the Middle Irish prose paraphrase, *Imtheachta Aeniasa*. In the thirteenth century appeared Guido da Pisa's

I Fatti d'Enea; in the fourteenth, Andrea Lancia's prose *Istoria di Eneas*; in the fifteenth, the French *Livre des Eneydes*. This was the source of Caxton's *Eneydos* (*c*.1490).[63] These and other works were versions of the *Aeneid* rather than translations. In them Virgil's poem was adapted, abridged, abbreviated, translated only in the same sense as the unfortunate Bottom. Sometimes Virgilian passages or whole books were omitted, sometimes material from other sources was inserted; sometimes the order of the books was changed so that an *ordo naturalis* was substituted for Virgil's *ordo artificialis*; important changes of emphasis and interpretation occurred, particularly in the characters of Aeneas and Dido.[64] The best parallel perhaps is with the changes that occur today when a work of art is transferred from one medium to another; when a novel, for instance, is transferred to stage, screen or television.

Douglas was undoubtedly interested in the 'matter of Troy'. He devoted a substantial section of his *Palice of Honour* (1594ff.) to Trojan legends and history, and placed Dares and Dictys along with Lucan at the court of the Muses (900). His two references to Raoul Lefevre's popular *Recueil des Histoires de Troye* (fifteenth century) are both respectful (1 Prol 205–6; 1.v.2n). (I suspect that he read this in Caxton's translation, in the 1503 edition printed by Wynkyn de Worde.)[65] Nonetheless, Douglas is at pains to assert that his version of the Troy story will be new and different from that told by his predecessors in the vernacular:

> The drery fait with terys lamentabill
> Of Troys sege wydequhar our all is song,
> Bot followand Virgil, gif my wit war abill,
> Ane other wys now salt that bell be rong
> Than euer was tofor hard in our tong.
> (II Prol 8–12)

The novelty, however, will consist not in his re-shaping of the story but in 'followand Virgil'.

The same concern with fidelity to the Virgilian tradition informs Douglas's well-known attack on Caxton:

> Thocht Wilȝame Caxtoun, of Inglis natioun,
> In proys hes prent ane buke of Inglys gros,
> Clepand it Virgill in Eneados,
> Quhilk that he says of Franch he dyd translait,
> It has na thing ado tharwith, God wait,
> Ne na mair lyke than the devill and Sanct Austyne.
> Haue he na thank tharfor, bot loys hys pyne,
> So schamefully that story dyd pervert.
> (1 Prol 138–45)

Uncharitable readers might interpret this as a piece of knocking copy
—an attempt to denigrate a dead rival's work. Undoubtedly it contains an element of 'flyting', as Douglas acknowledges, but the
attack is mounted on Caxton not just as an individual but as a representative of a whole tradition. Through Caxton's *Eneydos* Douglas is
criticizing popular medieval treatments of the *Aeneid* and popular
notions of translation. Douglas's criticisms are largely justified, if we
judge the *Eneydos*, or its French original, as a translation of the
Aeneid. (Caxton to some extent forestalled critics by making it clear
in his Prologue that he was not translating directly from Virgil.)
Douglas is not content with vague denunciation, but makes precise
and detailed charges. He pours scorn on Caxton's 'febil proys' (v Prol
51), mis-spellings and factual errors; but what most offends him—
and most strikes a modern reader—are the insertion of non-Virgilian
material and the major omissions, such as the similes or the whole of
book vi. In this way the proportions of the *Aeneid* are quite falsified:

> Me lyst nocht schaw quhou thystory of Dydo
> Be this Caxtoun is haill pervertit so
> That besyde quhar he fenys to follow Bocas,
> He rynnys sa fer from Virgill in mony place,
> On sa prolixt and tedyus fasson,
> So that the ferd buke of Eneadon,
> Twichand the lufe and ded of Dido queyn,
> The twa part of his volume doith conteyn
> That in the text of Virgill, trastis me,
> The twelt part scars contenys, as ʒe may se.
>   (1 Prol 163–72)

(It is true that Caxton's *Eneydos* devotes 24 out of 65 chapters to the
Dido story.)

According to Douglas, Caxton offered his readers not a version
but a perversion of the *Aeneid*. By contrast, Douglas offers his
readers something directly based on Virgil:

> Bot my propyne com from the pres fute hait,
> Onforlatit, not iawyn fra tun to tun,[66]
> In fresch sapour new from the berry run.
>   (v Prol 52–4)

The image vividly contrasts the unadulterated wine offered by
Douglas with the stale, secondhand product retailed by Caxton. In
Prologue 1 Douglas expresses very forcibly his sense of the integrity
of the work of art, and of the translator's duty to be as faithful as
possible to his original:

> Rycht so am I to Virgillis text ybund.
>   (1 Prol 299)

(More will be said in the next chapter of the extent to which Douglas puts his principles into practice.)

Douglas is concerned to defend the structure of the *Aeneid* against its mutilators and manglers. He is also concerned to defend the character and reputation of Aeneas. At the end of the *Eneados* Douglas says:

> Be glaid, Ene, thy bell is hiely rong,
> Thy faym is blaw, thy prowes and renown
> Dywlgat ar, and sung fra town to town,
> So hardy from thens, that other man or boy
> The ony mair reput traytour of Troy,
> Bot as a worthy conquerour and kyng
> The honour and extoll, as thou art dyng.
> (Directioun, 128–34)

Douglas here rebuts one of the major charges against Aeneas, that it was he, together with Antenor, who betrayed Troy to the Greeks. This charge was widely accepted by many medieval readers, but it was not a medieval invention. Discrepant traditions about Aeneas already existed in classical times. Indeed the conception of Aeneas as *proditor Troiae* seems to be pre-Virgilian;[67] it was transmitted to the Middle Ages by the Virgil scholiasts as well as by Dares and Dictys. In the later medieval period it owed its wide currency to Guido, who described the conspiracy to betray Troy in books 28–30 of his immensely popular *Historia Destructionis Troiae*.[68] Douglas directly challenged Guido on this point:

> Becaus ther is mension of Anthenor, quham many, followand Gwydo De Columnis, haldis tratour, sum thing of him will I speyk, thocht it may suffis for his purgation that Virgill heir hayth namyt him, and almaste comparit him to the mast soueran Eneas, quhilk comparison na wys wald he haf maid for lak of Eneas, gif he had bein tratour. Bot to schaw his innocens, lat vs induce the mast nobill and famus historian and mylky flud of eloquens, gret Tytus Lyuius. . . . Now I beseik ȝow, curtes redaris, considdir gif this be punctis of traison, or rather of honour, and wey the excellent awtorite of Virgill and Tytus Lyuius wyth ȝour pevach and corrupt Gwido.
> (I.v.28n)[69]

'Pevach and corrupt Gwido'—the scorn is far removed from Lydgate's panegyric on 'maister' Guido, 'Whiche had in writyng passyng excellence' (*Troy Book*, Prol 361), or the respectful references to the authority of the 'clerk' Guido in the Asloan Manuscript.[70] Douglas was certainly going counter to much contemporary Scottish opinion both in criticizing Guido, and in attempting to remove the label

'traitors of Troy' from Aeneas and Antenor. One of the insults that
Kennedie hurled at Dunbar was that he was not only descended from
Herod and Mahomet but had as 'trew kynnismen, Antenor and
Eneas' (*Flyting*, 539). For the Scots, after all, this belief furnished
useful ammunition against the English, who—unlike the Scots—
boasted of their descent from Brutus, and ultimately therefore from
the 'tressonabile tratouris of troye Of quhais wikit fals deidis all þe
warld reidis'.[71]

Douglas defends Aeneas from a second charge often made by
medieval writers: that he abandoned Dido callously and treacher-
ously. Such an attitude, although it can be seen to derive partly from
the dramatic and sympathetic presentation of Dido in *Aeneid* IV, was
clearly not Virgil's. It springs from the medieval tendency to isolate
the love story from the context of the whole *Aeneid*, and to see it
chiefly from Dido's angle—a tendency which was encouraged by
the popularity of Ovid's version of events in *Heroides* VII. For many
medieval people Aeneas had become a type of the treacherous lover,
and frequently appeared in lists of false lovers, along with Jason,
Theseus, and Demophon.[72] This is Chaucer's attitude in the *House of
Fame* (267 ff.) and in the *Legend of Dido*:

> This Eneas, that hath so depe yswore,
> Is wery of his craft withinne a throwe;
> The hote ernest is al overblowe.
>   (*Legend of Good Women*, 1285 – 7)[73]

Indeed this is how Aeneas appears in the *Palice of Honour* (564),
where we read of 'Quene Dido with hir fals lufe Enee'. By the time
he came to translate the *Aeneid*, however, Douglas had abandoned
this position, and mounted a respectful attack on Chaucer, presumably because he was the most influential exponent of the 'medieval'
view of Aeneas:

> My mastir Chauser gretly Virgill offendit.
> All thoch I be tobald hym to repreif,
> He was fer baldar, certis, by hys leif,
> Sayand he followit Virgillis lantern toforn,
> Quhou Eneas to Dydo was forsworn.
> Was he forsworn? Than Eneas was fals—
> That he admittis and callys hym tratour als.
>   (I Prol 410– 16)

Douglas then defends Aeneas in terms of his destiny and his duty to
obey the will of the gods. Although he deals briefly and superficially with the problem, he shows something of the complexity of
Virgil's purpose in the *Aeneid*. That such an approach was new and
uncongenial to some at least of Douglas's Scottish readers can be

seen in the marginal note to I Prologue 425:

> This argument excusis nocht the tratory of Eneas na his mayn-
> sweryng . . . He falit than gretly to the sueit Dydo, quhilk falt
> reprefit nocht the goddes diuinite, for thai had na diuinite, as
> said is befoir.[74]

Douglas thus attempts a rehabilitation of the character of Aeneas.
He not only defends him from the stock charges, he presents him
more positively as a model of virtuous conduct:

> For euery vertu belangand a nobill man
> This ornate poet bettir than ony can
> Payntand discryvis in person of Eneas—
> Not forto say sikane Eneas was
> ȝit than by hym perfytely blasons he
> All wirschip, manhed and nobilite,
> With euery bonte belangand a gentill wycht,
> Ane prynce, ane conquerour or a valȝeand knycht.
>
> (I Prol 325–32)

Such a conception of Aeneas was not yet widely popular, but it
would have been acceptable to many humanists, such as Landino,[75]
or Maphaeus Vegius, who called Aeneas 'man endowed with every
virtue'.[76] Ascensius similarly in the dedication of his Virgil to Louis
of Flanders called Aeneas *speculum atque exemplum perfecti viri*.[77] It
was not the attitude that was new but its expression in the vernacular.
Douglas anticipated Sidney both in the idealization of Aeneas, and
in discriminating between Aeneas, the historical person, and Aeneas,
the exemplary figure, as the poet 'feigns' or 'blasons' him to be.[78]

Some sixteenth-century readers of the *Aeneid* saw Aeneas specifically as the ideal prince:

> In iustice, wysdome, and magnanimitye A myroure to all
> Prynces, Quhas verteous, gif the Prynces of our dayis, wyll
> folow, thay schal not onely be fauored of god, bot also weil
> beloued of al gud men.

This comes from a passage immediately following Prologue VII in
the 1553 edition of the *Eneados*. This edition is notorious for its
alterations to Douglas's text,[79] and since this passage is without
manuscript authority I can see no justification for taking it necessarily to express Douglas's own views. It seems to me that in the
lines quoted earlier Douglas presents Aeneas less as a model prince
than as a model man. The tone is certainly aristocratic—'nobill' and
'gentill' are perhaps ambiguous—but if the stress lies anywhere it is
not on 'prynce' but on 'knycht'. So too in Prologue IX Douglas presents the *Aeneid* as a work of 'prowes and hie chevelry' (90), written
for a knightly audience in a heroic or 'knychtlyke style' (31). Some

scholars, however, have laid great stress on Douglas's political interpretation of the *Aeneid*. To Coldwell the *Aeneid* is a 'political tract'; translating it 'a political act'; and 'the harvest that a Renaissance reader barned from Vergil was political'.[80] This seems an enormous over-simplification both of the *Aeneid* and the 'Renaissance' response to it. Douglas was undoubtedly aware of the political implications of the *Aeneid*; Prologue IX.57–8 and his note to I.v.102 show that he knew something of the historical context in which it was written. But in the Prologues and Comment to his translation he is concerned above all to show the richness and variety of the *Aeneid*. For a Scottish translator with a political message we must turn to John Bellenden. His *Livy* was commissioned by James V, and dedicated to him in a Prologue which far more explicitly than anything in Douglas presents his work as a 'mirror for princes':

Ʒe may also be mony stories see
Quhat besynes may proffitt or avance
Ʒoure princely state with ferme continuance.[81]

If Douglas lays particular stress on any one aspect of the poem he is translating, it is moral and ethical rather than political.

It would be mistaken to think that Douglas was interested solely in the moral content of the *Aeneid*. As a poet himself Douglas responded to the poetic artistry of Virgil. He speaks admiringly of his 'craft' or workmanship:

Nane is, nor was, ne ʒit salbe, trow I,
Had, has or sal haue sic craft in poetry.
    (1 Prol 55–6)
So crafty wrocht hys wark is, lyne by lyne
    (v Prol 31)

(cf. also 1 Prol 11 and 335, and 1.i.62n.) Douglas singles out the economy of Virgil's writing—'sa wysly wrocht with nevir a word invane' (1 Prol 30); his vividness—'feilabill in all degre / As quha the mater beheld tofor thar e' (1 Prol 13–14); and, above all, the beauty of his style, which he conceives chiefly as verbal ornament—'polyst termys redymyte' (1 Prol 34),

quent and curyus castis poeticall,
Perfyte symylitudes and exemplis all,
Quharin Virgill beris the palm of lawd.
    (1 Prol 255–6)

Such stylistic felicities are summed up for Douglas in the key term, *eloquence*. Douglas returns again and again to the theme of Virgil's eloquence, opposing it to his 'sentence' in a dualism similar to that between body and soul:

> The bewte of his ornate eloquens
> May nocht al tyme be kepit with the sentens

(1 Prol 393–4; see also 1x Prol 53–4, and Directioun 95–6.) Douglas repeatedly uses the same image to characterize Virgil's eloquence. He speaks of it as a 'flude' (1 Prol 4 and 310), and later elaborates still further:

> of eloquens the flude
> Maste cheif, profund and copyus plenitud,
> Surs capitall in veyn poeticall,
> Soverane fontane, and flum imperiall.

(Directioun, 55–8)

Dante similarly addressed Virgil as 'quella fonte/Che spande di parlar si largo fiume' (*Inferno*, 1.79–80), and Beroaldus called him *alter ingeniorum fons, alter eloquentię torrens.*[82] The image was traditional (probably originating in the classical *flumen verborum, orationis*),[83] but it is none the less apt and well chosen. It suggests both Virgil's creative abundance, and Douglas's ingrained love of 'fouth'. Douglas was familiar with the first critic to lavish praise on Virgil's *eloquentia*. He quotes directly from Macrobius's 'gret volume clepit Saturnaill':

> Thy sawys in sic eloquens doith fleit
>
> . . . .
>
> That na lovyngis ma do incres thy fame,
> Nor na reproche dymynew thy gud name.

(1 Prol 69 ff.)

(cf. *haec est quidem . . . Maronis gloria ut nullius laudibus crescat, nullius vituperatione minuatur.*)[84] Eloquence is a term closely linked with the art of rhetoric. The connection between poetry and rhetoric, a commonplace in Douglas's time, was inherited from antiquity. When Douglas praises Virgil's 'rethorik flowris sweit' (1 Prol 70) and says that 'Na lusty cast of oratry Virgill wantis' (1 Prol 308) he is writing in a tradition that many centuries earlier had produced a treatise with the title *Vergilius orator an poeta?*[85]

For Douglas, as for most of his contemporaries, style chiefly consisted in the choice and arrangement of words. Yet the Prologues and Comment reveal that he had some interest in the larger aspects of style. Prologue 1 shows his concern for the structure and proportions of the *Aeneid*, and his awareness that the Dido-story was part of a larger whole. Elsewhere he briefly discusses the relationship between the order of some books in the *Aeneid* and the order of events (1.i.62n). Again, he shows interest in Virgil's methods of characterization. He is concerned not only with *what* Aeneas stands for, but *how* Virgil presents him to the reader:

Her fyrst namys Virgill Eneas. This cald, sais Seruyus, coym of
dreid; nocht that Eneas dred the ded, bot this maner of ded;
and alsso he that dredis na thyng, nor kan haf na dred, is not
hardy, but fuyll hardy and beistly.

(1.iii.1n = *Aeneid* 1.92: *extemplo Aeneae soluuntur frigore mem-
bra.*)

Ʒe sall ondirstand Virgill in all partis of his proses, quhat maner
or fasson he discrivis ony man at the begynnyng, sa continewys
he of that samin person all thro, and Eneas in all his wark
secludis from all vylle offyce; bot as twychand materris of pyety
or devotion thar labowris he euer wyth the first.

(1.iv.41n = *Aeneid* 1.180: *Aeneas scopulum interea conscendit.*)

That Eneas heyr commendis his self, it is not to be tayn that he
said this for arrogans bot forto schaw hys styll . . .

(1.vi.125n = *Aeneid* 1.378: *sum pius Aeneas*)

These passages, as Douglas acknowledges, partly derive from the
Commentary of Servius. What Douglas says is not strikingly original,
yet it shows him to be interested in the continuing critical controversy about Aeneas, and grappling with the implications of
Virgil's portraiture. The pertinence of some of his remarks even
today may be illustrated by the comments of a modern editor of
Virgil, R. G. Austin, at the same points of book 1. Professor Austin
comments on the 'first naming of Aeneas, almost casually', and the
human aspects of his fear (1.92), and says of *sum pius Aeneas* (1.378):
'this is not a boast; "non est hoc loco adrogantia, sed indicium"
(Servius)'.[86] Another example shows how Douglas's response to
Virgil's 'craft' can be rooted in tradition, and still relevant today.
His remark about the famous first simile in the *Aeneid* (1.148 ff.) displays an interest in iterative imagery which may strike us as curiously
modern:

> Noyte Virgill in this comparison and symilytud, for therin and
> in syk lyke baris he the palm of lawd . . . It is to be considderit
> alsso that our all this wark, he comparis batell tyll spayt or
> dyluge of watyr, or than to suddan fyr, and to nocht ellis.
>
> (1.iii.92n)

Although Coldwell provides no source, this was inspired, I think,
by Servius's comment not on these lines but on *Aeneid* XII.524:
bellum semper incendio et fluminibus comparat.

Douglas's interest in Virgil was not confined to the *Aeneid*. He
knew and admired the *Eclogues* and the *Georgics*. He knew also some
of the spurious poems still thought to be Virgil's, and included in
most contemporary editions: *De Musis*, which he paraphrased in the
Palice of Honour; and *De Venere et Vino*, which he incorporated in IV

Prologue 92–9.[87] Douglas often quotes from Virgil, buttressing his argument with the weight of an esteemed authority: 'O Lord, quhat writis myne author of thi fors in hys Georgikis' (iv Prol 57–8), or 'Myne author eyk in Bucolykis endytis' (v Prol 22). The tone and method resemble his Scriptural citations.

Douglas's admiration for Virgil's shorter poems sometimes led him not to quote but to imitate. Macrobius had devoted books v and vi of the *Saturnalia* to illustrating Virgil's indebtedness to earlier poets, and the doctrine of 'imitation', particularly of classical authors, was advocated by many humanists. Bembo, its foremost champion, said that in poetry Virgil should be one's chief model.[88] Douglas, too, called Virgil the 'patroun' (i.e. pattern or exemplar) of poetry (i Prol 5), and occasionally imitated what he thought, at times mistakenly, was the practice of Virgil. The four lines of verse that list Virgil's three major poems (*Ille ego, qui quondam gracili modulatus auena, etc.*) are the model for Douglas's 'Mensioun of thre of hys pryncipall warkis':

> Lo thus, followand the flowr of poetry,
> The batellys and the man translait haue I;
> Quhilk ʒoir ago in myne ondantit ʒouth,
> Onfructuus idylnes fleand, as I couth,
> Of Lundeys Lufe the Remeid dyd translait;
> And syne off hie Honour the Palyce wrait:
> 'Quhen paill Aurora, with face lamentabill,
> Hir russet mantill bordowrit all with sabill, &c'.
>
> (iv, p. 139)

But Douglas also had an authentic passage of Virgil in his mind. He quotes here the opening lines of his *Palice of Honour*, rather as Virgil half-quoted the opening line of his first *Eclogue* at the close of the *Georgics*:

> illo Vergilium me tempore dulcis alebat
> Parthenope studiis florentem ignobilis oti,
> carmina qui lusi pastorum audaxque iuuenta,
> Tityre, te patulae cecini sub tegmine fagi.
>
> (iv.563–6)

The resemblances between *audaxque iuuenta* and 'ondantit ʒouth', and between *studiis florentem ignobilis oti* and 'Onfructuus idylnes'— Douglas medievalizes the sentiment—confirm that he was indeed 'followand the flowr of poetry'. Virgil's linking of the *Eclogues* and *Georgics* may too have prompted Douglas's cross-reference, already mentioned, between the *Palice of Honour* and the *Eneados*. Douglas's occasional repetition of lines, and transference of lines or half-lines from one work to another (most evident in the relationship between the *Palice of Honour* and Prologue XII) may perhaps be modelled on Virgil's practice.[89]

This type of imitation was usually considered desirable, but the close copying of another poet's phrasing, though often practised, was sometimes condemned. Douglas himself depreciated the 'beggit' (i.e. borrowed) terms in the *Palice of Honour* (131), and condemned the poem as 'bot stouth' and 'thift' (2167). Yet like many others who poured scorn on such 'pilfring' he nonetheless practised close verbal imitation—of other poets besides Virgil—and seemed to regard it as a way of enriching his own style. Douglas acknowledges his indebtedness to Virgil in I Prol 57–61:

Of Helicon so drank thou dry the flude
That of thy copios fouth or plenitude
All mon purches drynk at thy sugurit tun;
So lamp of day thou art and schynand son
All otheris on fors mon thar lycht beg or borrow;

Several of the Prologues shine with a light borrowed from that of Virgil. There are occasional reminiscences of the *Eclogues*, as in

Thy fury, luf, moderis taucht, for dispyte,
Fyle handis in blude of thar ȝong chyldering lyte.
(IV Prol 55–6; cf. *Eclogue* VIII.48–9)

But it is the *Georgics* that Douglas seems to have particularly admired. Virgil's idealized description of the Italian spring in *Georgic* II clearly influenced Prologue XII. Both the idealistic tone and the theme of this Prologue—a celebration of natural rebirth and fecundity—owe something to Virgil. But small details are also closely imitated. Virgil's

parturit almus ager Zephyrique tepentibus auris
laxant arua sinus; superat tener omnibus umor,
inque nouos soles audent se gramina tuto
credere
(II.330–3)

is echoed first in Douglas's

The sulȝe spred hir braid bosum on breid,
Ȝephyrus confortabill inspiratioun
Fortill ressaue law in hyr barm adoun.
(74–6)

and later in

And blisfull blossummys in the blomyt ȝard
Submittis thar hedis in the ȝong sonnys salfgard.
(95–6)

Some earlier lines of Virgil's

et quantum longis carpent armenta diebus

> exigua tantum gelidus ros nocte reponet.
> (11.201−2)

are closely followed in Douglas's

> For callour humour on the dewy nyght,
> Rendryng sum place the gers pilis thar hycht,
> Als far as catal, the lang symmyris day,
> Had in thar pastur eyt and knyp away.
> (91−4)

Douglas shows his familiarity with all four books of the *Georgics*, but he seems to have had a special fondness for this book, alluding to it also in VI Prol 108−9, and 113−18.

In the Middle Ages the *Georgics* seem to have been far less well known than the *Aeneid*. There is no definite evidence, for instance, that they were known to Chaucer.[90] But from the second half of the fifteenth century onwards, particularly among Italian writers, there was a growing appreciation of the *Georgics*, fostered, it has been suggested, by the increasing interest of the age in botany and gardening.[91] Douglas was sensitive to this change in literary taste, and in his admiration for the *Georgics* anticipated Continental poets, such as Luigi Alamanni and Pierre Ronsard. He was well in advance of English poets, who in this respect at least 'followed in the wake of France and even of Scotland'.[92] In England the *Georgics* had their greatest vogue in the eighteenth century. It is striking that several passages that Douglas most admired—if we can judge from echoes and allusions—made a similar appeal to Ronsard, and over two centuries later to James Thomson. These were chiefly splendid set-pieces of description, such as the *laus veris* already referred to; the storm and weather-portents in book 1.311 ff., which are recalled in Douglas's Prologue VII; and the celebration of the power of *saeuus amor* over man and beast (111.209 ff.), which accounts for several stanzas in Prologue IV.

I have tried to illustrate the variety of Douglas's response to Virgil, and the way in which his ideas were often shaped by tradition or directly indebted to other writers. Douglas was not an original thinker, yet he should not be dismissed as commonplace or wholly derivative. In the context of the learned tradition he perhaps has nothing very new to say. Where he is an innovator is in the context of the vernacular tradition: in attempting to correct or inform popular taste, and voice in his own tongue things still usually said only in Latin. This is a role very congenial to him: that of translator. Chaucer and Lydgate before him had lavished praise on Virgil 'Mantuane', but no earlier English poet, as far as I know, discusses Virgil in such detail, or cares to talk about his iterative imagery. No earlier English poet shows such interest in the *Georgics*, or tries at times to transpose into his own poetry something of Virgil's own style. Furthermore, there shines through the sometimes conventional themes and phrasing a genuine warmth and enthusiasm for Virgil: what Douglas himself calls a 'naturall lufe and frendely affectioun' (1 Prol 36). At the end of the *Eneados* Douglas writes

>   And, set that empty be my brayn and dull,
>   I haue translait a volum wondirfull:
>   So profund was this wark at I haue said,
>   Me semyt oft throw the deip sey to waid;
>   And sa mysty vmquhile this poecy,
>   My spreit was reft half deill in extasy,
>   To pyke the sentens as I couth als playn,
>   And bryng it to my purpos, was full fayn;
>   And thus, becaus the mater was onkowth,
>   Not as I suld, I wrait, bot as I couth.
>   (Directioun, 101–10)

This is not just mock-modesty. The lines convey very touchingly the sense of humility and awe instilled in one poet by a far greater one.

The Eneados: *'Text' and 'Sentence'*

In the Prologues to the *Eneados* Douglas, like many other writers of
the fifteenth and sixteenth centuries, lavishes praise on his patron,
voices contempt for his critics, and proclaims that his work will be
'plesand and eyk profitabill' to his readers, enabling them 'To pas
the tyme, and eschew idylnes' (Directioun, 37 and 40). These were
the 'stock motives of a hundred prologues and epilogues'.[1] There is
a conventional element in Douglas's Prologues, but we should not
therefore dismiss all that he says as empty or meaningless. It is
characteristic of Douglas not to flout convention, but to embrace it
and use it meaningfully. What he says about his aims and methods
as a translator of Virgil seems to me largely convincing. Douglas is
not always completely consistent, but there is a reasonable degree
of harmony between what he says and what he does. His practice
does not fundamentally belie his principles. It is important, however, not to take everything he writes at its face value, to read judici-
ously, and to note differences of emphasis and tone. Douglas tells us
the truth, if hardly the whole truth, about the origins of the *Eneados*.

Douglas was well aware that it might be asked 'quhy I dyd this
buke translait' (Directioun, 17), and one answer was that he did it
at the request of his kinsman, Henry, lord Sinclair:

> Quhilk with gret instance diuers tymys seir
> Prayt me translait Virgill or Homeir,
> Quhais plesour suythly as I vndirstude
> As neir coniunct to hys lordschip in blude
> So that me thocht hys request ane command,
> Half disparit this wark I tuke on hand
> Nocht fully grantand nor anys sayand 3ee,
> Bot only to assay quhou it mycht be.
> (1 Prol 87–94)

At the end, Douglas similarly dedicated the *Eneados* to Sinclair, with
the remark, '3he war the caus tharof, full weill 3he wait' (Directioun,
18). This 'request'-theme has a long history—it is found in Quintilian's Epistle to Tryphon, prefixed to the *Institutio Oratoria*—and
it is very common in medieval Prologues. Henryson too professed
to write not from 'vane presumptioun,/Bot be requeist and precept
of ane Lord' (*Fables*, 33–4). The device was partly a 'sort of free

insurance against rebuke',[2] partly a means of proclaiming one's modesty as a writer. Yet it is striking that Douglas does not adopt what E.P.Hammond called 'the regulation tone of humility towards patron or master'.[3] Douglas's tone towards Sinclair is that of one equal to another. There is nothing of Lydgate's self-prostration before Humphrey of Gloucester:

> I shal procede in this translacioun,
> Fro me auoidyng al presumpcioun,
> Lowli submyttyng eueri hour and space,
> Mi reud language to my lordis grace.
> (*Fall of Princes*, 1 Prol 438–41)

Again, there seems to have been some basis for Douglas's portrait of Sinclair as an ardent book-lover:

> Bukis to recollect, to reid and se,
> Has gret delyte as euer had Ptholome.
> (1 Prol 99–100)

Sinclair's ownership of the manuscript containing the *Kingis Quair* has already been mentioned, and he seems to have belonged to a book-loving family, several generations of which contained patrons of letters or book-collectors. Gilbert of the Hay made his translation of the *Buke of the Law of Armys* for Sinclair's grandfather, the 'hye and mychty Prince and worthy lord, William erle of Orknay and of Cathnes, lord Synclere and chancelare of Scotland'.[4] In the mid-sixteenth century another Henry Sinclair, bishop of Ross, assembled a learned library, over a hundred volumes of which still survive.[5] It is plausible therefore that the idea for a translation of the *Aeneid* should have occurred in a friendly conversation with Sinclair. Douglas probably hoped also for some material reward from his patron, who was a prominent landowner; this he is unlikely to have received, since Sinclair died on the field at Flodden.

Sinclair may indeed have been the first 'caus' of the *Eneados*, but Douglas clearly had a wider audience in mind and a more complex purpose:

> Go, wlgar Virgill, to euery churlych wight
> Say, I avow thou art translatit rycht . . .
> Now salt thou with euery gentill Scot be kend,
> And to onletterit folk be red on hight,
> That erst was bot with clerkis comprehend.
> (Exclamatioun, 37 ff.)

The form of this is highly traditional, but the words are carefully chosen, and it is worth considering some of their implications. Douglas's *Eneados* was a 'wlgar Virgill', that is, a 'vernacular Virgil'. He was not writing for 'clerkis', like John Major or Hector Boece, who could express themselves fluently in Latin and had no need of such a translation; nor was he writing principally for the unlettered, though he seems to have hoped that his version might be read aloud to them. Douglas was addressing himself chiefly to 'euery gentill Scot', and what he understood by this phrase may be illustrated by earlier lines addressed to Sinclair in which he hoped

> That Virgill mycht intill our langage be
> Red lowd and playn be ʒour lordschip and me,
> And other gentill companʒeonis, quha sa lyst;
> Nane ar compellit drynk not bot thai haue thryst.
>
> (Directioun, 85–8)

The desire for a select and responsive audience is evident elsewhere:

> Greyn gentill ingynys and breistis curageus,
> Sik are the pepill at ganys best for ws;
> Our werk desiris na lewyt rebalddaill.
>
> (1 Prol 321–3)

Douglas was writing for the cultivated readers of his own language, those who read Chaucer or Dunbar with ease and pleasure, but who were less at home in the world of Virgil, even if they had some acquaintance with Latin. Their picture of the *Aeneid*, in Douglas's opinion, was liable to distortion, and he wrote in order to correct that picture and supply what he thought a truer conception of the *Aeneid*.

Douglas's motives for translating Virgil seem to me interlinked: a deep respect for the *Aeneid*, and a desire to communicate this to a wider audience. Douglas thus shared something of the spirit that inspired the translations of Greek works into Latin, that prompted popular editions of the Latin classics, and that is evident in Erasmus's famous remark about the Scriptures: 'I wish that they might be translated into all tongues. . . . I wish that the countryman might sing them at his plough, the weaver chant them at his loom'.[6] At the beginning of the sixteenth century no major classical work had been translated into English, yet translations from the classics into the vernacular had begun to appear in France and other European countries.[7] In 1500 Octavien de Saint Gelais, like Douglas a courtier and churchman, dedicated his translation of the *Aeneid* to Louis XII. (The date of the first printed edition, 1509, makes it possible that Douglas might have seen this work, but there is no conclusive proof that he used it.)[8] Douglas was among the first to see the need for such translation, and to respond to it. His *Eneados* was the precursor to a host of famous translations—among them Golding's Ovid, North's Plutarch, and Chapman's Homer. Many other Scots contemporary with Douglas must have shared his range of literary experience, but Douglas was unusually responsive to the popularizing mood of the time, acting as a bridge or intermediary between the world of learning and the world of the court and vernacular poetry. His 'wlgar Virgill' attempted to convey to the less learned how Virgil was read and interpreted by the 'clerkis' of his time. In order to achieve this Douglas tried to give his readers, in so far as it was possible, a Scottish equivalent not simply of the *Aeneid* but of the learned apparatus which accompanied it in most contemporary editions of Virgil.

Virgil was consistently one of the most popular of the classical poets. His works were printed and re-printed; over a hundred separate editions are listed in Mambelli's *Gli Annali delle Edizioni Virgiliane* (Florence 1954) between the *editio princeps* (? 1469) and 1512. Moreover, manuscripts continued to be copied and illuminated long after the introduction of printing.[9] The editions of this time differ strikingly from modern editions of Virgil. On the most elementary level, they have no line-numbering, and in some of the earliest editions there is no pagination either. The pampered modern reader does not find them at all easy to consult. Their canon, too, is different. The *Opera Virgilii* at this time included not only the three major works and the Virgilian Appendix, but a number of short poems no longer regarded as authentic. As for the text of the *Aeneid*, this is often surprisingly different from that we read today in scholarly editions, such as those of H.R.Fairclough (Loeb Classical Library 1934), R.Sabbadini (Rome 1937), and R.A.B.Mynors (Oxford Classical Texts 1972). Modern editions base their text of the *Aeneid* on three main authorities, the Codex Mediceus (fifth century), the Codex Palatinus (fourth or fifth century), and the Codex Romanus (fifth century); this is supplemented by fragments (such as the Schedae Vaticanae), by a group of later manuscripts, and by readings preserved in the grammarians and the commentary of Servius. Modern editors record the most important early variants in their textual apparatus, but it is no part of their purpose to indicate the host of further variants, many of them obvious corruptions, which over the centuries have entered the textual tradition of Virgil. Early printed editions incorporate many of these variants into their text, usually without comment. In addition, they sometimes insert or omit whole lines, or complete Virgil's famous half-lines; they sometimes punctuate differently from modern editors; they may run together words which should be separate, or break up words which should be united; and they often spell place names and personal names in a manner very different from that accepted today.

This clearly has an important bearing on our evaluation of

Douglas's skill and accuracy as a translator. Many apparent mis-translations in the *Eneados* can be shown to originate not in Douglas's ignorance but in the peculiarities of his Latin text. Douglas's eccentric-seeming spelling of Virgilian names—'Thersander' (II. v.22) for *Thessandrus* (11.261), 'Athamas' (II.v.23) for *Acamas* (11.262), 'Lacon' (x.vii.125) for *Ladona* (x.413), 'Choreus' (xi.xv.1) for *Chloreus* (x1.768)—often derives from the spelling customary in the editions of his time (e.g. *Thersandrus, Athamas, Lacona, Choreus*). Again, some of the words and phrases that seem to a modern reader to be interpolated by Douglas in fact reveal Douglas's fidelity to the text he had in front of him. Douglas's line describing Polyphemus, 'About hys hals a quhissil hung had he' (111.x.11), corresponds to *de collo fistula pendet*, a 'completion' of Virgil's half-line at 111.661. So too with 1x.iii.104–5:

> Quhou mony steill stammyt bargis that ayr
> Stude by the costis syde, or thai war fyryt.

Douglas is here translating *Quot prius aeratae steterant ad litora prorae* (1x.121), a line usually preserved by sixteenth-century editors, but relegated by most modern editors to the footnotes. Some examples from book x11 will illustrate how Douglas, when he diverges from the text of a modern edition of the *Aeneid*, is often translating readings that had scholarly acceptance in the sixteenth century. The Latin text is that of the o.c.t. edition. The variant that Douglas seems to have had before him is placed in square brackets; it may be found in editions of widely different character (e.g. Ascensius, 1501; Brant, 1502; Aldus, 1505).[10] Italics are used to identify the words or phrase being compared.

> *Rutilianys*, hynt 3our wapynnys and follow me
> (xII.v.98)
>   me, me duce ferrum
> corripite, o *miseri* [*rutuli*].
> (xII.260–1)
> *Quham* tho (allace, gret piete was to se!)
> The quhirland quheill and spedy swyft extre
> Smate doun to grond.
> (xII.vi.167–9)
> *cum* [*quem*] rota praecipitem et procursu concitus axis
> impulit effunditque solo.
> (xII.379–80)
> For feir the bestis dum all standis by,
> And all in dowt squelys the 3ong ky,
> Quha salbe master of the *catal* all.
> (xII.xii.59–61)

stat pecus omne metu mutum, mussantque iuuencae
quis *nemori* [*pecori*] imperitet.
   (XII.718–19)
And tharon eik the clathis *bekend* vpstent.
   (XII.xii.185)
   et *uotas* [*notas*] suspendere uestis.
   (XII.769)
For, *gif I mortal war, now, now* suythly,
Thir sa gret dolouris mycht I end inhy,
And with my reuthfull brother go withall.
   (XII.xiii.207–9)
   possem tantos finire dolores
nunc certe, et misero fratri comes ire per umbras!
immortalis [*iam mortalis*] [11] ego?
   (XII.880–2)

Douglas professes great concern for textual accuracy. It is this which underlies all his criticisms of Caxton; and the word 'text' occurs repeatedly in Prologue I (e.g. 171, 243, 314, 347, 352, 357, 485). He asserts the duty of a translator to follow his original as closely as possible:

Quha is attachit ontill a staik, we se,
May go na ferthir bot wreil about that tre:
Rycht so am I to Virgillis text ybund,
I may nocht fle les than my falt be fund.
   (I Prol 297–300)

It is very important therefore to recognize—and all too easy to forget—how different from ours was Douglas's text of Virgil. Again and again, when he appears to mistranslate, he is making an accurate translation of a defective text. I have here provided only a small sample of the evidence which elsewhere I have discussed and illustrated far more fully. [12]

These early editions of Virgil differed also among themselves. The best known and most admired today are those published by the Venetian scholar-printer, Aldus Manutius. [13] His Virgil of 1501 was the first of a celebrated series of editions of the Greek and Latin classics. His famous italic type is clear and visually attractive, and his text is considered good for its time. Aldus introduced the idea of smaller, less expensive, more portable editions of the classics. His Virgils were not provided with commentaries. They were pocket editions for those who knew Virgil well, and were not primarily intended either for beginners or for learned scholars. Aldus, however, was an innovator. The most characteristic edition of this time was a large and bulky folio. The text of Virgil, in the centre of the page, was surrounded by a mass of commentary which takes up far more room than the text. The closest modern parallel is perhaps the Variorum edition of Shakespeare. Although these large folio Virgils have a generic likeness, it should not be assumed that they are identical either in text, choice of commentaries, or the audience for whom they were designed. Many were *Opera cum quinque commentariis*, that is, they were furnished with the ancient commentaries of Servius and Tiberius Donatus, and the 'modern' commentaries of Landino, Mancinelli, and Calderini. Some editions, however, were intended specially for beginners. Ascensius's Virgil, first published at Paris in 1501, was of this type. The text of the *Aeneid* was accompanied not only by the commentaries of Servius, Donatus, and Beroaldus's annotations on Servius, but by Ascensius's own combination of commentary and paraphrase, which he referred to disparagingly (on the title-page of the *Aeneid*) as *familiarissima . . . elucidatione atque ordinis contextu*. Ascensius's commentary was indeed elementary, yet its popularity in the first half of the sixteenth century shows that it supplied a need. Ascensius was a teacher before he became a printer-publisher, and the prefaces to some of his other works, together with his *commentarii familiares*, reveal his conscious efforts to bring the Latin classics to a wider audience. P. Renouard, contrasting him with Aldus, says that he was 'surtout un divulgateur, et son effort tendait à faciliter aux débutants l'étude des auteurs classiques pour leur permettre d'apprendre le latin aux meilleures sources de latinité'.[14] Sebastian Brant, the poet and humanist, adopted another method to help the less learned reader of Virgil. In 1502 he published the first illustrated edition of Virgil (printed at Strasbourg by Johann Gruninger). The numerous highly detailed woodcuts that accompanied the *Aeneid* were more than embellishment. They illustrated nearly every important event in the poem, and were intended, as Brant makes clear, to elucidate the text:

> Virgilium exponant alii sermone diserto
> Et calamo pueris tradere et ore iuvet.
> Pictura agresti voluit Brant atque tabellis
> Edere eum indoctis rusticolisque viris.[15]

Can we identify the particular text of the *Aeneid* that Douglas translated? The task might seem impossibly difficult, considering the large number of manuscripts and editions available when Douglas was writing. Douglas never mentions what text he used, yet various clues exist which serve to narrow the field considerably. He tells us that he worked on the translation for approximately eighteen months, and completed it in July 1513 (Tyme, space, and dait). It seems unlikely therefore that Douglas used an edition published later than

1512. Furthermore, he translated the 'Thirteenth' Book of Maphaeus Vegius, a fifteenth-century supplement, which is frequently but not invariably found in the Virgils of this period. Douglas says also of his Virgil that 'the volum was so huge' (Exclamatioun, 22), which seems to exclude the pocket-sized Aldines. The most valuable clue, however, is Douglas's approving mention of Ascensius (vɪ Prol 73), and the fact that he made close and continuous use of Ascensius's commentary on Virgil.[16] This commentary was not published separately; to begin with, it was found only in Ascensius's editions of Virgil. It seems likely therefore that if Douglas used the commentary he would also use the text to which it was so intimately related.

Ascensius's edition of Virgil was extremely popular. First published in 1501, it was re-printed at Paris for Ascensius himself in 1507 and 1512. In 1517 a pirated edition was published at Lyons, in which the printer Jacques Sacon combined Ascensius's text and commentary with the fine series of woodcuts that had first appeared in Sebastian Brant's Virgil of 1502. (It is this edition of 1517 to which Coldwell refers in his Introduction and Notes, and, taking it to be printed in 1507, mistakenly implies was early enough to have been used by Douglas.)[17] It is important to be accurate in such matters, because Ascensius's editions of Virgil differ in pagination and spelling, and—more significantly—in actual readings. If Douglas finished his translation in 1513 there were available to him three editions printed for Ascensius himself: 1501, 1507, and 1512. It seems unlikely that he used 1512, if (as he asserts) he spent 18 months on the translation. The colophon of 1512 is dated June, which would give Douglas barely a year, even if one assumes that he received a copy straight from the press. My study of the variant readings in 1501, 1507 and 1512, although far from exhaustive, points to 1501 as being the edition that Douglas used. At several places in his translation Douglas's choice of words suggests that he had in front of him a Latin reading that may be found in *some* but not *all* of Ascensius's editions. The reading that corresponds to Douglas's wording is invariably found in 1501, but only in one or other of 1507 and 1512. One of these variants accounts for the peculiar form *Cymynyk* in

> And thai that in Flavynya feildis dwell,
> Or that wonnys besyde the layk or well
> Of Cymynyk, vndre the montane bra,
> Or ʒit amang the schawys of Capua—
>   (vɪɪ.xi.137–40)

This corresponds to

> hi Soractis habent arces Flauiniaque arua
> et *Cimini cum* monte lacum lucosque Capenos.
>   (VII.696–7)

Small thought Douglas's form was an error and normalized it to 'Cymynus', but the error was Ascensius's, who read *Ciminicum* in 1501 and 1507. At another point Douglas translates *eductum Martis luco* (IX.584) as 'Fostyrrit he was and vpbrocht tendirly/Within his *moderis* hallowyt schaw' (IX.ix.129–30). This seems to be a case where Ascensius changed his mind about the correct reading: in 1501 and 1507 he printed *matris* (which Douglas translates), but 1512 and later editions have *martis*. Douglas also seems to mis-translate Virgil's

> pedes et Lycius processerat Agis
>   (X.751)

as

> Aganys hym than went a *man of Arge*,
> Hait Lycyus, bodyn with speir and targe.
>   (X.xii.153–4)

But Douglas is translating a text which had *Argis* (so 1501 and 1512) instead of the reading *Agis* (so 1507). There is another piece of evidence, which seems to point, even more definitely, to 1501 as being Douglas's text. This is the form *Lybibe* in

> The dangerus schaldis and cost vppykit we,
> With al hys blynd rolkis, of Lybibe.
>   (III.x.99–100)

This corresponds to

> et uada dura lego saxis *Lilybeia* caecis
>   (III.706)

The error, however, is not Douglas's. The peculiar spelling *libybeia* occurs in 1501, although it is corrected to *lilybeia* in subsequent editions of Ascensius's Virgil.

Some scholars have argued that Douglas used Brant's Virgil of 1502. As first expounded by Edmund Schmidt this argument was unconvincing, since the readings that he cited to prove Douglas's dependence on Brant were present also in Ascensius.[18] More recently scholars have modified the argument. O. L. Jiriczek was aware that Douglas had used Ascensius's commentary and that this was not included in Brant's edition; he suggested that Douglas might 'well be credited with having had access to more than one edition'.[19] This is plausible, but convincing evidence has yet to be put forward that Brant's edition was one that Douglas used. Miss Florence Ridley, who has discussed the subject recently, suggests that in book IV at least Douglas used Brant as well as Ascensius.[20] Her chief piece of evidence, however, is that Douglas translated a line omitted from Ascensius's editions, *instauratque choros mixtique altaria circum* (IV.145):

> Renewand ryngis and dansys, mony a rowt;
> Mixt togiddir, his altaris standing about.
>
> (IV.iv.31–2)

This might be construed as an argument against Douglas's use of Ascensius, but why should it point so specifically to his use of Brant, when many other editions, if correct, must have contained this line? In fact, although Virgil's line is omitted from Ascensius's text, it is found in his commentary together with an explanatory paraphrase. Douglas seems to be following the commentary at this point, even when discrepant with the text, as he occasionally does elsewhere in his translation. There are numerous other divergencies between the texts of Ascensius and Brant, some far from 'insignificant'.[21] After studying these variants and relating them to Douglas's translation, I see no clear evidence that he used Brant. I have found no reading in Douglas that could have originated only in Brant, whereas again and again he is clearly translating a reading that is not in Brant although it occurs in all editions of Ascensius. Only a selection of the evidence can be given here. Speaking of Polyphemus, Douglas says:

> For he is vgsum and grysly forto se,
> *Hutyt to speke of,* and *aucht not nemmyt be.*
>
> (III.ix.61–2)

This corresponds to Virgil's

> nec uisu facilis nec dictu adfabilis ulli.
>
> (III.621)

The italicized words appear to mistranslate *adfabilis*; what they translate is Ascensius's reading *effabilis* (Brant has *affabilis*). Again, Douglas's lines on Discord,

> Quham followit Bellona of batell,
> With *hir kynd cosyng,* the scharp scurgis fell.
>
> (VIII.xii.71–2)

appear to be a lamentable mistranslation of

> et scissa gaudens uadit Discordia palla,
> quam *cum sanguineo* sequitur Bellona flagello.
>
> (VIII.702–3)

Douglas is translating Ascensius's *consanguineo* (a misreading shared also by the Aldines); Brant has the correct *cum sanguineo*. Virgil's *uolat igneus aequore Tarchon* (XI.746) appears in Douglas as

> This Tarchon, ardent as the fyry levyn,
> Flaw furth swyft as a fowle vp *towart hevyn.*
>
> (XI.xiv.51–2)

Brant has the correct *aequore*; the italicized phrase in Douglas translates Ascensius's reading, *ethere*. The illustrations I have chosen may suggest that Ascensius's text is always inferior to that of Brant. This is not so. But it is necessary to do a partial injustice to Ascensius in order to be fair to Douglas; to show how the oddities in his translation sometimes result from his very faithfulness to his text.

It seems unlikely that Douglas used one edition of Virgil and no other. There are signs of his familiarity with the *Aeneid* in the *Palice of Honour*, and a man with his education and interest in poetry would probably have possessed a copy of Virgil long before Ascensius's edition of 1501 appeared. There is indeed one definite piece of evidence that he consulted, possibly at a late stage, an edition other than Ascensius's, since he quotes from Landino's commentary in his own Comment.[22] In the translation itself there are a few cases where Douglas seems to translate readings that are not present in Ascensius's text of 1501. Sometimes the difficulty is resolved by consulting the commentary; Douglas found variant readings there which he preferred. In 11.x.99 Douglas speaks of the 'weirlyke weid' of Pallas Athene. This may seem an odd translation of *nimbo*, 'cloud enveloping a god or goddess' (Ascensius's reading at 11.616); in fact it corresponds not to this but to *chlamyde militari*, Ascensius's gloss for the variant *limbo*, which he mentions immediately after *nimbo* in his commentary.[23] This practice of Douglas's does not solve all the problems. At XIII.xi.17, for instance, Douglas's 'faderis' corresponds to Ascensius's *partes* (XIII.601), and it looks as if Douglas is translating a form with transposed consonants, *patres*. Nonetheless there is a mass of evidence, to be found in all books of the *Eneados*, that leads me to conclude that although Douglas may have been acquainted with other editions of Virgil, when he came to translate the *Aeneid* he chose Ascensius's edition of 1501 as his working text. Many places in Douglas's own text hitherto dark are illuminated when set beside Ascensius's Virgil; many 'howlers' vanish, and Douglas emerges as a responsible, if not a perfect, translator, striving to make the best sense he could of a far from ideal text.

So far I have been principally concerned with the text of the *Aeneid* as Douglas would find it in contemporary editions, and more particularly those of Ascensius. I wish now to show how the *Eneados* was affected by other features of those editions: their contents, their lay-out, and above all, the bulky commentary that accompanied the *Aeneid*. All these influenced Douglas both in what he himself chose to include in his 'wlgar Virgill' and in the way he presented it. Most important of all, the practice of the commentators profoundly in-

fluenced Douglas in his understanding and interpretation of the
Aeneid, and even in his methods as a translator.

Immediately preceding the first book of the *Eneados* are thirteen
couplets describing 'the Contentis of Euery Buke Followyng':

> The first contenys quhou the prynce Ene
> And Troianys war dryve onto Cartage cite.

> The secund buke schawis the finale ennoy,
> The gret myscheif and subuersioun of Troy.

> The thryd tellith quhou fra Troys cite
> The Troianys careit war throu owt the see.

> The ferd rehersis of fair Queyn Dido
> The dowbill woundis and the mortale wo . . .
>   (11, p.18)

Douglas's editors have made no comment on these rather pedestrian
lines. They are not Douglas's invention, however—apart from the
thirteenth couplet—but a fairly close rendering of the so-called
monosticha argumenta, a set of twelve one-line summaries of the individual books of the *Aeneid*, which were regularly included in
contemporary editions, and usually placed in the same position as
Douglas's. Two versions of the *monosticha argumenta* occur; Douglas
translates the fairly common version printed by Ascensius:

> Quę contineant duodecim aeneidos libri.

> Primus habet libycam veniant vt troes in vrbem.
> Edocet excidium troię clademque secundus.
> Tertius a troia vectos canit ęquore teucros.
> Quartus item misere duo vulnera narrat elissę.
> Manibus ad tumulum quinto celebrantur honores.
> Aeneam memorat visentem tartara sextus.
> In phrygas italiam bello iam septimus armat.
> Dat simul ęneae socios octauus: et arma.
> Daunius expugnat nono noua moenia troiae.
> Exponit decimus tuscorum in littore pugnas.
> Vndecimo rutuli superantur morte camillae.
> Vltimus imponit bello turni nece finem.[24]

Douglas's desire to be faithful both to Virgil and to contemporary
scholarship is illustrated by his dealings with the four preliminary lines:

> Ille ego qui quondam gracili modulatus auena
> carmen, et egressus siluis uicina coegi
> ut quamuis auido parerent arua colono
> gratum opus agricolis, at nunc horrentia Martis . . .

Few classical scholars now think these lines were written by Virgil
himself; it has been suggested that they were intended as an inscription

beneath a portrait of Virgil forming a frontispiece to a copy of the *Aeneid*.[25] Douglas, however, probably accepted the story told by Aelius Donatus, that they were authentic but rejected by Virgil's literary executors. He therefore made a fairly close translation of the lines, and placed them not at the opening of his *Eneados* but at the end of the First Prologue (504–11): 'Me thocht Virgill begouth on this maner: / I the ilk vmquhile that in the small ait reid / Tonyt my sang. . .'. Douglas thus followed the lead of Servius, who had preserved the lines in his preface to the *Aeneid*, and of editors such as Ascensius, who printed them at a slight remove from the text itself. This double desire to include as much of Virgil as possible and to follow the pattern of the Latin editions is apparent also in Douglas's translation of Virgil's Epitaph, *Mantua me genuit*. This appears at the very end of the *Eneados*, after Book XIII (IV, p.195). It is placed similarly in many Virgils of the time.

In addition to the twelve books of the *Aeneid* Douglas translated the so-called Thirteenth book, a supplement describing the marriage of Aeneas and Lavinia and Aeneas's apotheosis, written by the Italian humanist, Maphaeus Vegius. This may be considered an inconsistency in Douglas—the First Prologue, after all, boasts of his determination to stay close to the text of Virgil—yet the decision is not surprising in the context of Douglas's time and what we know of his literary intentions. Maphaeus Vegius's *Supplementum* was included not only in Ascensius's editions but in most other printed editions of Virgil from 1471 (the Ambergau edition at Venice) until the middle of the seventeenth century.[26] The only other translation of the whole *Aeneid* into English during the sixteenth century — that started by Thomas Phaer and finished by Thomas Twyne (published between 1558 and 1584)—resembles Douglas's in including the Thirteenth book. Douglas translated this book—as he had translated the *monosticha argumenta*—because it regularly accompanied the *Aeneid* in the Latin editions of his day. Nonetheless, for Douglas to include it obviously involved a clash between his aim at scholarly completeness and his ideal of fidelity to Virgil. He takes great pains to make it clear that book XIII was not written by Virgil himself; the rubric states that it was 'ekit to Virgill be Mapheus Vegius'. There are signs that Douglas had a divided mind about the propriety of including it. Prologue XIII—in which Douglas dreams that Maphaeus appears to him—dramatizes his doubts and scruples most effectively. Maphaeus complains that 'to my buke ȝit lyst the tak na heid' (XIII Prol 106). Douglas replies

    syndry haldis, fader, trastis me,
  Ȝour buke ekit but ony necessite,

As to the text accordyng neuer a deill,
Mair than langis to the cart the fift quheill.
    (XIII Prol 115–8)
Douglas here recalls the criticisms of Ascensius; his last image is
lifted from Ascensius's Prologue to this book: *vnde frustra quidam
quadrigis rotam quintam addidit*. Douglas's hesitations recall the fluc-
tuations of a greater scholar than Ascensius. Aldus Manutius omitted
the *Supplementum* from his first edition of Virgil (1501), but included
it somewhat reluctantly in the 1505 edition— *Vegii praeterea libellum
diuinis Aeneidos libris inuiti adiunximus, sed obsequendum fuit quibusdam*.[27]
In his much-praised edition of 1514, however, he purged it and other
offending matter so that 'nothing alien should defile the majesty of the
divine poet.'[28] In his mixed reactions to the Thirteenth book Douglas
was thus very much a man of his time.

One striking characteristic of the *Eneados* is the division of each
book into what Douglas himself calls 'chapters' (see epigraphs to 11.ix;
v.vi and ix). The number of chapters a book contains may vary
between ten and seventeen, and their length varies considerably
(between 100 and 230 lines). This parcelling up of Virgil's text may
seem odd and insensitive today, yet it is in part a sign of Douglas's
consideration for his readers, a device to help them find their way
about a bulky volume. There is no line-numbering in the manuscripts
of Douglas's *Eneados*, any more than in contemporary editions of the
Aeneid. Anyone who has tried to locate a particular line in one of the
Scottish manuscripts is thus grateful for the existence of these
chapters.

Douglas must have been familiar with the way in which earlier
vernacular writers had divided large-scale works into books and
chapters. The practice is found in prose writers, such as John Ireland
or Caxton, and in poets such as Lydgate.[29] The French translators of
the fourteenth century, such as Nicholas Oresme, also divided their
work into chapters.[30] Nonetheless, I think Douglas had a model closer
at hand: Ascensius's treatment of the text of the *Aeneid*. Many
sixteenth-century editors of Virgil divided the text into 'blocks' or
sections, but they do not always divide the text at the same points.
Sebastian Brant's blocks are quite different from Ascensius's, and less
logical. Douglas's chapter divisions frequently—but not, it must be
stressed, invariably—correspond to Ascensius's divisions of the text.
The relationship is rarely one-to-one, since Ascensius's sections are
shorter than Douglas's chapters. Douglas most often uses two sections for a chapter, but sometimes when they are very short he uses
four. Book IV of the *Eneados* may illustrate this. Of its twelve chapters
two correspond exactly to single blocks in Ascensius; five correspond

to two blocks in Ascensius; one corresponds to four of Ascensius's blocks. Four chapters only do not correspond in this way, and break up Ascensius's units. It should be noted that Ascensius's sections are not arbitrary or meaningless. They represent sense-units in Virgil, and perhaps teaching-units also. In this respect Douglas, even when following Ascensius, is not necessarily distorting Virgil's sense. The logical nature of many if not all of Douglas's chapters can be seen from the way in which they frequently relate to the paragraphing in modern editions of Virgil. Thus in book iv of the *Eneados* all but two of its twelve chapters open at lines that start new paragraphs in the o.c.t. edition of Virgil. Yet it is undeniable that Douglas's chapters impose hard and definite divisions upon the different books of the *Aeneid*, thus weakening their continuous and unified effect. More will be said of these chapters later.

Douglas's chapters are preceded by couplets, which give a brief and rather bald summary of their contents. These chapter-headings have, of course, no equivalent in Virgil. They might be considered a form of medieval rubric—in several manuscripts of the *Eneados* the headings are made more distinctive by being written in red ink. It was not uncommon for the different sections of long narrative poems to be accompanied by prose explanations—they occur in several manuscripts of Lydgate's *Troy Book*;[31] but the use of verse for this purpose seems to have been less common. Douglas's headings may be compared to the quatrains that precede each canto of Spenser's *Faerie Queene*, but there is an earlier and closer parallel in Wyntoun's *Original Chronicle*, which similarly divides each book into chapters and summarizes their contents in octosyllabic couplets.[32] Douglas may thus be following a native tradition, yet it seems to me likely that here too he recalled the usage of the editors of Virgil, and in part modelled his practice on theirs. In them he would find that each book of the *Aeneid* was accompanied by a metrical summary: apart from the *monosticha argumenta* there existed the fuller ten-line summaries, or *decasticha argumenta*. In addition, Ascensius's commentary regularly provided at the beginning of each section of text a brief summary of its contents. Ascensius often began with the words *Docet quomodo*. . . . With this one may compare Douglas's frequent opening, 'Quhow':

> Quhou dame Iuno tyll Eolus cuntre went . . .
>
> Quhou that Ene was with the tempest schaik . . .
>
> (i.ii, iii, and passim)

It would be difficult to prove that Douglas was definitely indebted to Ascensius, because the prose summaries are much fuller than Douglas's brief couplets. Nonetheless, the following passages may illustrate how similar Douglas sometimes is to Ascensius in method

and contents. (In each case Ascensius is commenting on the section of
Virgil's text that corresponds to Douglas's chapter.)

> Quhou Eneas ambassatouris dyd send
> To Kyng Latyn with rewardis and commend.
> (VII.iii)

> Docet quomodo legationem instituit ęneas et missis centum
> oratoribus ad Latinum regem...
> (Ascensius on VII.152 ff.)

> Heir comptis Virgill the pepil of Tuscane,
> Quhilkis with Eneas com to the bargane.
> (x.iv)

> Recitat hoc loco quos Aeneas ex Ehtruria secum aduexerat
> socios ...
> (Ascensius on x.163 ff.)

> Eneas feghtis and Turnus, hand for hand,
> And Turnus fled, for he had brokkyn his brand.
> (XII.xii)

> Recitat congressum Turni et Aeneę in quo gladio turni effracto
> in fugam versus est ...
> (Ascensius on XII.697 ff.)

Douglas clearly wished also to give his readers something similar
to the commentaries that he found in the Latin editions. One way of
doing this was to incorporate such material in his Prologues. I have
already discussed how Douglas uses some Prologues to correct what
he considered false opinions concerning Virgil. Such interpretative
material is found in the Latin commentaries, beside more strictly
grammatical notes. Douglas sometimes alludes to specific remarks
made by Ascensius (VI Prol 73) or Servius (VI Prol 27–30).
Douglas's moralizing Prologue IV, with its reflections on the 'fors'
of love, its attack on the 'subtell wilis' of lust, and its allusion to
Augustine weeping over Dido, has a train of thought very similar
to Ascensius's introductory remarks on *Aeneid* IV:

> In hoc quarto libro ... describit poeta vim amoris ... Id autem
> facit prudens et commodus poeta, quo mortales animos ab
> amorum illecebris auertat, cum nemo sit a venereis laqueis tutus,
> nisi qui omne obiectum procul habuerit et carnis luxum
> domuerit: Cum ergo in toto opere tum hic poeta et delectat et
> prodest plurimum ... iucunda est huius libri lectio, vt diuus
> Augustinus sese ad lachrymas compulsum Didonis querela
> confiteatur.

The closest approximation to the form of the Latin commentaries, however, is the brief series of marginal notes that accompany
Prologue I and the first seven chapters of book I. This appears in

full only in the Cambridge Manuscript of the *Eneados*, but I think there can be no doubt that it is the work referred to by Douglas himself:

I haue alsso a schort comment compilyt
To expon strange histouris and termys wild.
        (Directioun, 141–2)

There is ample internal evidence that this Comment was composed by Douglas himself. The hortatory tone—'Now I beseik ȝow, curtas redaris'—resembles that of Douglas's more didactic Prologues; and phrases such as 'my Palyce of Honour' (1.i.13 n), 'my proheme' (1.iii.92 n), or 'my proloug of the x buyk' (1.v.2 n) bear the mark of the author not of a scribe or later reader. The only evidence inconsistent with this is found in two notes on 1 Prologue 425 and 437, which criticize Douglas's 'argument' and refer to him in the third person: 'Heir he argouis better than befoir'. These might be interpreted as showing Douglas engaged in debate with himself. I am inclined to regard them as an interpolation, perhaps the reaction of Matthew Geddes, the scribe of the Cambridge Manuscript. Some scholars have regarded this commentary as Douglas's holograph addition;[33] to me it appears written in the same hand as the text itself, careful and orderly, and in the same colour of ink. As to the date of the Comment, I take it to have been composed before the Directioun, but after Douglas had finished the translation of the *Aeneid*, since it contains many references to the later books and Prologues.

Although brief and perhaps unfinished, Douglas's Comment is clearly modelled on the line-by-line Latin commentaries. He discusses much the same range of topics. He uses it, as I have already shown, to interpret the hidden 'sentence' of Virgil. He devotes much space to explaining historical and geographical allusions. He also comments on the pronunciation of words: 'Iulus is thre sillabis, spellit with i per se and v per se' (1.v.68 n); on their etymology—he follows Servius in his explanation of the meaning of *oppetere* (1 Prol 350 n) and *Achates* (1.vi.15 n); and on the significance of a complex word such as *pius* (1.vi.125 n). Many notes have specific sources, and Douglas sometimes takes pains to point out his debts: 'as sais Seruius' . . . 'as sais Boccas' (1.iii.85 n). Yet although some notes follow the wording of Ascensius very closely, Douglas at no point in the Comment mentions Ascensius, as if he perhaps did not regard his name as sufficiently authoritative. Sometimes indeed Douglas cites an esteemed author, such as St Augustine, and makes no mention of the commentator who seems to be his real source. Thus he comments on Jupiter's prophecy that the Roman *imperium* would be eternal:

Sanct Augustyn in his volum clepit De Verbis Domini, in the
xxix sermond, mokkis at this word, sayand: 'ȝit is not the end,
and the empyr is translat to the Almanys. Bot Virgill was crafty,'
sais he, 'that wald not on his awyn byhalf rehers thir wordis, bot
maid Iupiter pronunce thaim—and as he is a half fenȝeit god,
swa is his prophecy.'

> (1.v.85 n)

This particular note seems to have been supplied to Douglas by
Ascensius, who in his discussion of *Aeneid* 1.278–9 wrote:

numerus nondum completus est cum iam imperium in ger-
manos translatum videamus . . . De qua re diuus augustinus, de
verbis domini ser. xxix ita loquitur . . . [Augustine imagines Virgil
to reply when taunted with the inaccuracy of his prophecies]
ego scio. Sed quid facerem, qui romanis verba vendebam, nisi
hac adulatione aliquid promitterem, quod falsum erat? Et
tamen in hoc cautus fui: quando dixi imperium sine fine: iouem
ipsorum induxi qui hoc diceret: non ex persona mea dixerim
falsa: sed ioui imposui falsitatis personam. Sicut deus falsus
erat: ita vates mendax erat.

So too Douglas purports to be quoting direct from Varro (1.vi.
132n), when his note derives from Servius on *Aeneid* 1.382. We
should not be over-contemptuous of Douglas for practices which
are not unknown today. Sometimes they provide a scholarly short
cut, and do not necessarily prove that Douglas was without firsthand
acquaintance with the work to which he alludes.

Douglas refers to another commentator, Cristoforo Landino:

Landinus sais also of this Anthenor that, for his sone Glaucus
followit Paris, he depechit him of him, and for that sam caus,
quhen he was aftyr slan by Agamenon, he maid na duyll for his
ded.

> (1.v.28 n)

This translates fairly literally Landino's note on Antenor (1.242):
*Glaucum filium: quia sequebatur Paridem abdicauisse: eundemque ab
Agamemnone cęsum non fleuisse.*[34] Landino's commentary on Virgil was
quite separate from his *Quaestiones Camaldulenses*. It was one of the
quinque commentarii, and from 1487 appeared in many editions of
Virgil, including Brant's. Ascensius occasionally quotes Landino's
opinions in his own commentary, but does not print him in full.
Douglas's references to this commentary thus constitute the most
definite evidence that he indeed consulted an edition other than
Ascensius's. Since Landino was so popular it is difficult to track
down the particular edition that Douglas used; and since the Comment appears to have been something of an afterthought or 'extra',

it does not necessarily follow that Landino was available to Douglas when he made the translation.

Lastly but most important of all, the translation itself incorporates much that in the Latin editions of Douglas's time appeared in the commentaries. (A modern translator would probably be more likely to put such material in his Notes.) Douglas's *Eneados* thus sometimes appears to be translation and running commentary, all in one. This is no accident. It springs from Douglas's central concern with rendering as accurately as possible not just the 'text' of the *Aeneid* but the 'sentence' or inner meaning. By 'sentence' here I mean not the larger moral or allegorical significance of the *Aeneid* (which Douglas scrupulously reserves for discussion in the Prologues or Comment), but the meaning of individual words or phrases, which Douglas professes to translate as precisely, fully, and unambiguously as possible:

> Sum tyme the text mon haue ane expositioun,
> Sum tyme the collour will caus a litill additioun,
> And sum tyme of a word I mon mak thre,
> In witnes of this term 'oppetere' . . .
> God wait in Virgill ar termys mony a hundir
> Fortill expone maid me a felloun blundir.
> To follow alanerly Virgilis wordis, I weyn,
> Thar suld few vndirstand me quhat thai meyn.
>   (1 Prol 347–50; 389–92)

This approach to translation seems to have sprung ultimately from classical and medieval methods of tackling a text in the classroom, a combination of paraphrase, translation, and explanatory gloss.[35] Douglas himself connects his concern with 'expositioun' with the methods used in the schools. At one point he addresses directly those who 'wald Virgill to childryn expone':

> For quha lyst note my versys, one by one,
> Sall fynd tharin hys sentens euery deill,
> And al maste word by word, that wait I weill.
>   (Directioun, 44–6)

Douglas here alludes to the old dictum, traditionally associated with the names of Jerome and Gregory, that one should translate not word for word, but sense for sense: *non verbum e verbo, sed sensum exprimere de sensu.*[36] This principle was often invoked by medieval translators, usually to justify a fairly free translation.[37] In Prologue 1 395 ff. Douglas, too, had vigorously rejected the 'word for word' method, yet this later passage is not necessarily inconsistent with what he said earlier. As a translator, he rejected the extremes of

The Eneados: 'Text' and 'Sentence'

literalism yet tried to stay close to his text. His *Eneados* was an attempt to convey something of the wealth of 'sentence' implicit in the words of Virgil.

Douglas was certainly familiar with the classroom procedures of his time. He probably knew earlier translations, such as Nicholas Oresme's *Aristotle* or Chaucer's *Boethius*. But the major influence upon his *Eneados*, apart from Virgil himself, was the commentary of Ascensius. It would be difficult to over-state the importance of this work to Douglas; without it his translation would be very different, and might well have not come into existence. The extent to which it influenced his understanding of the *Aeneid*, and subsequently the diction and phrasing of his own *Eneados*, is still, I think, insufficiently recognised, although we owe Dr Coldwell a debt for publicizing and illustrating Douglas's use of Ascensius. Ascensius's influence upon the *Eneados* is continuously apparent, and ranges from single-word glosses to the adoption of whole sentences. It was an influence both for the good and the bad. Undoubtedly, Ascensius helped to clarify the sense of Virgil for Douglas; sometimes when he mis-translated (as at III.vii.9–10) he disregarded a warning from Ascensius: *caueat autem explanator*. At other times, however, Ascensius misled Douglas by perverse and completely inaccurate glosses. We know that Douglas sometimes made use of the commentary of Servius. It may therefore surprise classical scholars that he should so often prefer to use the greatly inferior work of Ascensius. But Ascensius was a contemporary of Douglas. There were many links between Scottish scholars and Ascensius's press in Paris, and it is possible that Douglas knew him. Ascensius's Latin was of the sort that Douglas himself must have used at university and on legal and ecclesiastical business; to cope with the Latin of Virgil he may even have needed a fuller and more elementary commentary than was provided by Servius. Above all, Ascensius's aims as an editor were in harmony with Douglas's aims as a translator: to bring out the 'sentence' of his author and make it 'braid and plane' (1 Prol 110) to not very learned readers. It would be an exaggeration to say that Ascensius was solely responsible for Douglas's approach to trans-lation (in so far as he has a consistent approach), but he undoubtedly encouraged and reinforced some of the most striking features of Douglas's style and technique.

Douglas, like Ascensius, explains and clarifies Virgil's geographi-cal allusions. When a place-name is mentioned he regularly specifies whether it is town, river, lake or mountain. In III.x.63 ff. Aeneas sails past 'Pelorus the mont', 'flude Pantagyas', 'Tapsum ile', 'the flude Plemyrion', 'the loch Cameryna', and the 'hyl and cite'

Agragas. Douglas presumably did not need always to consult Ascensius on such points; but his practice is very similar to Ascensius's, whose commentary on the relevant passage of the *Aeneid* (III.687 ff.) is studded with such glosses as *illius promontorii, illam insulam, mons ille in Sicilia,* or *scilicet urbs.* Sometimes Douglas follows Ascensius's phrasing closely, as when he calls *Erymanthus* (v.448) 'the mont of Archade' (cf. Ascensius's *idest in illo monte Arcadiae*), or speaks of 'The flude Tybir, throu Lawrent feildis slydis' (v.xiii.71); cf. Ascensius who comments on Virgil's *Laurentem . . . Thybrim* (v. 797): *i. per agros laurentes defluentem.* Douglas adopts the same explanatory technique with Virgil's many allusions to ancient history and myth. Even today translators do this occasionally, but it is clear that Douglas felt a special need to clarify Virgil's geography and history because of the ignorance of his readers—an ignorance that he confesses partly to sharing:

> This text is full of storys euery deill,
> Realmys and landis, quharof I haue na feill
> Bot as I follow Virgill in sentens;
> Few knawis all thir costis sa far hens;
> To pike thame vp perchance ʒour eyn suld reill—
> Thus aucht thar nane blame me for smal offens.
>
> (III Prol 31–6)

That Douglas's misgivings were justified can be seen from the way Virgil's names were strangely mangled by some copyists of the *Eneados.*[38]

The same desire to simplify and clarify is seen in Douglas's treatment of persons' names. He regularly unravels patronymics—Virgil's *Atridae* (II.104) becomes 'Agamenon als, and Menalay' (II. ii.83); and he uses the one term 'Greikis' or occasionally 'Gregiounis' for the varied poetic names employed by Virgil, such as *Danai, Achivi, Argolici, Pelasgi.* (An illustration of this may be seen at the beginning of book II.) Douglas sometimes, but by no means invariably, substitutes a more familiar name, such as Diana or Mars, where Virgil had used the less common *Triuia* or *Gradiuus.* Occasionally, following the lead of Ascensius, he provides an explanatory parenthesis:

> And sic wordis spak to Iulus ʒyng,
> That otherwys is hayt Ascanyus.
>
> (IX.x.142–3)

Douglas sometimes attempts to clarify Virgil's battle-scenes in a way that owes more to the promptings of Ascensius than to Virgil. In IX.571 ff. Virgil's close-packed lines present a scene of confusion, where 'ignorant armies clash by night':

> Emathiona Liger, Corynaeum sternit Asilas,
> his iaculo bonus, hic longe fallente sagitta,

Ortygium Caeneus, uictorem Caenea Turnus,
Turnus Ityn Cloniumque, Dioxippum Promolumque ...

But Ascensius sorts out the two sides in his commentary: *troianus ille ... scilicet rutulum ... italum*, etc.; and so does Douglas:

Liger a Troiane from the wall also
Doun bet a Rutiliane hait Emathio.
A Phrigiane eik, Asylas, stern and stowt,
All tofruschit Choryneus withowt ...
(ix.ix.99 ff.)

Douglas regularly had recourse to the commentators in his translation of technical terms and phrases, particularly those concerned
with religious belief or with war. He translated Virgil's *chlamydem*
(viii.167), for instance, as 'knychtly weid' (viii.iii.167) because
Ascensius had rendered it as *vestem militarem*. When Douglas was
faced with what he called a 'subtell word' (1 Prol 305), that is, a rare
and difficult word, he similarly consulted Ascensius. An illustration
is afforded by some lines from Anchises' famous speech about the
experience of souls in the underworld:

penitusque necesse est
multa diu concreta modis inolescere miris.
(vi.737–8)

Douglas translates this as

And thus, aluterly, it is neidfull thing
The mony vycis lang tyme induryng,
Contrackit in the corps, be done away,
And purgit on seir wonderfull wys to say.
(vi.xii.35–8)

Douglas misunderstood the unusual word *inolescere*, which means
'grow into, as an engrafted plant'. He translated it as 'be done away',
because Ascensius had glossed it as *aboleri* in his comment on the
lines:

multa. scilicet mala. concreta. idest contracta cum corpore.
inolescere. idest aboleri. miris. idest mirabilibus modis. scilicet
purgandi.

Douglas here followed Ascensius very closely indeed, and it is clear
that he needed the help of a commentator with the whole of Anchises' difficult speech.

It is understandable that Douglas consulted a commentator over
difficult or highly allusive passages in the *Aeneid*. What is surprising
is the way he so often followed Ascensius at points where Virgil's
text seems reasonably clear and straightforward. Again and again
Douglas follows Ascensius in spelling out the contextual implications of a word. Thus Virgil's *ramis* (viii.250) is translated as

'branchis *rent of treis*' (VIII.iv.149) because of Ascensius's gloss: *scilicet detractis arboribus*. So too *domus* (V.638) is translated as 'dwelling place *for euermar*' (V.xi.76) because of Ascensius's *idest perpetua mansio*. *Imaona* (X.424) appears as '*Imaonus . . . That was to hym hys frend and fallow deir*' (X.vii.152–3), because of Ascensius's explanation *scilicet consocium suum*. Virgil's *iussi* (III.697) is translated as 'at command *of my fader*' (III.x.83) because of Ascensius's *a patre*.

A particularly clear illustration of Douglas's method and its dependence upon Ascensius may be seen in his treatment of certain adverbs. Virgil's *tandem* (IV.304) is glossed by Ascensius as *post longam cogitationem*; at VII.259 it is similarly glossed as *post longiusculam cogitationem*. At the same points in the *Eneados* we find that Douglas translates *tandem* as 'at the last . . . Eftir lang musyng' (IV.vi.47–8); and again, neatly filling a whole line, as 'And at the last efter ful lang musyng' (VII.iv.147). Virgil's *iamdudum* (VIII.153) is explained by Ascensius as *idest ab eo tempore quo loqui coeperat*. This supplies a whole line in Douglas: 'Fra tyme that he first forto speke began' (VIII.iii. 132). So too with *dehinc* (IX.480): in the light of the context Ascensius expands this to *idest postquam nati ora conspexit*. Douglas translates similarly: 'And as that from the wall hyr sonnys hede / Behaldis scho' (IX.viii.47–8). In somewhat the same way Douglas follows Ascensius in his expansion of Virgil's compressed syntax. Thus Douglas supplies a grammatical object unstated by Virgil in translating *textilibusque onerat donis* (III.485) as

> Hym and his feris of hir nedill wark
> And wovyn dowreis furnyst.
> (III.vii.29–30)

'Hym and his feris' seems to reflect Ascensius's instruction to supply *eum aut ministros eius*. So too Virgil's *nec minor in terris . . . Aeneae mihi cura tui* (V.803–4) has the terms of its comparison spelt out in Ascensius's comment on *in terris: scilicet quam in mari*, and by Douglas after him:

> That I na les cuyr tuke of thine Ene
> To salue him on the land than on the see.
> (V.xiii.89–90)

Many of the most striking and rhetorical features of Virgil's language thus disappear in Douglas. He regularly simplifies figures of speech, such as litotes: *haud segnis* (III.513), for instance, becomes 'Not sweir bot . . . deligent' (III.viii.15). He follows Ascensius in completing Neptune's famous aposiopesis, *Quos ego—*(I.135), translating it as 'I sal ʒou chastys' (I.iii.69). He thus loses the disjointed and dramatic character of Neptune's angry speech. Douglas does more than translate rhetorical questions: he often supplies the answer to them. Virgil says of Aeneas as he hesitates on hearing the message of Mercury: *heu! quid agat?* (IV.283) Douglas renders this as 'Allace! quhat suld he do? oneth he wist' (IV.vi.8). So too with Dido's passionate questioning of Aeneas's behaviour: *num fletu ingemuit nostro? num lumina flexit* . . . (IV.369ff.) Douglas translates fairly closely, 'Quhiddir gif he murnyt . . .', and then concludes 'Na, not to ȝeir' (IV.vii.15–18). At the same point Ascensius had commented similarly: *quasi dicat non.* In the course of a similar series of questions addressed to herself by Dido Douglas again supplies an emphatic 'Na, wyll I not!' (IV.x.28).

This explicitness is one of Douglas's most striking characteristics as a translator. Again and again, where Virgil is brief, succinct, or allusive, implying far more than is actually stated, Douglas turns hints or ambiguities into definite statements. This largely though not entirely derives from his concern with making the 'sentence' plain. At IV.448 Virgil does not specify what emotion Aeneas felt after Anna pleaded with him on Dido's behalf: *magno persentit pectore curas.* But Douglas tells us precisely what the *curas* were— 'Of reuth and amouris felt the perturbance' (IV.viii.85)—probably because he had read Ascensius's gloss: *idest sollicitudines amoris et miserationis.* So too with Douglas's translation of *Ascanius curuo direxit spicula cornu* (VII.497) as

> With nokkyt bow ybent all reddy bown,
> Wenand hym wilde, leyt sone ane arrow glide.
>   (VII.viii.46–7)

'Wenand hym wilde' corresponds to nothing in Virgil but to the motive suggested by Ascensius: *putantis videlicet siluestrem esse.* Douglas's greater explicitness over mental processes may be seen in his translation of the famous lines on Daedalus:

> bis conatus erat casus effingere in auro,
> bis patriae cecidere manus.
>   (VI.32–3)
> In gold to grave thi fall twys etlyt he,
> And twys, for rewth, failȝeis the faderis handis.
>   (VI.i.56–7)

Virgil felt no need to state explicitly the emotion felt by Daedalus. Douglas, in his mention of 'rewth', is probably following Ascensius: *quia prae pietate paterna effingere non potuit.* Another example occurs in the description of Lavinia:

> accepit uocem lacrimis Lauinia matris
> flagrantis perfusa genas, cui plurimus ignem
> subiecit rubor et calefacta per ora cucurrit.
>   (XII.64–6)

Conington comments on this passage that Virgil never informs us as to the feelings of Lavinia,[39] but Douglas is not so reticent:

> Lavinia the maid, with soir smert,
> Hyr moderis wordis felt deip in hyr hart ...
> The fervent fyre of *schame* rysys on hie,
> Kyndland mar large the red culloryt bewte.
>   (xii.ii.27 ff.)

Douglas is presumably following Ascensius, who twice mentions *pudor* in his discussion of these lines.

Part of a word's latent 'sentence' was its etymology, real or fanciful. It was common for commentators to discuss etymologies, and Douglas observes tradition in his own Comment, where, following Servius, he offers a rather misguided explanation of *oppetere* as

> ore terram petere ... quhilk to translate in our tung is with mowth to seik or byte the erd. And, lo, that is ane hail sentens for ane of Virgillis wordis.
>   (1 Prol 35 on)

Consistently enough, when Virgil uses *oppetere* at 1.96 Douglas translates it as 'Deit ... bytand the erd' (i.iii.6). At other points in the *Eneados* Douglas similarly inserts a phrase bringing out what he thought to be the etymology of the Latin word. He translates Virgil's *Lugentes campi* (vi.441) as 'boundis of Complaynt, all voyd of lycht' (vi.vii.39), because both Servius and Ascensius supplied an erroneous explanation of *Lugentes* as *quasi lucis egentes*. Douglas's etymologies are not invariably mistaken. He translates Virgil's *falcati ... enses* (vii.732), for instance, as 'crukyt swerdis, bowand as a syth' (vii.xii.69). Coldwell's Note says 'this comparison is the translator's', but Douglas—quite justifiably, it seems to me—is trying to convey the vividness of *falcati*, which literally means 'scythe-shaped'. Douglas's interest in etymology is sometimes apparent in the Prologues, as in vii Prol 14: 'tha schort days that clerkis clepe brumaill'. Douglas had just translated Virgil's *brumali* (vi.205 = vi.iii.93), but the etymological explanation of *bruma* as a shortened form of *brevissimus* [*dies*] could have been supplied to him by 'clerkis' such as Isidore or Macrobius.[40]

Douglas's preoccupation with conveying the full sense of even the smallest word in Virgil often led to the practice of what might be called 'double translation': an attempt to render in his own words both the *litera* and its *sententia*, the literal sense of a word or phrase as well as its 'sentence'. This double effect may have been noted in some of the examples quoted earlier. Thus *tandem* appears as both 'at the last' and 'eftir lang musyng'; and *Lugentes campi* as 'boundis of Complaynt' and then as 'voyd of lycht'. Another illustration is

provided by Douglas's translation of some lines at the point just
before Sinon releases the Greeks from the Wooden Horse:

> flammas cum regia puppis
> extulerat.
>
> (11.256–7)
>
> And quhen the takynnyng or the bail of fyre
> Rays fro the kyngis schip.
>
> (11.v.13–4)

Douglas translates *flammas* literally, but he also indicates that they
formed a signal or 'takynnyng' to Sinon: Ascensius comments *id enim
signum dederant Sinoni*. So too Douglas sometimes tries to render the
double aspect of Virgil's metaphors. Dido exclaims:

> hauriat hunc oculis ignem crudelis ab alto
> Dardanus . . .
>
> (iv.661–2)

Douglas translates this as

> Now lat ʒone cruel Troiane swelly and se
> This our fyre funerale from the deip see.
>
> (iv.xii.35–6)

'Swelly and se' is designed to convey first the literal then the figurative meaning of *hauriat*. So too with another passage:

> Ne suffir not thy hyd sorrow, I pray,
> Na langar the consume and waist away,
> That I na mar sik wofull thochtis se
> *Schyne nor appeir* in thy sweit face,' quod he.
>
> (xii.xiii.25–8)

This corresponds to

> ne te tantus edit tacitam dolor et mihi curae
> saepe tuo dulci tristes ex ore *recursent*.
>
> (xii.801–2)

Douglas's translation may seem widely aberrant, until we find that
Ascensius's text read not *recursent* ('come back') but *coruscent*, and
was accompanied by the gloss: *idest cum coruscatione quadam emineant*.
Douglas's 'schyne nor appeir' thus gives first the literal then the
figurative meaning of *coruscent*.

An impression similar to that of 'double translation' is produced
by Douglas's occasional habit of adopting the word actually used by
Virgil (sometimes in a slightly altered form), and accompanying it
with an explanatory gloss. Thus Virgil's *recentibus* (11.395) becomes
'recent . . . warm' (11.vii.59); elsewhere the same Latin word appears
as 'recent . . . fresch and callour' (vii.xii.110 = vii.748), or 'recent
. . . newly sched' (viii.iv.28 = viii.195). Virgil's *facilis* (vi.126)
becomes 'facil and eith' (vi.ii.101); *gubernaclum* (vi.349) becomes

'helmstok or gubernakil of tre' (VI.v.113); *praecordia* (VII.347) becomes 'hartpipis or precordialis' (VII.vi.14); and *exilium* (Ascensius's reading at X.850 for *exitium*), 'exill...and banysyng' (X.xiv.44). Sometimes the explanatory gloss, native and homely, may well have originated with Douglas, but often the choice of word betrays the influence of Ascensius. Thus Virgil's *numero* (11.424) is glossed by Ascensius as *multitudine ingruentium*, and appears in Douglas as 'multitude and nowmyr' (11.vii.109). So too Virgil's *aeterna* (VII.609) is glossed as *inconsumptibilia*, and in Douglas appears as 'eternal and inconsumptive' (VII.x.23).

This practice is closely related to the technique of multiple glossing, used both by commentators on the classics and teachers in the classroom. (Often they were the same people.) A generation after Douglas made his translation Pierre de la Ramée (Ramus) described how his master Toussaint taught Greek by translating it into Latin:

> when he could not render a Greek expression by a single Latin term which conveyed all its energy he used several, wishing to leave nothing obscure, and always anxious to bring light to his hearers' minds.[41]

The method is still a familiar pedagogic one. Douglas was probably acquainted with it from an early age, and did not need to learn it from Ascensius. Yet we can often see a direct relationship between Douglas's phrasing and the use of such multiple glosses in Ascensius's commentary. Thus Virgil's *nobilis* (VII.564) is glossed by Ascensius as *famosus et multum notus*, and this appears in Douglas as 'famus . . . weil beknaw' (VII.ix.50). Similarly Virgil's *infelix* (X.850), glossed as *durum et intolerabile*, becomes Douglas's 'hard and insufferabill' (X.xiv.45); *aequa* (XII.569), glossed as *aequalia et aeque plana*, becomes 'plane and equale' (XII.x.38); and *uerius* (XII.694), glossed as *'iustius et equius*, becomes 'mair iust and equale' (XII.xi.179). As with adjectives, so too with nouns: Virgil's *clienti* (VI.609), glossed by Ascensius as *familiari et domestico*, becomes in Douglas 'seruandis or famyliaris' (VI.ix.167); and *missilibus* (IX.520), glossed as *iaculis et sagittis*, becomes 'ganჳeis, arrowis . . . and dartis' (IX.viii.145). Verbs are sometimes treated in the same way. Virgil's *prodiderim* (XII.42) glossed by Ascensius as *prostituerim et exposuerim ac porro dederim*, becomes in Douglas 'expone or offer' (XII.i.103); and *edit* (XII.801), glossed as *rodat et consumat*, becomes 'consume and waist away' (XII.xiii.26).

It will already be evident that the practice of the commentators, and particularly of Ascensius, had a further influence on Douglas's style; it affected not only his balanced phrasing and piling up of near-synonyms but his very diction, what Douglas himself called the 'bastard Latyn' (1 Prol 117) element in it. It is Ascensius, not only Virgil, who is responsible for many of the Latinate words in the *Eneados*. This is not to deny that a large number have been adopted directly from the *Aeneid*—sometimes simple words, like *duces*, sometimes technical terms, like *pronuba* or *indigites*. But a surprisingly large number of the learned, polysyllabic words that Douglas uses— abstract nouns or adjectives with suffixes in *-ive, -ible*, or *-able*— clearly derives not from Virgil's own words but from the commentators. Thus Douglas's 'prosperite' (I.vii.65) derives from *prosperitas*, Ascensius's gloss on Virgil's *fortuna* (1.454); 'progenitor' (IX.i.11) derives from *progenitoris*, the gloss on *parentis* (IX.3); 'obstakill' (X.vii.41) from *obstaculo*, the gloss on *obice* (X.377); 'violens' (X.xii.17) from *violentiam*, the gloss on *uim* (X.695); and 'punitioun' (XII.xiv.148) from *punitionem*, the gloss on *poenam* (XII.949). So too Douglas's 'flexibill' (VI.ii.122), derives from *flexibili*, the gloss on *lento* (VI.137); 'invynsibill' (X.v.68) from *inuincibilem*, the gloss on *inuictum* (X.243); and 'detestabill' (XI.x.57) from *detestabilis*, the gloss on *improbus* (XI.512). Occasionally not just a word but a whole phrase is appropriated in a form very close to Ascensius's Latin. Virgil's *curae* (VIII.401), for instance, is glossed by Ascensius as *solicitę diligentę*; this appears in Douglas as 'solist diligens' (VIII. vii.71). So too at XII.317 Virgil's *sacra* is glossed as *sacrificia violata*, which appears in Douglas as 'sacrifice violate' (XII.vi.19). Sometimes Douglas keeps close to Virgil but slightly modifies the form of the word, adding or altering the prefix. Here too he is sometimes influenced by Ascensius: Virgil's *aspirate* (IX.525) appears as 'inspire' (IX.ix.2)—cf. the gloss *inspirate*; Virgil's *soluit* (XII.867) appears as 'dissoluyt' (XII.xiii.178)—cf. the gloss *dissoluit*. Ascensius's glosses also seem to underlie Douglas's translation of *firma* (11.691) as 'conferm' (II.xi.22); of *ueterum* (VI.739) as 'inveterat' (VI.xii.40); and of *tollunt* (IX.637) as 'extolland' (IX.x.109).

Sometimes one may feel that Douglas's practice was perverse and Ascensius's influence pernicious. Comparatively simple words are translated by Douglas in a way which seems unnecessarily formal, especially when there was no lack of equivalents in his native language. Virgil's *dabat* (1.507) is thus rendered 'pronuncis' (I.viii.24), presumably because of Ascensius's *pronunciabat*; *feram* (VII.549) is rendered 'induce' (VII.ix.21) because of *inducam*; *altus* (VIII.27) is rendered 'profund' (VIII.i.22) because of *profundus*; *tenet* (X.238) is rendered 'occupy' (X.v.61) because of *occupat*. Yet Ascensius's Latin may have been congenial to Douglas not only because it was more familiar to him than classical Latin, but because its vocabulary and grammatical structure were far closer to those of his own language and could perhaps be assimilated more easily. The grammatical differences between classical Latin and an analytic language such as modern English are well known, but the structure of medieval Latin had several features in common with the medieval vernaculars, including Middle Scots. Ascensius often substituted an abstract noun for Virgil's substantival adjectives, and is sometimes followed in this by Douglas. Thus in the description of Ripheus as *seruantissimus aequi* (11.427) *aequi* is glossed by Ascensius as *idest equitatis et iustitię*, and appears in Douglas as 'best kepand equite' (11.vii.115). So too Virgil's *uiuere rapto* (VII.749), glossed as *ex rapina*, becomes in Douglas 'on spulȝe to leif and on rapyne' (VII.xii.111). Douglas may have found Ascensius's rendering of Virgil's ablative constructions useful. In one such case he followed Ascensius's word-order so closely as to be unidiomatic: Virgil's *fatis auctoribus* (x.67), glossed by Ascensius as *fatorum autoritate*, appears awkwardly in Douglas as 'Of the fatys by the autoryte' (x.ii.12).

Douglas usually incorporates explanatory phrases into the text silently, but sometimes he calls the reader's attention to them:

in a byrd hym turnyt fut and hand
With sprutlyt weyngis, clepit a Speicht with ws,
Quhilk in Latyn hait Pycus Marcyus.
(VII.iii.90–2)

The gret gammys Circenses forto se,
Quhilk iustyng or than turnament cleip we.
(VIII.x.95–6)

            Iapigya sulȝe
That now on dayis Apulȝe clepyng we.
(XI.vi.45–6)

Douglas may have recalled Virgil's occasional use of this same device, as in VII.208: *quae nunc Samothracia fertur*. But it is the commentator's voice, I suspect, that sounded loudest in his ears. Ascensius speaks similarly of Virgil's *aulaeis* (1.697): *quae vulgo tapeta dicuntur*; and of *oratores* (VIII.505): *legatos quos vulgo ambasiatores vocant*. (It may be noted that at these points in his translation Douglas adopts 'tapetis' (1.xi.8) and 'ambassatouris' (VIII.viii.115).) Whatever its origin, the narrative flow is interrupted and the dramatic effect impaired when such explanations are placed in the mouth of Anchises (11.x.156) or Evander (VIII.vi.7).

At one point the tone and manner of the commentator become very obtrusive indeed in the lines upon Iuturna, the *uirago* (XII.468):

Quhilk term to expone, be myne avys,
Is a woman exersand a mannys offys.
(XII.viii.57–8)

(Servius—and Ascensius after him—explain *uirago* as *mulier, quae virile implet officium.*) Such unconcealed didacticism brings to mind very forcibly the master and pupils sitting on their 'benkis and stulys'. It is only fair to Douglas, however, to state that in such a blatant form it is extremely rare in the *Eneados*. More commonly there is a muted echo of the expositor's tone in the use of introductory phrases, such as 'that is to say', 'that is to knaw', or 'I meyn'. Their correspondence to the commentator's *idest* or *scilicet* is clear. Virgil's *primisque cadentibus astris* (VIII.59) is translated

First as the starris declynys, the addres,

I meyn into the dawyng rycht ayrly.

    (VIII.i.88–9)

This incorporates Ascensius's gloss: *hoc est cum prima luce*. Virgil's *sol medium caeli conscenderat igneus orbem* (VIII.97) is translated as

The fyry son be this ascendit evin

The myddill ward and regioun of the hevyn;

That is to knaw, be than it was myd day.

    (VIII.iii.1–3)

Line 3 follows not only the sense but also the phrasing of Ascensius: *idest iam meridies erat*. Virgil's *hic* (XII.529) is expanded to 'The tane of thame, that is to know, Enee' (XII.ix.69); this follows Ascensius's *idest alter eorum, scilicet eneas*.

What originated as a scholarly practice entered the traditions of vernacular poetry. Chaucer had used similar phrases—'that is to seyn' or 'as who seith'—to introduce glosses in his translation of Boethius's *Consolation of Philosophy*; in *Troilus and Criseyde* he also furnished explanations of words like *urn, Manes* or *ambages* (V.311, 892, 897–9). Late medieval poets do not seem to have regarded such encapsulated definitions as pedantic, but accepted them as a mark, and even an ornament, of serious poetry. A well-known example occurs in the *Franklin's Tale* (V.1016–18):

Til that the brighte sonne loste his hewe;

For th' orisonte hath reft the sonne his lyght—

This is as muche to seye as it was nyght!

Modern readers find this humorous and mock-pedantic, but there seems no such ambiguity about similar usages in Lydgate, in Douglas's *Palice of Honour* (30–31), or the imitation of Chaucer's lines in the *Kingis Quair* (stanza 72).[42] This particular practice of Douglas's seems to derive from a double tradition, both pedagogic and poetic.

Very occasionally Douglas uses another device, pedantic-sounding to modern ears, which is designed to signal that he is returning to a subject treated earlier: '. . . as heir abufe said we' (x.iii.64), '. . . as we said haue laitly heir tofor' (XI.vii.95), or '... as we haue said or this' (XII.xii.107). Such reminders recall the *ut supradiximus* of the commentators (cf. Servius on 11.296), but here too Douglas may have been indebted to the traditions of medieval narrative. In *Troilus and Criseyde* Chaucer uses similar phrases, such as 'of which I tolde' (1.261) and 'as I have seyd er this' (IV.29). The practice perhaps originated in the need for oral verse to make its structure and transitions as clear as possible.

Douglas sometimes faced the problem that all translators meet: a scholarly disagreement as to the exact meaning of a word or phrase. He says that in such a case he will choose one interpretation and stick to it:

> Eik weill I wait syndry expositouris seir
> Makis on a text sentens diuers to heir,
> As thame apperis, accordyng thar entent,
> And for thar part schawis ressonys euident.
> Al this is ganand, I will weill it swa be,
> Bot a sentens to follow may suffice me.
>
> (1 Prol 351–6)

This indeed is Douglas's normal practice. There is plenty of evidence that Douglas did not rely entirely on the easier and more elementary commentary of Ascensius, but at times consulted Servius directly and chose his interpretation of a word in preference to Ascensius's.[43] Thus Virgil's *laeua* (11.54) is glossed as *sinistra, inimica* by Ascensius but *contraria* by Servius, and appears as 'contrary' (11.i.75) in Douglas. Similarly Virgil's *insano* (VI.135), which is not glossed by Ascensius, is glossed as *magno* by Servius, and appears as 'huge' (VI.ii.119) in Douglas; *demens* (VI.172) receives no discussion in Ascensius but is glossed as *improvidus* by Servius, and appears in Douglas as 'onprovisitly' (VI.iii.28); *maligna* (VI.270), glossed as *exigua et sterili* by Ascensius but *obscura* by Servius, appears in Douglas as 'obscure' (VI.iv.72); and *notis* (VI.499), glossed by Ascensius as *sermone patrio aut proprio nomine* but by Servius as *amicalibus*, appears in Douglas as 'frendly' (VI.viii.46).

It is tempting to search for some difference in Douglas's employment of these two commentaries. One might expect that he would use Ascensius to aid him in his line-by-line construing, and turn to Servius at particularly difficult points or for explanation of Roman antiquity. This is not so. As far as I can see, Douglas's approach is very much an *ad hoc* one: sometimes he followed one commentary, sometimes (as he himself said) he followed the other. Again and again Douglas used Servius—as he had used Ascensius—to extract the 'sentence' as well as the literal sense of Virgil. He translated

Virgil's *nouus . . . hospes* (IV.10) as 'gret new gest' (IV.i.19) because
Servius had glossed *nouus* as *magnus*. He translated *buxus* (IX.619) as
'turnyt buschboun tre' (IX.x.67) because Servius, quoting the
Georgics, had commented: *torno rasile buxum*. Servius is sometimes
directly responsible for Douglas's characteristic pairs of near-
synonyms: Virgil's *numina* (VIII.78) is interpreted by Ascensius as
divina munera; Servius, however, has *oracula et promissa*, which appears
in Douglas as 'promys and orakill' (VIII.ii.27). More elaborate
renderings of the type which involves an explanatory phrase or line
often derive from Servius. Where Virgil describes Sinon as *turbatus*
and *pauitans* (II.67 and 107), Douglas stresses Sinon's dissimulation
and translates '*semyng* ful rad' and 'quakand . . . *as it had bene* for dreid'
(II.ii.18 and 88). In this he follows the hint of Servius, who had
commented: *quasi turbatus* and *quasi pavitans*. Virgil's *dixitque nouis-
sima uerba* (VI.231) is translated by Douglas as 'The lattir word, "Al
is done!" said he then' (VI.iii.146). This is not 'an echo of the phrase
"consummatum est"' (so Coldwell), but an adoption of Servius's
novissima . . . id est ilicet. In another instance a whole line derives from
Servius. Douglas renders Virgil's *non felicia tela* (XI.196) fairly literally as 'thair onsilly scheildis', and then continues with 'Quhilk
mycht thame nocht defend into the feildis' (XI.v.33–4). This drawing out of the meaning ͻ ᷑ ᷢ *non felicia* derives from Servius's *quibus se
defendere nequiverunt*.

Yet Douglas is not invariably selective. Occasionally, when he
encounters differing explanations of a word he includes both in his
translation, although what he is doing is not immediately obvious
without a knowledge of the commentaries. In book I, for instance,
Cupid begins to efface the memory of Sychaeus from Dido's heart

> And with *scharp amouris* of the *man alyve*
> Gan hir dolf spreit forto preveyn and steir.
> (I.xi.54–5)

The italicized words correspond to Virgil's *uiuo . . . amore* (I.721),
but their nature is determined by the alternative interpretations of
uiuo offered by Ascensius: *aut de vivente, aut vehementi*. Another example may show how what at first may appear sheer padding is really
Douglas's attempt to capture all the possible 'sentence' in Virgil's
text. In book IX Turnus slays

> the huge byg Troiane, hait Idas,
> Standand forto defend the towris hie.
> (IX.ix.112–13)

Virgil here has *summis stantem pro turribus Idan* (IX.575), which
Ascensius (following Servius) interprets in two ways: *idest pro
defensione summarum turrium . . . aut sic magnum vt pro turri haberi et*

putare possit. Sometimes the different interpretations are irreconcilable, and Douglas's indecision or desire to be as inclusive as possible is then betrayed by a tell-tale *or* (cf. the commentator's *aut . . . aut*). He speaks of Jupiter's 'tawbart, or his beknyt targe' (VIII.vi.96). This translates *aegida* (VIII.354), which when it is mentioned later by Virgil (VIII.435) is given conflicting glosses as *munimentum pectoris . . . lorica* (Servius) and *scutum* (Ascensius). In much the same way Douglas's translation of Virgil's *aclydes* (VII.730) as 'Round casting dartis, or macis with pikit hedis' (VII.xii.62) seems to show the influence of both Ascensius—*tela de longe iaci apta*—and Servius— *clavae . . . eminentibus hinc et hinc acuminibus.*

Another closely related practice should be mentioned here. Douglas sometimes translates *both* of two variant readings in Virgil's text; the more important variants were sometimes discussed by the commentators. Thus in XII.iv.159–60 Douglas describes Turnus

> With chekis walxin leyn, to thar semyng,
> Quharon the soft berd newly dyd furth spryng.

The chief source of this is *pubentesque genae* (XII.221), a reading preserved by the best manuscripts and found also in Ascensius, who glosses *pubentes* as *adhuc molli barba . . . tectae.* But what is the source of 'walxin leyn'? It translates *tabentes*, 'wasting away', a variant preserved by Tiberius Donatus and still preferred by some modern editors of the *Aeneid.* In another instance from the same book the clash of variants is quite obvious:

> With lynnyng valis or lyke apronys lycht
> Thai war arrayt . . .
> (XII.iii.17–18)

This clearly reflects the variant readings at XII.120; *lino*, 'linen', and *limo*, 'apron worn by priests'.[44]

Douglas boasts of his faithfulness to the *Aeneid.* Yet some modern scholars argue that he distorts or over-stresses certain aspects of Virgil's thought. B. Dearing, for instance, says that by his additions and expansions Douglas is 'deliberately emphasizing the political lessons to be gleaned by a sixteenth-century prince from the pages of Vergil'.[45] Coldwell goes further and says that he 'manipulated the poem to demonstrate clearly its political implications'.[46] Dearing quotes Douglas's rendering of a passage dealing with Lucius Junius Brutus (VI.817–23):

> Ples the behald the Tarquynys kingis two,
> And the stowt curage of Brutus alsso . . .
> Hys awin sonnys, movyng onkyndly wer,
> To punytioun and ded sal damp infeir,
> To kepe frensches and souerane liberte;

And thus onsilly fader sall he be,
Quhou sa evir the pepil hys fatel dedis
In tyme tocum sal blason, quha thame redis;
The feruent lufe of his kynd natyve land,
And excedand desyre he bar on hand
Of honour and hie glory to ressaue,
Mot al evil rumour fra his lawd byvaue.
      (VI.xiv.23–42)

Dearing says that this 'echoes the characteristic abhorrence of rebellion and civil strife found throughout sixteenth-century English literature'.[47] But has Douglas imported this feeling into Virgil? Douglas's method here seems little different from that employed throughout the *Eneados*. The undoubted diffuseness of his translation reveals a desire not to indoctrinate but to elucidate. Virgil's Latin is compressed and allusive, and Douglas is following the lead of Ascensius in attempting to explain technical terms like *fasces*, expanding *poenas* to 'punytioun and ded', and inserting a reference to 'evil rumour' (Ascensius has *rumores populi*). Douglas must have been aware that what Virgil said of 'onkyndly wer' and 'souerane liberte' was relevant to the Scotland of his own time. But I cannot find in this and the other passages cited by Dearing or Coldwell evidence that Douglas had a conscious political purpose in translating the *Aeneid*, or that he displays a special interest in Virgil's ideas on kingship and government.

Another critic implies that Douglas christianizes Virgil not only in the Prologues but in the translation itself: 'the whole Virgilian underworld is mapped out in circles and limbos on the Christian pattern . . . *Suos patimur manes* is rendered 'Ilk ane of us his ganand purgatory Maun suffir'.[48] Douglas has more respect for his original than this suggests. Despite his interest in Virgil's apparent anticipations of Christian thought, he does not give a specifically Christian colouring to the underworld apart from applying to it the term 'hell'. The word 'limbo' appears in VI Prologue 92–3, but never in the translation of book VI. Douglas's use of the word 'circle' to describe the divisions of the underworld (heading to VI.vii and VI.vii.7) may remind us of the structure of Dante's *Inferno*, but it is not a peculiarly medieval idea. Douglas probably derived it from Servius's comment on VI.426: *novem circulis inferi cincti esse dicuntur.* The charge that Douglas foists onto Virgil the doctrine of purgatory deserves closer examination. Superficially, it might appear to be supported by the removal in the 1553 edition of the word 'purgatory' from the heading to VI.xii. In this chapter of the *Eneados* (which corresponds to *Aeneid* VI.724–55) Douglas uses words such as 'purgatory', 'purgit', and 'purefyit', but it seems to me that he does so with propriety. Virgil is undoubtedly describing a purgatorial experience, which Servius (on VI.741) calls *purgatio animarum*. The notion of purgatory did not exist among the earliest Christians, and seems to have been introduced into Christian thought by the platonizing theologian, Origen. Douglas is here using the words available to him to bring out something genuinely present in Virgil. It may be questioned whether Douglas distorts a specific line, such as *quisque suos patimur manis* (VI.743). The meaning of this has been long debated, but Douglas's reference to 'purgatory' in his translation accords with the interpretation not only of Ascensius (*i. purgamur apud manes*) but that of a scholar such as Mackail ('we pass through our several purgatorial experiences').[49] In the *Eneados* Douglas tends to emphasize and make more explicit other ideas congenial to some medieval Christians, such as the prison of the body—'in the dyrk mansioun and preson blynd / Of thir vyle bodeis yfettyrit and bynd' (VI.xii.27–8); but he does not, I think, radically distort the sense of Virgil.[50]

This is true also of the way Douglas handles the theme of fate or destiny in the *Aeneid*. Virgil is insistent on the role of fate in shaping events: the second line of the poem introduces Aeneas as *fato profugus*, and there are references throughout the *Aeneid* to the part played by fate not only in the history of Aeneas, but in the protracted siege of Troy, its ultimate fall, and in the foundation of Rome itself. Douglas frequently speaks of fate and 'fatal destany'—the latter may seem a pleonasm, but is common in Chaucer—and these words usually render accurately what is present in the text of the *Aeneid*. Sometimes, however, Douglas makes more explicit what is only hinted at in Virgil. When Aeneas speaks of his decision to leave Troy, his simple but momentous *cessi* (II.804) is rendered as 'My purpos I left, obeyand destanye' (II.xii.83). The last phrase may seem intrusive, yet R. G. Austin comments that *cessi* here 'combines the idea of departure with that of yielding to circumstances'.[51] So too with the translation of Jupiter's *uoce* (X.628) as 'wordis of fatale destane' (X.xi.60). Douglas is here trying to bring out the 'sentence': Ascensius had glossed *uoce* as *fato*, and Servius had noted *vox enim Iouis fatum est*. Sometimes Douglas inserts lines which have no strict equivalent in Virgil but are appropriate in the context: he says of the fall of Troy, 'The fatis wil na mair it induryng' (II.v.78); and of Pallas's death, 'Seand the fatys wald haue hys endyng' (X.viii.68). Very occasionally Douglas clothes Virgil's references to fate in traditional Christian phrasing: 'purviance dyvyne' (III.vi.42 = *auspiciis*); 'purvyance' (V.ii.28 = *numine*); 'fatale ordinans, Thar destyne and goddis purvians' (XII.ii.151–2 = *fata*). But Douglas does not impose upon Virgil a specifically Christian conception of destiny and its relation to the divine purpose; rather he tends to stress and expand those ideas that he could reconcile with his own religion.

Douglas invited his readers to compare the *Eneados* with its original:

> Bot, gyf I le, lat Virgyll be owr iuge,
> Hys wark is patent, I may have na refuge;
> Tharby go note my faltis on by on . . .
> (Exclamatioun, 19–21)

It is not difficult to note Douglas's 'faltis'—his occasional failure to observe distinctions of case or quantity, and other small grammatical errors or mistranslations. Yet again and again what may at first appear a blunder turns out to be a correct translation of a corrupt reading in Douglas's Latin text, or to derive from the mistaken interpretation of a commentator. If we wish to make a fair judgment of Douglas's accuracy as a translator, we must view the *Eneados* in the context of contemporary classical scholarship. Again, faithfulness to Virgil, for Douglas, often entailed a fullness of expression that few translators would seek today. Yet Douglas does not distort the proportions of the *Aeneid* nor fundamentally alter Virgil's thought. Unlike Caxton, he makes no major omissions or insertions. He preserves a balance between the different elements in Virgil's poem, and much, if not all, of its complexity.

[6]

The Eneados: *'Eloquence'*

Dryden felt that the English language was inadequate to render Virgil's 'almost inexhaustible' stock of 'figurative, Elegant, and sounding Words';[1] and a modern translator, C. Day Lewis, has remarked that 'though there is no great difficulty about putting into English what Vergil meant, it is almost impossible to convey how he said it'.[2] Douglas used the critical vocabulary of his time to voice a similar thought:

> The bewte of his ornate eloquens
> May nocht al tyme be kepit with the sentens.
>   (1 Prol 393–4)[3]

For Douglas as a translator, 'sentence' took priority over 'eloquence'; he was a far less deliberate and consistent stylist in the *Eneados* than he had been in the *Palice of Honour*. His intense concern for the 'sentence' often led him to approach the *Aeneid* in the spirit of a teacher or a *grammaticus*, explaining, glossing and paraphrasing. Yet Douglas was a poet as well as a 'clerk'; sometimes he sought less to explain Virgil than to re-create him, translating the *Aeneid* not only into his own language, but into his own culture and poetic traditions. A distinction of this kind is clearly an over-simplification—the *Eneados* cannot be neatly parcelled up into sections, illustrating now one approach, now the other. The styles of the commentator and the late medieval poet sometimes conflict, but sometimes, as I have already illustrated, they have much in common. Indeed, Douglas even extracts a kind of poetry from the dry commentary of Ascensius. Douglas is far more ready to talk to his readers about the first approach than the second. He says little about his own style, and, apart from praising Chaucer, says even less of his debt to native traditions of poetry. This chapter will be largely concerned with the *Eneados* as a poem, and above all with the question of 'eloquence'—the extent to which Douglas conveys something of Virgil's eloquence, or substitutes for it an eloquence of his own.

A fifteenth-century Italian, Antonio Filarete, criticized those who made figures of Caesar and Hannibal and dressed them in 'the clothes that we wear today'.[4] In the *Eneados*, however, Douglas frequently translates Virgil's world into terms of contemporary experience.

Merum is rendered as 'Ypocras' (i.xi.67). Dido wears a wimple and a 'quayf of fyne gold wyrin threid' (iv.iv.19). Amata wears a 'quafe' (vii.vi.26), and Ascanius a 'tawbart' (iii.vii.27). At the entry of the horse within the walls of Troy, the young people rejoice by 'syngand karrellis and dansand in a ryng' (ii.iv.70). When Douglas speaks of ships it is clear that he visualizes them like the ships of the Discoverers or those which appear in the woodcuts of Sebastian Brant, with 'forcastell' (v.xiii.25) and 'eftcastellis' (iii.viii.41 or v.iii.58). When he describes armour, Douglas regularly translates Virgil's *aes* by 'steill' (viii.x.60), 'stelyt' (xi.i.25), 'irne graith' (xi.vii.79), 'plait of steill' (xii.ix.99), or 'steill weid' (xii.xii.45). So too *aeratae* (of ships' prows) is translated as 'stelyt' (x.iv.138; x.v.18). Douglas knew well enough the literal meaning of *aes*, and could translate it accurately in other contexts, but he has here transposed the bronze age world of the *Aeneid* (already archaic in Virgil's time) into the experience of his own age. This he did with many of his other military terms: in the *Eneados* the soldiers wear 'basnet', 'curace', 'gorget', 'hawbrik', 'habergeon', and 'sallet'; and Aeneas's helmet has a 'vental' (xii.vii.123). They defend themselves with 'buclaris' and 'pavys'; they fight with 'awblastir' (cross-bow), 'gisarme', 'glaive', and 'pollax', and Camilla even bears a Turkish bow (xi.xiii.11). Douglas does not, however, put firearms into the hands of the Trojans, although he introduces an un-Virgilian image in his account of the Cyclops at their forge:

> Syne to thar wark, in maner of gun powder,
> Thai myddillyt and thai myxit this feirful sowder.
> (viii.vii.139–40)

(This may seem odder to us than to Douglas, since some humanists believed that gunpowder was known to the ancients and invented by Archimedes.)[5] Such usages may be justifiably regarded as anachronistic, yet they should be distinguished from other phrases, superficially quaint, such as 'ammyral of our flote' (used of Anchises in iii.viii.37) or the 'toppyt hattis' worn by the *Salii* (viii.xi.52). We must dismiss from our minds irrelevant images of gold braid, and remember too that top hats were quite unknown to Douglas and that 'toppyt' simply means 'pointed'.[6] Quaintness of this kind is not anachronism but a patina conferred upon Douglas's language by the passage of time.

Douglas had to grapple with one of the central problems faced by any translator: that of rendering not simply words but unfamiliar objects or practices, or ideas and beliefs that were alien and sometimes considered dangerous. The problem of translating a culture is implicit in translating a language. One method that Douglas used to

cope with this difficulty has already been mentioned—the paren-
thetic explanation, for instance, of Jupiter's thunderbolt—

> That we intill our langage clepe fyreflauch
> (II.x.156)

But what is the effect? To emphasize the gulf between the 'they' of
the *Aeneid* and the 'we' of Douglas and his readers; between 'then'
and 'now on dayis'; between 'thair leid' and 'our langage'. It creates,
if fleetingly, a sense of the remoteness of the *Aeneid* from Douglas's
world. The other method that Douglas uses, more frequently and
probably far less consciously, telescopes the first, and is the one we
tend to call anachronistic. Some of the differences are apparent in
Douglas's two versions of the same Virgilian line, *Arcturum pluui-
asque Hyadas geminosque Triones*, first as

> The rany Hyades, quhilk ar the sternys sevyn,
> And eik Arcturus, quhilk we cal the laid stern,
> The dowbill Vrsys weil couth he decern.
> (I.xi.100-2 = I.744)

and later as

> Arthuris Huyf, and Hyades betakynnand rayn,
> Syne Watlyng Streit, the Horn and the Charle Wayn.
> (III.viii.21-2 = III.516)

In the first passage we hear two voices: Douglas's superimposed on
that of Virgil. In the second Douglas gives the vernacular names for
stars and constellations, names with un-Virgilian associations:
Arthur (the confusion of *Arcturus* and *Arthurus* seems to have
occurred long before Douglas),[7] and Charlemagne, and Watling
Street (the popular term for the Galaxy, which is not indeed mentioned by Virgil). Douglas's search to find native equivalents for
Virgil's astronomy produces an imaginative jolt, a sense of incongruity.

Yet it is this second approach, concrete, specific, and local, which
is responsible for Douglas's greatest triumphs as a translator. At his
best 'he makes the world of the *Aeneid* seem almost contemporary;
Virgil's characters might be just round the corner; they are young
and glowing'.[8] Douglas describes Aeneas, 'lyke till ane ʒongker with
twa lauchand eyn' (I.ix.19). He catches the informal beauty of Venus:

> As scho had bene a wild hunteres,
> With wynd waving hir haris lowsit of tres,
> Hir skyrt kiltit til hir bair kne.
> (I.vi.25-7)

and the weird, uncanny aspect of Charon:

> Thir ryveris and thir watyris kepit war
> By ane Charon, a grisly ferryar,

Terribil of schap and sluggart of array,
Apon his chyn feil cannos harys gray,
Lyart feltrit tatis: with burnand eyn red,
Lyk twa fyre blesys fixit in his hed;
Hys smottrit habyt, owr his schulderis lydder,
Hang pevagely knyt with a knot togiddir,
Hym self the cobill dyd with hys bolm furth schow,
And, quhen hym list, halit vp salys fow.
    (VI.v.7–16)

Douglas had an imaginative sympathy with many different aspects of the *Aeneid*, ranging from the brief mention of

    a valle in a crukyt glen,
Ganand for slycht till enbusch armyt men . . .
    (XI.x.83 ff.)

to the richly caparisoned horses prepared for the Trojans by Evander:

Thar brusyt trappuris and patrellis reddy bovne,
With goldin bruchis hang from thar brestis dovne;
Thar harnessing of gold rycht deirly dicht;
Thai runge the goldin mollettis burnyst bright.
    (VII.iv.193–6)

We may say that here and elsewhere Douglas Scotticizes or medievalizes Virgil, or sometimes adds details of his own invention, but this does not mean that he invariably 'lowers' Virgil or makes him more rustic.[9] Douglas was alert to Virgil's variety, and his own style was sufficiently flexible to convey the distinctive tone of these very different passages. What is most important is that in each case Douglas transmits the vitality present in Virgil's words.

Our difficulty in judging this aspect of Douglas's translation is heightened by the fact that the relationship between one culture and another is not fixed and unchanging. In some respects even unlearned readers today know more about antiquity and the world of Virgil than did the audience envisaged by Douglas. Few modern readers of a translation of the *Aeneid* require an explanation of the Sirens (Douglas compares them to mermaids, in v.xiv.71). Few people today need to have the word *trident* explained; the word and what it represents have long been assimilated into English, and when it occurs in the *Aeneid* a modern translator feels no need either to explain it or to hunt for a native equivalent. But the position in Douglas's time was quite different. The word *trident* is not recorded in English till towards the end of the sixteenth century. Douglas's repeated efforts to find a satisfactory translation—'thre granyt ceptour . . .lyk a crepar [grappling hook] or a graip [pitchfork] with thre granys' (I.iii.54n), 'thre granyt ceptour wand' (I.iii.75), 'mattok havand granys thre' (11.x.90)—may strike a modern reader as comical, but they reflect a real difficulty, and are understandable in the context of his time.[10] In other respects Douglas's first readers were closer to Virgil than we are. We have adopted many Latin words into our own language; they lived more similar lives. In social organization and methods of warfare, for instance, the sixteenth century had more in common with the world of the *Aeneid* than we do. The dynastic significance of the marriage between Aeneas and Lavinia would need no explaining to the subjects of James IV and Margaret Tudor. Virgil's portrait of the malicious Drances well fits several of the Scottish noblemen in Douglas's own circle:

> Bot ane seditioun or a brek to make
> Sa masterfull, tharin was nane hys mayk;
> The nobill kynrent of hys moderis syde
> Maid hym full gret of blude, and full of pryde.
> (xi.vii.105–8)

Sometimes indeed Douglas can render Virgil more exactly than a modern translator. Virgil's *bidentis* (iv.57, v.96), a ritual term for 'a sheep two years old', is succinctly translated by Douglas as 'twyntris', which has the literal meaning 'of two winters' (iv.ii.10 and v.ii.105). Modern translators usually render it more generally as 'sheep'. In this case Douglas's vocabulary and Virgil's had something in common, whereas the standard English of our urbanized society no longer contains such a technical term.

It is with religion that the gap between Virgil and Douglas is greatest, and sometimes becomes a chasm. Here we are most aware of the historical distance between the translator and his material. Douglas applies phrases like these to pagan ritual and sacrifice: 'eftir thar gys' (vii.iii.60), 'on thar gys' (viii.iii.16), 'as tho was the gys' (xii.iv.35). Sometimes, it is true, these originate in Virgil's own *de more* or *rite* (as in v.ii.71 or vi.xvi.12). At other times they serve chiefly as couplet-fillers; it is amusing to note how often 'gys' rhymes with 'sacrifice' (as in iii.ii.137 and passim). Yet the sense of distaste for pagan ritual is clearly Douglas's in comments such as these: 'Eftir the serymonys of thar payane gys' (iv.ii.7); 'eftir thar payane ryte and gys' (v.ii.71); and 'by thar gentil law' (vii.iii.56). Dido, most inappropriately self-aware, invokes Proserpina 'by our gentile lawys' (iv.xi.50). At such points Douglas reminds us of his medieval predecessors, Chaucer and Lydgate, who spoke similarly of 'payens corsed olde rites' (*Troilus and Criseyde*, v.1849) or

> þe custom vsed in þo dawes
> And þe ritys of her paynym lawes.
> (*Troy Book*, iv.521–2)

Yet such interposed comments are comparatively rare. Douglas usually shows more historical imagination in referring to the pagan religion. He had available many words that a translator would use today — *temple, priest, sacrifice, gods*. In other cases he chose what seem acceptable, even if less familiar terms — 'franches or sanctuary' (VIII.vi.69) for Virgil's *asylum* (VIII.342), or 'spamen' (IV.ii.29) for *uatum* (IV.65). Where modern readers feel most disquiet is at Douglas's rendering of the *sacerdos* referred to by Dido, whom he variously calls 'ane haly nun', 'prophetes', 'religyus', and 'religyus nun' (all in IV.ix); and of the *Sibyl* of book VI, who appears as 'nun', 'sant', and 'holy religyus woman clene'. Attention has focused chiefly on the term 'nun' — there seems a particular incongruity in the phrase 'nunnys of Bachus' (IV.vi.41), which refers to *Thyias* (IV.302).[11] Yet it is important to see this in historical perspective; one may thus sympathize with Douglas's problems, even if not applauding his solution. *Priestess*, the neutral word commonly used by modern translators in these contexts, did not exist in the sixteenth century; according to *O.E.D.* it is not recorded in English until 1693. Douglas's term, *nun*, then possessed a wider range of meaning than it has today, and had been used in Old and Middle English to signify a 'priestess of some pagan deity'. In the sixteenth century it was still current in this sense, and so used not only by Douglas but by later writers, such as Surrey, and Drayton, who speaks similarly of 'Bacchus raging frantike Nunnes'.[12] Douglas seems indeed to betray much less sensitivity as a translator when he refers to Latinus's *diuos* (XII.286) as 'mawmontis', literally, 'Mahomets' (XII.v.165). This introduces the scorn of Douglas's own age for heathen gods and idols.

Douglas was highly responsive to the story-telling aspect of the *Aeneid*; I suspect that he enjoyed the battles of the later books far more than do modern readers. The *Aeneid* was a tale, excitingly told, and in order to tell it himself he adopted a style that owed much to earlier narrative poets, both Scots and English. With one or two exceptions, he made little attempt to imitate the more rhetorical features of Virgil's style at all closely. It is characteristic that at the very opening of the *Eneados* Douglas summoned the attention of his readers in the peremptory manner of the romances:

> Quha list attend, gevis audiens and draw neir!
> (I Prol 503)

Part of the purpose of this chapter is to show the strength and diversity of the native poetic traditions that Douglas inherited, and the way in which they influenced the *Eneados*, both for good and ill.

Douglas's choice of verse-form illustrates his readiness to work within an existing tradition. Surrey, in his translation of *Aeneid* II and IV, was to introduce into English the 'straunge metre'[13] of blank verse, possibly modelled on Virgil's own hexameters. Douglas was no such innovator, metrically. He used the decasyllabic couplet, which in the fifteenth century had virtually replaced the octosyllabic couplet as a suitable form for narrative, although it does not seem to have been as highly esteemed as stanzaic verse. Among English poets the form had been successfully used by Chaucer in the *Legend of Good Women* and in many of the *Canterbury Tales*; it was also used by Lydgate, in the *Troy Book*, and by a number of other fifteenth-century writers. Among Scottish poets Douglas's chief predecessor in this form was the author of the *Wallace*. Apart from Chaucer, Douglas's models were not very sophisticated; it is hardly surprising that his own use of the couplet is competent, rather than distinguished. Douglas lacks the metrical consistency of Dunbar or Henryson, and does not give the same impression of being wholly in control of his medium. Saintsbury says aptly that he is 'the only one [of these Scottish poets] in whom the Thistle rather bristles itself up against the Rose'.[14] Douglas himself is apologetic about his 'corruppit cadens imperfyte' (1 Prol 46), yet the very skill of that cadence and of the surrounding verse should make one wary of taking the remark too literally. At the end of the *Eneados* Douglas values his own verse highly enough to follow Chaucer in admonishing his scribes:

> Зhe nother maggill nor mysmetyr my ryme!
>
> (Tyme, space and dait, 24; IV, p. 194)[15]

I shall not here attempt a detailed examination of Douglas's versification, but mention some of the salient points.[16] First, he clearly had a firm notion of metrical regularity. Again and again, he writes lines like these:

> To meys the flude or rays with stormys hie
>
> (I.ii.30)
>
> Belive Eneas membris schuk for cald
>
> (I.iii.1)
>
> Now fletis the mekil holk with tallonyt keyll
>
> (IV.vii.74)

To achieve this regularity Douglas employed a variety of devices. Like other Scottish poets of his time he took advantage of permitted variations in pronunciation. The grammatical endings *-is* and *-it* (*-id*) could be syllabic or not, as the verse required. (In the lines above, 'stormys' is two-syllabled, but 'fletis' is a monosyllable.) Douglas sometimes used the shortened pronunciation of words with intervocalic /v/, such as 'euir' or 'euin', although this is not always apparent in the spelling. Sometimes a shortened, colloquial form of other words is used, to supply the rhyme, as in 'befaw' (= befall), which rhymes with 'schaw' (ix.i.47–8); so too the rhyme with 'spak' indicates that the shortened pronunciation of 'contract' is used in xii.ii.157–8.[17] Douglas frequently varies the form of names to suit the metrical context: 'Achill' as well as 'Achilles'; 'Enee' as well as 'Eneas'; 'Mercur' as well as 'Mercurius'. Like other poets Douglas sometimes uses periphrastic forms of the verb to aid his verse:

And murnand baith his handis vp *did hald.*

(i.iii.2)

This construction with *did* is familiar in English verse of the period, but is extended to other parts of the verb, such as the infinitive and present participle, by Scottish poets.[18] Douglas has another method of forming the past tense, employing *gan*, or its variant, *can*:[19]

The firmament *gan* rummylling, rair and rout

(i.ii.64)

Thus said Ilioneus, and sa *can* he ces.

(i.viii.116)

This construction is particularly associated with Scottish narrative poets, such as Barbour, Hary and Henryson. It occurs chiefly in the third person, and functions as a device for lengthening the line or placing the infinitive in rhyme position. Douglas seems to have 'exercised a great deal of freedom with the idiom. He used more compound infinitives than his predecessors, and he more frequently placed the auxiliary in one line and the infinitive in the next.'[20]

Douglas often departs from the metrical norm. His occasional reversion to octosyllabics has been noted by Coldwell,[21] and he sometimes writes lines that are hypermetrical:

Quhat wikkit counsale, fader, has turnyt thi thocht?

(i.v.21)

Quhat fors and violens drave the hyddir till ws

(i.ix.67)

Lines often begin with a heavy stress on the first syllable:

Myghty of moblys, full of sculys seyr

(i.i.23)

Warp all thar bodeis in the deip bedeyn

(i.ii.33)

This might be regarded as an inversion of stress in the first foot, or, more plausibly, as an inheritance from the stress-patterns characteristic of the older, alliterative verse. Whatever the metrical analysis, such variations from the norm seem in most cases to be acceptable and even desirable. But it cannot be denied that Douglas's verse also contains rough and clumsy-sounding lines, which have a metrical structure difficult to analyse and which sometimes resemble the 'broken-backed' lines of Lydgate.[22]

Douglas's couplets are often end-stopped, and we are sometimes over-conscious of redundant phrases inserted to complete them .Yet his deployment of these couplets has more variety than is always realized. Sometimes they are woven together by enjambement, as in

> Quha sal the harmys of that woful nycht
> Expreme? Or quha with tong to tell hes mycht
> Sa feil ded corsis as thar lyis slane?
> Or thocht in cace thai weip quhil teris rayn
> Equaly may bewail tha sorowis all?
> (II.vii.1–5)

Sometimes, however, the couplet is split apart into a series of separate lines. This staccato, even stichic, effect is characteristic of scenes of action, and is particularly clear in this expansion of a single line in Virgil (v.429):

> Now, hand to hand, the dynt lychtis with a swak;
> Now bendis he vp hys burdon with a mynt,
> On syde he bradis fortil eschew the dynt;
> He etlys ʒondir hys avantage to tak,
> He metis hym thar, and charris hym with a chak;
> He watis to spy, and smytis in al hys mycht,
> The tother keppys hym on hys burdon wycht;
> (v.viii.10–16)

At other times Douglas piles up the clauses in long and rather loosely articulated structures:

> Amyd a four quhelit char Latyn that thraw
> With huge pomp by stedis fowr was draw,
> *Quhais* haris and hys tymplis war weil dycht
> With ryall crown of fyne gold burnyst brycht,
> *Quharon* stud turrettis twelf, lyke bemys scheyn,
> As it ane rych enornament had beyn
> Of cleir Phebus, *that* was hys grandschir hald:
> Nixt *quham* furth rollyt was Prynce Turnus bald
> Within a twa quhelyt chariot of delyte
> *That* drawyn was with stedis twa mylk quhyte.
> (XII.iv.3–12)

(A similar use of relative pronouns and other connectives may be seen in VII.vii.5 ff., XI.x.83–93 and XIII.i.27–50.) It would be an exaggeration to apply the term 'verse paragraphing' to this unwieldy sentence, yet it shows Douglas striving to sustain and prolong the momentum of his verse in a way that may owe something to the practice of Virgil.

It seems to me, however, that Douglas tends to see Virgil in terms of single lines—again and again his basic unit, the couplet, corresponds exactly to one line of Virgil's. It is not easy to determine how far Douglas understood the structure of Virgil's hexameter. Some of his mistranslations betray an ignorance of Latin quantities, and therefore of the scansion of Virgil's verse. In IV.252 Virgil describes Mercury as *nītens*, 'poising, balancing', but Douglas's translation, 'schynand' (IV.v.144), suggests that he read it as the different verb *nĭtens*. Sometimes Douglas mistakes the case of adjectives and thus their grammatical agreement, confusing ablatives in *-ā* with nominatives or accusatives in *-ă*. Virgil's

> ipse inter primos correpta dura bipenni
> limina perrumpit
> (II.479–80)

is mistranslated as

> Bot first of al, ane stalwart ax hynt he,
> The stern Pyrrus, to hew and brek the ʒet.
> (II.viii.70–1)

I suspect that Douglas paid more attention to the proximity of *dura* to *bipenni* than to the fact that *dura* forms part of a dactyl. Douglas similarly confused *mănus* with *mānes*, when he mistranslated Virgil's

> manibus et cineri, si qua est ea cura, remitto
> (X.828)

as

> 'Onto thy parentis handis and sepulcre
> I the belief to be entyrit', quod he.
> (X.xiii.163–4)

It is difficult to say whether such errors resulted from carelessness, or a failure to perceive that the ancient pronunciation of Latin differed considerably from that employed by Douglas himself.[23] He certainly appreciated some of Virgil's sound-effects, as I shall show later in the chapter. Yet there is no sign that Douglas possessed the interest in Latin metres that characterized many English poets in the latter half of the sixteenth century.[24] He differs from Richard Stanyhurst, who discussed the prosodies of Latin and English in the preface to his *First Foure Bookes of Virgil his Aeneis* (1582), and attempted to emulate the hexameter in his own eccentric verse.

I have said something already of the way in which Douglas divides each book of the *Eneados* into chapters. These chapters often follow Virgil's own hints as to the smaller units or paragraphs into which the books of the *Aeneid* are disposed. Many begin with phrases such as 'in the meyn tyme' (I.vii; I.x), 'in the meyn quhile' (III.vii; v.i), 'the meyn sesson' (x.vi; xI.xi), 'dvryng this quhile' (xI.xii), or 'wyth this' (II.v; II.vi). These are transition-formulas, and they usually, if not invariably, correspond to Latin words with a similar function, such as *interea* or *iamque*. In Virgil, too, these words are often signposts, introducing a new piece of narrative (as at 1.180 and 1.223), or marking a fresh stage in the action. Douglas sometimes follows Virgil's lead in other respects, as when he opens new chapters with invocations (in 1x.iii and ix; x.iv).

Yet Douglas's chapters also reflect medieval methods of composition. His favourite way of opening a chapter is to refer to the passage of time, more particularly the coming of night or of dawn:[25]

Cummyn is the nycht . . .
    (III.iii.1)
The secund day be this sprang fra the est,
Quhen Aurora the wak nycht dyd arest
And chays fra hevyn with hir dym skyis donk.
    (III.ix.1-3)
Furth of the sey, with this, the dawyng spryngis.
    (IV.iv.1)

Douglas did not invent these passages; Virgil had punctuated his narrative similarly—with *Nox erat* (III.147), *Postera iamque dies primo surgebat Eoo* (III.588), and *Oceanum interea surgens Aurora reliquit* (IV.129). But in placing such descriptions so often at the beginning of his chapters Douglas was clearly influenced by the popularity of the season-opening with medieval poets. Chaucer, Lydgate, and some romance-writers used this same device to introduce a new stage in their narrative.[26] Douglas is so fond of the practice that he sometimes gives a season reference far greater prominence than it has in the *Aeneid*. Modern editors do not place Virgil's

interea magnum sol circumuoluitur annum
et glacialis hiems Aquilonibus asperat undas
    (III.284-5)

at the opening of a paragraph. But Douglas makes it the emphatic beginning of a new chapter:

Be this the son had circulit his lang 3er,
And frosty wyntir scharpit the watir cleir
With cald blastis of the northin art.
    (III.v.1-3)

(The same is true of Douglas's opening to VIII.iii.)
    Douglas begins another chapter in this way:

The nycht approchis, with hir weyngis gray
Ourspred the erd and put all lycht away.
(VIII.vii.1–2)
This translates
nox ruit et fuscis tellurem amplectitur alis
(VIII.369)
Modern editors usually treat this line not as a beginning but an end;
they start a fresh paragraph with line 370. But Virgil's line is surely
transitional, pointing back to Aeneas, falling asleep in the humble
dwelling of Evander, and forward to Venus and Vulcan in their
golden nuptial chamber. This illustrates the dangers of breaking up
Virgil's text into sections of any kind; it makes sharp and discrete
what is continuous and interwoven. A similar effect is produced
when Douglas ends a chapter with a striking and emphatic line:
Thai fewter fut to fut, and man to man.
(x.vi.166)
This derives from Virgil (x.361), but occasionally Douglas inserts
a punchline of his own:
'Delay no more, bot manfully go to it.'
(xi.vii.198)
(cf. also IX.ix.142; x.xiv.193 ff.; and XI.viii.166).

Sometimes Douglas's fondness for the season-opening leads him
to split a Virgilian line. Virgil's
Dixit, deinde lacu fluuius se condidit alto
ima petens; nox Aenean somnusque reliquit.
(VIII.66–7)
is spread over two chapters. The first sentence concludes VIII.i; the
second opens chapter ii:
The nycht fled, and the sleip left Ene.
A more gross example occurs at the beginning of Douglas's book
VII, which opens not with Virgil's first line (the apostrophe to
Caieta) but with line 25—*Iamque rubescebat radiis mare et aethere ab
alto:*
Tho gan the sey of bemis walxin red,
And heich abuf, dovn from the hevinly sted,
Within hyr rosy cartis cleirly schane
Aurora vestit into brovn sanguane.
Such a practice does not show Douglas's customary respect for
Virgil's text, and it is not an isolated occurrence. In three other
places—and without the excuse of the season-opening—Douglas
alters Virgil's book-divisions: he begins book II with *Aeneid* II.13,
thus breaking Virgil off in mid-line; book VI with *Aeneid* VI.9; and
book VIII with *Aeneid* VIII.18. These changes must be attributed to

Douglas himself, since they are found in all manuscripts of the
Eneados. Only the 1553 edition re-arranges the text in the correct
Virgilian pattern. (If Douglas's copyists were responsible, it seems
unlikely that they would have inserted the extra explanatory line
at vi.i.i.) Coldwell regards these changes as 'an act of textual
criticism',[27] but I find them perhaps the most puzzling feature of
Douglas's translation, and by no means 'minor textual adjustments'.
It is true that a kind of logic may be discerned in the changes; in
his edition of the *Aeneid* Mackail speaks of vi.1–8 as 'connecting
lines', and says that some scholars regard viii.1–17 as a 'stop-gap'.[28]
Douglas may have possessed a scholarly authority for so reorganiz-
ing the text, similar perhaps to Servius's comment that the first two
verses of book vi were originally at the end of book v. Yet, whatever
his justification, Douglas is here modifying the structure of the *Aeneid.*

The style and diction of the *Eneados* demonstrate Douglas's familiarity with the traditions of vernacular poetry. Much of his phrase-
ology came from a common stock, drawn upon by poets who in
other respects differed greatly from one another—Scots and English,
courtly and popular, alliterative and non-alliterative. One small
instance of this is Douglas's taste for fixed epithets: blood is red
(xii.i.125); tears are salt (x.viii.69); grass and herbs are green
(i.iv.97; and ix.iii.205); clouds are grey (xii.xiii.161), as is marble
also (vii.i.7). We read again and again of 'fludis gray' (vi.v.66 and
passim), and of 'assys cald' (iv.i.69 and passim). These adjectives
usually have no equivalent in Virgil. Sometimes they are appropriate, but add little to the sense; in v.ii.64–6 Helymus is 'great',
Acestes 'old', and Ascanius 'bold'. Douglas often inserts adjectives
which intensify and add colour: Virgil's *lampade* (vii.148) becomes
a 'goldin lamp bryght' (vii.iii.1); horses that are *nitidi* (vii.275) in
Virgil are 'mylk quhite' (vii.iv.189) in Douglas. Virgil is vivid, but
Douglas sometimes makes him more obviously bright and pictorial—'as quha the mater beheld tofor thar e' (i Prol 14). Sometimes this is pleasing, as in this image of the sea –

> the lippyrrand wallys quhyte
> War pulderit full of fomy froith mylk quhite.
> (viii.xi.73–4)

But Virgil's restrained picture of the dead Lausus—*sanguine turpan-
tem comptos de more capillos* (x.832)—is coarsened by Douglas:

> The ded body vplyftis fra the grond,
> That with red blude of his new grene wond
> Besparklyt had hys ȝallow lokis brycht,
> That ayr war kemmyt and addressyt rycht.
> (x.xiii.175–8)

Douglas frequently inserts short similes and comparisons into his translation. Sometimes these have been sparked off by a Virgilian metaphor: Virgil's *rosea* (1.402) lies behind Douglas's description of Venus—'Hir nek schane lyke onto the roys in May' (1.vi.163). So too *flammato* (1.50) lies behind 'byrnyng as fyre' (1.ii.1), and *ardet* (XII.3) behind 'byrnand hait as fyre' (XII.i.10). Virgil's bold *aquae mons* (1.105) becomes 'heich as a hill' (1.iii.21). In VIII.659 Virgil's *aurea* means literally 'golden, carved out of gold', but Douglas seizes the chance to introduce an image much favoured by courtly poets:

> Thar haris schane as doith the brycht gold wyre.[29]
> (VIII.xi.41)

Most of these similes, however, have a popular and proverbial character. Douglas uses some repeatedly, such as 'dolf as led' (v. viii.95 and XI.vii.102) or 'drunk as swyne' (IX.v.28). He sometimes plays several variations on a well-known formula: 'blak as pyk' (v.xii.56); 'blak as ony craw' (VI.iv.7), and 'blak as hell' (VIII.iv. 154). Yet Douglas also supplies imaginative comparisons of his own, as when he describes Turnus fleeing from Aeneas:

> turnyng heir and thar,
> Lyke as befor the hund wiskis the hair.[30]
> (XII.xii.171-2)

At other times Douglas's image is not original but is still vivid and appropriate, as when he expands *lacrimas* to 'salt terys . . . Furth ʒetting our hys chekis thyk as rayn' (x.viii.69-70). Douglas describes the flight of weapons as 'thik as haill schour' (x.xii.12), and says of a warrior—'Than as wod lyon ruschit he in the fight' (x.ix. 8). Chaucer had used each of these comparisons in very similar contexts.[31] The resemblance seems to me coincidental, but is still revealing. Neither Chaucer nor Douglas disdained to draw their imagery from the common stock, and the effect is not necessarily trite but contributes to the concrete, down-to-earth element in their style.

Douglas frequently uses phrases that call attention to the mood or emotion of a scene. When Andromache is reminded of Hector, she 'walit so that piete was to heir' (III.v.61). Elsewhere occur lines such as these:

> O soverane preist, *quhat reuth was it of the!*
> (VII.xii.130)
> And of hys mouth, *a petuus thing to se,*
> The lopprit blude in ded thraw voydis he.
> (x.vi.135-6)
> The wemen bet thar breistis, *was reuth to se.*[32]
> (XI.xvii.24)

Phrases similar to those italicized occur in Chaucer also—in the *Knight's Tale* (2345) Emily 'weep that it was pitee for to heere'. But they are part of the stock in trade of most medieval poets, and their formulaic character is evident.³³ With them should be linked similar phrases expressing astonishment: 'a wondir thing to se' (VIII.iv.35); or horror: 'grysly forto tell' (II.iii.44) and 'grysly for to se' (VII. ix.61). Such formulaic expressions are not without precedent in Virgil; he too uses *miserabile uisu* (I.111), and it is his *mirabile dictu* that lies behind Douglas's 'wonderfull to tell' (II.iii.57 = II.174) and 'a wondrus thing to tell' (VIII.iv.153 = VIII.252). But Douglas often inserts such phrases, particularly those which emphasize the 'reuth' and 'pietie' of a scene, where they have no literal equivalent in the text of the *Aeneid*. They do not usually go counter to Virgil's tone, but they make the pathos more insistent.

Interjections, such as *allace, allaik, harro*, and others, give a similar guidance to the reader's sympathies. These sometimes translate Virgil's *heu*, but more frequently are the responsibility of Douglas. In the following lines from Dido's passionate speech to Aeneas (IV.318 ff.) the italicized words are inserted by Douglas:

> Quhat! wilt thou fle from me? *allace! allace!*
> . . . .
> My sweit gest, quhamto thou me leif will?
> My gest, *ha God!* quhou al thyng now invane is,
> Quhen of my spows nane othir name remanys!
> . . . .
> Than semyt I nocht, thus wys, *allace! allace!*
> Aluterly dissauyt nor dissolate.
> (IV.vi.65 ff.)

In keeping with this is Douglas's piling up of the adjectives in 'petuus rewthfull complantis sayr' (IX.viii.49), which translates *questibus* (IX.480), or 'wofull wyfly cry' (XI.xvii.25), which translates *femineum clamorem* (XI.878). Such explicitness as to mood and emotion is, as noted earlier, highly characteristic of the *Eneados*. It has justly been regarded as characteristic of much medieval verse.³⁴

Very occasionally, Douglas recalls another habit of medieval poets: he slips into the *Eneados* asides, such as 'as that thai tell' (IV.v.125), 'I the tell' (VI.ii.101), and even 'the story tellis thus' (X.xii.40).³⁵ With these may be linked other vestiges of medieval narrative technique, such as the brevity-formula—'schortlie to conclude' (VIII.iii.105, XI.xiii.44);³⁶ or interjections with a similar flavour, such as 'Quhat nedis mair?' (II.i.49), 'Quhat wil ʒe mair?' (II.iv.61), and 'Quhat nedis proces mar?' (XII.xiv.110).³⁷ Once Douglas calls himself back from a slight digression in the traditional way: 'Bot to our purpos' (xii.vi.109).[38] Such interjections are scattered and in-frequent, but they show Douglas viewing his material from the angle less of the strict translator than of the medieval storyteller.

It will be apparent that many of these traditional phrases occur in the second half of the line. Clearly they often had a further pur-pose—they were metrical make-weights, or were designed, as Douglas himself disarmingly remarks, 'to lykly my ryme' (1 Prol 124). In the *Eneados* Douglas often employs the conventional tags, so frequent in medieval poetry: 'y-wis', 'but weir', 'I ges', 'God wait', 'traist me'; and the longer but equally stereotyped phrases: 'as it [he] war wod' (ii.vi.16; iii.ix.71); 'or he wald ces' (x.vii.45); 'or evyr he stynt' (x.x.118). In the *Eneados* one of the commonest and emptiest of these phrases is 'quhar he stude'. Its expletive character is clear from its recurrence at the end of the line, usually rhyming with such words as *flude* or *blude* (e.g. in ii.v.51, viii.i.104, viii.ii.5, and passim). Its flexibility appears in the small variations that Douglas plays on it—'quhar *that* he stude' (iii.x.26); '*thar as* he stude' (v.iv. 4); 'quhar *scho* stude' (viii.xi.23); 'quhar *thai* stude' (ix.iv.1).[39] Douglas also uses inclusive formulae, such as 'est and west' (vii. viii.90), 'man and page' (vii.viii.68), and the well-known 'al and sum'; a bathetic example occurs in 'the thousand schippis al and sum' (ii.iii.104).

The presence of this element in Douglas's language cannot be ignored: conventional, formulaic, the common property of in-numerable medieval poets. Yet it is equally important to realize that it is not the only element in his eclectic and far-ranging vocabulary. It is arguable that in a narrative poet the presence of such familiar and easily-comprehensible phrases may be less of a drawback than an asset; compressed and too close-packed language may slow down the telling of a story. The skill with which such phrases are used can also greatly alter their poetic effect. In Lydgate, for instance, they are far more obtrusive than in Chaucer. 'The medium in which Chaucer's padding formulae and expletives are carried is of so firm and flavored a quality that our attention is not diverted by them. They are not only less frequent than in Lydgate, but often seem formulae only when we have disengaged them from their context.'[40] Douglas's position, in this respect, seems to me midway between these two poets; he is not so clumsy as Lydgate, nor so subtle as Chaucer.

Chaucer's impact on the *Eneados* is difficult to assess.[41] Sometimes what appears 'Chaucerian' to the modern reader might better be termed 'medieval'. At other times the direct influence of Chaucer himself cannot be clearly distinguished from that of his fifteenth-century imitators. Precise and striking echoes of Chaucer's phrasing and imagery are far rarer in the *Eneados* than in the *Palice of Honour* or the Prologues. Yet it is arguable that Chaucer had a pervasive if indirect influence upon Douglas's translation. It was for his language that Chaucer was most admired, and Chaucer seems ultimately responsible for two striking and inter-related features of Douglas's style: his anglicisms and his archaisms. Douglas himself refers to the 'southern' element in his pronunciation:

> Nor ȝit sa cleyn all sudron I refus,
> Bot sum word I pronunce as nyghtbouris doys.
> (1 Prol 113–14)

Anglicized spellings with *o* instead of the usual Scots *a*, *ai* or *ay* (= o.e. ā) are common in the *Eneados*, usually for the sake of the rhyme: 'one' (iv.viii.128) beside the normal 'ane'; 'hote' (viii.viii.10) beside 'hait'; 'gone' (iv.vi.46) beside 'ga'; 'mor' (vi.i.116) beside 'mair'. Anglicisms also appear in the form or choice of isolated words: 'sche' (iv.v.7) beside the more usual 'scho'; 'morrow' (iv.iv.84) beside 'morn'; 'mych' (i.xi.8) beside 'mekill' or 'meikill'.

The syntax of the *Eneados* sometimes recalls uncommon usages in Chaucer and Lydgate: 'cled with the spulȝe of *hym* Achillys' (ii.v. 47) or 'all the famyl of *hym* Iulius' (vi.xiii.75).[42] But Douglas's tendency to archaism is most apparent in the morphology of verbs. He frequently uses *bene* as the present indicative plural of 'be' instead of the regular Scots *ar*: 'the sawlis beyn' (vi.iv.57). This has a precedent in the usage of Chaucer and southern poets, but Douglas occasionally uses it as a form of the third singular—'as beyn the gys' (v.iii.19)—where it has no such justification. Douglas also uses past participles with prefixed *y-* or *i-* : 'ybaik' (xi.xi.47), 'ybe' (xi.i.73), 'yberyit' (ii.v.28), 'yfettyrit' (vi.xii.28), 'ywymplyt' (viii.viii.15), and many more. J. A. H. Murray noted Douglas's use of 'peculiarly Southern forms which retain the prefix and drop the terminations', as in 'ybaik'.[43] This prefix (which represents o.e. *ge-*) had virtually become a 'poetical addition';[44] it was archaic even in 'sudron' speech.

Douglas also uses infinitives ending in *-in* (with spelling variants in *-en*, *-yn*, *-ing*, etc.). Infinitives had regularly become uninflected in northern dialects and Scots by the fourteenth century, but Douglas employs, side by side with the regular forms, infinitives like 'helpyn' (ii.iv.29), 'granting' (iii.iii.44), 'spekyn' (iii.vi.37), and 'thynk-yng' (iii.vii.33). Douglas often uses this *-in* ending with other parts of the verb, such as the present indicative—'thai makyn' (v.iv.41) or 'thai sekyng' (iv.ii.9). The preterite plural *warryn* occurs often

(III.ii.130, v.x.32, etc.). Douglas is fond also of archaic, intensive prefixes like *for-*, *to-*, and *alto-*, as in 'forfeblit' (XII.xiv.59), 'to-schaik' (IV.v.139), and 'al to torn' (II.viii.46).[45]

These forms and usages differ greatly, but none is characteristic of everyday Middle Scots, such as we find it in the records and other prose documents. Yet their use is peculiar neither to the *Eneados* nor to Douglas. They are found in the *Palice of Honour*;[46] and they are found also in the more courtly writings of other Scottish poets such as Dunbar, Lindsay and Bellenden. Such forms had a lustre conferred upon them by their presence in the poetry of Chaucer and his English followers. Their rather restricted circulation may have made them seem appropriate to a high and courtly style. But they also had a highly practical value to Douglas and other Scottish poets: a variation in pronunciation was useful for rhymes, and an extra unstressed syllable, either at the beginning or end of a word, was clearly a metrical aid. The *Eneados* is remarkable, however, for the freedom and variety of its grammatical usage; archaic and anglicized forms do not replace the normal Scots ones, but co-exist beside them. Douglas seems ready to use whatever variant forms or pronunciations of a word are known to him: both 'drive' (I.vi.49) and 'drevyn' (IV.x.38) occur as past participles of 'drive'; 'drynt' (VI.v.97) occurs as well as 'drond' (I.iii.42); 'daw' in the fossilized phrase 'brocht of daw' (II.ii.58) as well as the regular 'day'; pronouns like 'hym selwyn' (II.ii.133), 'hir selwyn' (XI.xv.30), and 'thame selwyn' (IV.iii.65), beside the regular forms ending in *-self*. I suspect, indeed, that Douglas invented some forms to suit his metrical needs, such as the shortened participles 'call' (X.ix.92), or 'cary' (VI.ii.24 and XIII.i.57). Middle Scots itself had great variety of usage, yet this medley of forms contributes largely to the 'poetic' and artificial effect of Douglas's language. Chaucer was ultimately the great sanction for this element in Douglas's style, but the poetic result is far closer to Spenser than to Chaucer. It seems possible indeed that some of Douglas's first readers might have said of him, as Ben Jonson said of Spenser, that Douglas 'in affecting the Ancients, writ no Language'.[47]

From the courtly poetry of Chaucer and his fifteenth-century followers—above all, from poems such as the *Knight's Tale* and *Troilus and Criseyde*—Douglas inherited a chivalric attitude to love. Prologue IV criticizes this tradition from the angle of the moralist, yet shows how well Douglas is acquainted with the conventions, the paradoxes, and the vocabulary of the 'ioly wo' (IV Prol 5). Traces of its phrasing and imagery sometimes creep into his translation. Venus resolves 'this queyn first forto cawch in luffis lace' (I.x.33).[48] In

IV.ii.31 the seers are unable to divine the strength of 'luf with hys hard bandis' (cf. IV Prol 37). Whereas Virgil speaks of Vulcan as *aeterno . . . deuinctus amore* (VIII.394), Douglas describes him as 'lokkyt in the eternal cheyn of luf' (VIII.vii.52). This may be simply an attempt to bring out the meaning of *deuinctus*, yet to me it recalls IV Prologue 36, and Theseus's speech on the 'faire cheyne of love' (*Knight's Tale*, 1.2988 ff.). The idealistic approach to women that forms part of this tradition is to be seen in Douglas's description of Venus, Lavinia, and above all, Dido. Douglas, like Chaucer, loves the epithet 'bright'. He speaks of 'Venus the goddes brycht' (IV.iii. 73). In the heading to XIII.viii. he writes 'Heir Eneas, that worthy nobill knycht,/Was spowsyt with Lauinia the brycht'. He says of Dido

> the brycht teris onon owtbrist
> And fillyt all hir bosum or scho wist.
>
> (IV.i.61–2)

He describes Dido's grief when she finds that Aeneas has left her:

> Hir fayr quhite breist, thar as scho dyd stand,
> Feil tymys smate scho with hir awyn hand,
> And ryvand hir bricht haris petuusly . . .
>
> (IV.xi.9–11)

This may remind us of Criseyde upon hearing that she must leave Troy:

> Hire white brest she bet, and for the wo
> After the deth she cryed a thousand sithe.
>
> (*Troilus and Criseyde*, IV.752–3)

Yet such resemblances suggest Douglas's adherence to the courtly mode of writing rather than direct indebtedness to Chaucer.

Chaucer's direct influence upon the *Eneados* is to be seen chiefly in scattered echoes of words and phrases—such as the rare word 'besmottyrit' (V.vi.124)—and is most evident in two books, IV and XIII. It may seem surprising that Chaucer influenced the translation of *Aeneid* IV, since in Prologue I Douglas had sharply criticized Chaucer's handling of the Dido and Aeneas story. Yet Douglas's very criticism of the *Legend of Dido* shows how attentively he had read it, and although he departs from Chaucer in his interpretation of the characters of Dido and Aeneas, in the translation his attitude to Dido is almost as sympathetic as Chaucer's and is certainly not one of moral censure. Douglas was far from being what he said of Chaucer—'all womanis frend' (I Prol 449)—but he responded to the pathos of Dido's situation. He is good at conveying the pity and tenderness latent in Virgil's words, as in the account of Anna after Dido's death (IV.xii.60–88), or in Dido's

Bot, at the leist, tofor thi wayfleyng,
Had I a child consavyt of thyne ofspryng,
Gif I had ony ӡong Eneas small,
Befor me forto play within my hall,
Quhilk representit by symylitude thi face,
Than semyt I nocht, thus wys, allace! allace!
Aluterly dissauyt nor dissolate.
   (IV.vi.93–9)

Douglas was clearly impressed by many features of the *Legend of Dido*, notably the descriptive passages. These seem to have lingered in his mind and occasionally coloured his translation, particularly of the hunt in book IV:

Nobillys of Cartage, hovand at the port,
The queyn awatys that lang in chawmyr dwellys;
Hyr fers steyd stude stampyng, reddy ellys,
Rungeand the fomy goldyn byt gynglyng;
Of gold and pal wrocht hys rych harnasyng.
And scho at last of palyce yschit owt,
With huge menӡe walking hir abowt,
Lappyt in a brusyt mantill of Sydony,
With gold and perle the bordour al bewry,
Hyngand by hir syde the cays with arowis grund;
Hir bricht tressis envolupyt war and wond
Intil a quayf of fyne gold wyrin threid;
The goldyn button claspyt hir purpour weid—

. . . .

And eftyr thai ar cummyn to the chace,
Amang the montanys in the wild forest,
The rynnyng hundis of cuppillys sone thai kest,
And our the clewys and the holtis, belyve,
The wild beistis doun to the dail thai dryve.
Lo! thar the rays, rynnyng swyft as fyre,
Drevyn from the hyghtis, brekkis out at the swyre;
Ane othir part, syne ӡondyr mycht thou se
The herd of hartis with thar hedis hie,
Ourspynnerand with swyft cours the plane vaill,
The hepe of duste vpstowryng at thar taill,
Fleand the hundis, levand the hie montanys.
   (IV.iv.8–20; 44–55 = *Aeneid* IV.133–9; 151–5)

Douglas keeps fairly close to his text, and even at times tries to catch something of Virgil's sound-effects, as in lines 10–11, with their alliteration on *f* and *st*, which translate Virgil's *stat sonipes ac frena ferox spumantia mandit* (135). Yet Douglas often recalls Chaucer's

Legend of Dido not only in the general mode of writing but in specific echoes. Douglas's 'hovand' in line 8, for instance, seems to derive from Chaucer's use of this unusual and archaic verb in the same context:

> And upon coursers, swift as any thought,
> Hire yonge knyghtes hoven al aboute.
> (*Legend of Good Women*, 1195–6)

Douglas's line 16 expands Virgil's *picto . . . limbo* (137) in a way very similar to Chaucer's:

> Sit Dido, al in gold and perre wrye.
> (*Legend of Good Women*, 1201)

Despite these and other reminiscences of Chaucer, Douglas's style is individual. He draws upon his distinctive northern vocabulary — 'clewys', 'swyre', 'vpstowryng'—and even seems to coin the striking 'ourspynnerand' (= 'spinning or lightly skimming over'). The first passage conveys the visual richness and magnificence of the scene; the second is alive with movement. The whole chapter is a vivid and successful piece of translation.

Douglas's book XIII has several Chaucerian features. The very decision to translate the Thirteenth book shows Douglas departing from the most strict and rigorous conception of translation. Just as his jocular tone towards Maphaeus Vegius differs from his reverent attitude to Virgil, so Douglas takes more liberties with the text of Maphaeus than with that of Virgil. His translation of book XIII seems to me more free and expansive, and possibly more careless. Chaucer's influence is unmistakable in Douglas's handling of certain passages, and more frequently than elsewhere in the *Eneados* colours his narrative tone. One instance of this is the account of the marriage of Aeneas and Lavinia:

> Tharwith the bruyt and noys rays in tha wanys,
> Quhill all the large hallys rang attanys
> Of mannys voce and sound of instrumentis,
> That to the ruyf on hie the dyn vp went is;
> The blesand torchys schayn and sergis brycht,
> That far on breid all lemys of thar lycht;
> The harpys and the githornys plays attanys;
> Vpstart Troianys and syne Italianys
> And gan do dowbill brangillys and gambatis,
> Dansys and rowndis traysyng mony gatis,
> Athir throu other reland, on thar gys;
> Thai fut it so that lang war to devys
> Thar hasty fair, thar revellyng and deray,
> Thar morysis and syk ryot, quhil neir day.

Bot forto tellyng quhou with torch lycht
Thai went to chalmer and syne to bed at nycht,
Myne author list na mensioun tharof draw—
Na mair will I, for sik thingis beyn knaw;
All ar expert, eftir new mariage,
On the first nycht quhat suldbe the subcharge.
(XIII.ix.99–118 = XIII.530–5)

Douglas's translation is remarkably free: he re-arranges the order of events in Maphaeus; he considerably enlarges the description of the dancing, and makes it more specific, adding 'dowbill brangillys and gambatis' and 'morysis'; and the last six lines have no parallel in their original. The humorous *occupatio*, the light irony, the reference to 'myne author', all are in Chaucer's manner; more specifically, Douglas's line 115 directly recalls Chaucer's disclaimer at a very similar point in the *Legend of Dido*, after Dido and Aeneas enter the cave:

I not with hem if there wente any mo;
The autour maketh of it no mencioun.
(*Legend of Good Women*, 1227–8)

A little later in book XIII Douglas describes Venus's re-ascent to the heavens:

From thens scho went away in the schyre ayr,
I wait nocht quhidder, for I com neuer thar.
(XIII.x.111–12)

The flippant second line has no equivalent in Maphaeus, but recalls Chaucer's account of the death of Arcite:

His spirit chaunged hous and wente ther,
As I cam nevere, I kan nat tellen wher.
(*Knight's Tale*, 1.2809–10)

In the translation of the *Aeneid* itself such jocular insertions are rare, though not completely absent. In book VI Douglas describes the spirits waiting to pass in Charon's boat:

Waverand and wandrand by this bankis syde;
Than, at the last, to pas owr in this boyt
Thai beyn admyt, *and costis thame not a grote*.
(VI.v.70–72)

At such a point the jest seems inapposite. At I.xi.91–2, however, Douglas broadens a comedy implicit in Virgil's own words (1.738–40):

Syne al the nobillis tharof drank abowt—
I wil nocht say that ilkman playt cop owt.

This seems true of the description of the boat race in book V:

'Quhar, dysmall, wilt thou now?' gan Gyas cry,
'Hald to the crag agane, Meneyt, fast by.' . . .

> Bot than, God wait, quhat payn in hart gan dre
> The ʒong Gyas—hym thocht al brynt hys banys!
> The watir bryst from baith hys eyn atanys;
> Forʒet was wirschip and hys honeste thar,
> Forʒet was of hys fallowschip the weilfar,
> The ancyant treuth of Meneyt forʒettis he,
> And swakkyt hym our schipburd in the see.
> Hym self, as skyppar, hynt the steir in hand,
> Hym self, as mastir, gan maryneris command,
> And threw the ruddyr to the costis syde.
> Be than the auld Meneyt our schipburd slyde,
> Hevy, and al his weid sowpyt with seys,
> Skars from the watir grond vpboltyt he is,
> Syne swymmand held onto the craggis hycht,
> Sat on the dry rolk, and hym self gan dycht.
> The Troianys lauchys fast seand hym fall,
> And, hym behaldand swym, thai keklyt all,
> Bot mast, thai makyn gem and gret ryot,
> To se hym spowt salt watir of hys throte.
>   (v.iv.15–42)

The humour here is crude but vigorous. The swift pace, the use of direct speech, and the homely yet precise vocabulary—'swakkyt', 'keklyt', 'spowt'—recall the narrative tradition of the fabliau, whose best English examples are Chaucer's 'cherles tales'. But Douglas had no need to go to Chaucer to acquire this comic technique; e could have learnt much from native Scottish poets, such as Dunbar or the author of the *Freiris of Berwik*. Yet the rather slapstick comedy is not Douglas's invention. It derives, like the *repetitio* in lines 31–2, from Virgil himself; the last four lines amplify but do not distort Virgil's own climax:

> illum et labentem Teucri et risere natantem
> et salsos rident reuomentem pectore fluctus.
>   (v.181–2)

Douglas's translation of this episode and of the games in book v skilfully convey the lightened tone of Virgil in this part of the *Aeneid*.

Douglas seems to have felt that the more heroic subject matter of Virgil—especially in the last six books of the *Aeneid*—was best rendered in a style which owed less to Chaucer and the courtly tradition associated with his name than to the traditions of alliterative poetry, and to the diction and phrasing of native 'epics' on the deeds of such Scottish heroes as Robert Bruce and William Wallace.

Douglas's acquaintance with the Scottish alliterative revival has
already been noted (in chapter 2), and his fondness for alliteration
is apparent in all his poetry, not only in the *Eneados* but in the Prologues and the *Palice of Honour*. This has been remarked by some
critics yet seldom studied in any detail.[49] As an occasional ornament
of style alliteration was congenial to most medieval poets, particularly the Scottish ones, but Douglas's practice in the *Eneados*
sometimes resembles that of the alliterative romances, such as *Sir
Gawain and the Green Knight*, the *Destruction of Troy*, and the *Morte
Arthur*, or the Scottish *Rauf Coilȝear* and *Golagros and Gawane*. The
closest parallel, however, to the style of the later books of the *Eneados* is provided by Hary's *Wallace*: this is not technically an alliterative
poem, but it is frequently if sporadically alliterative in a way very
similar to Douglas's poem. Moreover it treats somewhat similar
subjects to the later books of the *Aeneid*: knights and their armour;
sieges and pitched battle; it celebrates the bloody and horrific side
of war as well as moods of patriotism and heroic courage. The style
and contents of this poem—and to a smaller extent that of the *Bruce*
—'hamelie' and 'barbar' though they must have seemed beside Virgil,
provided Douglas with the nearest native equivalent to the *Aeneid*.

The use of alliteration in the *Eneados* cannot be called strict or
systematic. It does not provide the metrical basis of the line, as in
Old English poetry or a poem such as *Sir Gawain*. Few of Douglas's
lines fall into the regular four-stress scheme, with alliteration in the
pattern A A / A X, such as we find it in

> Langaberde in Lumbardie lyftes vp homes
> (*Sir Gawain*, 12)

Yet Douglas's taste for alliterative patterning is apparent in lines
such as these:

> Of giltyn geir dyd glytter bank and bus
> (IX.i.63)
> Thar bustuus bowys keynly do thai bend
> (IX.xi.3)
> Quhill clowdis clattris, and all the lyft ourcastis.
> (IX.xi.20)

The alliteration here coincides with the most emphatic syllables in
the line; the rhythm is therefore sharply defined, and verges on the
traditional four-beat scheme. Douglas shares with many alliterative
poets a taste for starting the line with a strong stress, for parallelism,
and (if less frequently) for paratactic syntax:

> Hynt of the hydis, maid the bowkis bair,
> Rent furth the entralis, sum in tailȝeis schare
> (I.iv.91–2)

Alliteration of this kind is used at intervals throughout the *Eneados*. Its density tends to increase in passages describing noise or violent activity of any sort, and rises to a crescendo in battle scenes. (Chaucer employed alliteration similarly in two descriptions of battles.)[50] Critics have spoken of the 'vigour' of Douglas's translation,[51] and this impression of 'vigour' seems to me often to spring from his alliteration. Something of his practice may be seen in the following:

> Our all the planys brays the stampand stedis,
> Full galȝart in thar bardis and weyrly wedis,
> Apon thar strait born brydillis brankand fast,
> Now thrympand heir, now thar, thar hedis can cast:
>
> . . . .
>
> And furth thai streik thar lang speris weill far,
> Drew in thar armys with schaftis chargit on far,
> Tasyt vp dartis, taclys and fleand flanys;
> The contyr or first tocome for the nanys
> Full ardent wolx, and awfull for to se,
> The men byrnand to ioyn in the melle,
> And furour grew of stedis sterand on stray.
>
> . . . .
>
> Thai meit in melle with a felloun rak,
> Quhil schaftis al to schuldris with a crak;
> Togiddir duschis the stowt stedis atanys,
> That athyris contyr fruschyt otheris banys.
> (XI.xii.5 ff. = XI.599 ff.)
>
> hys swift stedis hovys, quhar thai went,
> Spangit vp the bludy sparkis our the bent,
> Quhil blude and brane, in abundans furth sched,
> Mydlit with sand vndir hors feit was tred.[52]
> (XII.vi.75-8 = XII.339-40)

These describe the onset of battle between Trojans and 'Latines', and Turnus riding over the field. Yet if one omits, as I have done, the clues provided by context and classical names, they might well be extracts from a medieval romance.

These passages illustrate how alliteration sometimes binds lines together in an interlacing of repeated sounds. They illustrate also how the alliterative tradition affected Douglas's diction and phrasing. His fondness for alliterative epithets is evident in phrases like 'stampand stedis' or 'fleand flanys', and he has recourse to many highly conventional phrases: 'douchty dynt', 'felloun fa', 'burnyst brand'. A *brand* is regularly 'burnyst' or 'bricht' or 'bytand' (IX. xii.49), or even 'bytand brycht' (VI.iv.119).[53] 'Weyrly' (or 'weirlyke') is regularly applied to *wedis* (as in IX.i.62 or XI.v.26). The alliterative pairing of syntactically balanced words—'bank and bus', 'blude and brane'—is also extremely frequent in the *Eneados*. Many examples might be given: 'ballyngar and barge', 'hors and harnes', 'fers and furius', 'stern and stout', 'styth and stuyr', 'war and wys', 'rug and reif', 'rummill and rout'. This is a well-established feature of alliterative verse, although not peculiar to it, and most of these pairs are traditional collocations. Their formulaic character, and the way in which they can be slightly varied to suit different contexts may be seen from Douglas's permutations on the familiar 'blood and bone':

> War done to ded, and brytnyt blude and bone
> (x.viii.81)
> Twa biggast men of body and of banys
> (XI.xiii.91)
> The dedly hed throu gyrd his body and banys
> (XI.xvi.68)
> Baith byg bonys and brawnys maid al bair.
> (v.vii.108)

The second passage employs another formula, 'our the bent'. Douglas uses many other phrases of this kind—'battaile to abyde', 'bargane to abyde', 'bownand to battale', 'batale bown'—which will be familiar to readers of alliterative verse.[54]

A word like 'duschis' illustrates how Douglas drew upon a specialized poetic diction associated with battle-description. The word was not perhaps peculiar to alliterative poetry, but tended to occur in alliterative collocations, often of rather a stereotyped kind. In the *Eneados* occur many lines like these:

> To ded he duschis down bath stif and cald
> (IX.vi.95)
> The bustuus body down duschit of the dynt
> (IX.xi.94)
> Down with the dynt duschit the steil blaid keyn
> (IX.xii.55)

With these may be compared

> Dreidles to ground derfly he duschit dede
> (*Wallace*, v.109)

and—since this is not a feature exclusively of Scottish verse—

> He dusshyt of the dynt, dede to the ground
> (*Destruction of Troy*, 6410)

It is this same heroic descriptive tradition that lies behind Douglas's choice of other verbs denoting swift, violent and often noisy action: *frusch* and the intensive *to-frusch*, often (as in the first extract) linked with *dusch*:

> Can with a ramrays to the portis dusche,
> Lyke with thar hedis the hard barris to frusch.
>> (XI.xvii.49–50)

schudder, as in

> Twys ruschit in, and schuddrit the melle
>> (IX.xiii.48)

or

> And with sa swift fard schot throu the melle
> That the myd rowtis and wardis schuddris he.
>> (XII.xi.151–2)

and *brusch*, which Douglas uses regularly of blood pouring out of a wound:

> a flude
> Furth bruschit of the blaknyt dedly blude.
>> (IX.xi.77–8)
> Furth bruschit the sawle with gret stremys of blude.
>> (X.xiv.192)

Hary's usage in the *Wallace* is very similar: 'Aboue the fyr bruschit the blud so red' (x.649); and 'Blud fra byrneis was bruschyt on the greyn' (XI.28).[55]

Some of the adjectives used by Douglas were similarly restricted to a poetic currency: *darf* in the twice repeated phrase 'darf and bald' (VIII.i.21 and IX.ix.22); and *stith*, which occurs chiefly in alliterative collocations, such as 'styth and stuyr' (XI.xi.45) or 'stith to stand' (XI.xiii.9). Douglas also employed some of the ancient synonyms for a hero or warrior, most of which derived ultimately from Old English poetic diction. Some he used only in the heavily demanding Eighth Prologue—'leyd' (118), 'freik' (123), 'grome' (165) and 'sege' (4, 19)—all in the weakened sense of 'man'. A few occur in the text of the *Eneados*, such as 'bern' (VIII.iii.61), 'wy' (III.ix.7), 'kempys' (v.vii.68), and 'heris' (IV.i.75, and passim).

The archaism of some of these words is suggested by the way Douglas's copyists at times altered them to other words, presumably more familiar and commonplace. 'Stith' is frequently altered to 'stif' (see Coldwell's textual notes to v.iv.64; v.viii.5; and XI.xi.45); so too 'birstand' is substituted for 'bruschand' at IX.vii.144 in the 1553 edition and the Ruthven manuscript. The Ruthven copyist also misinterpreted *heir* (= Virgil's *heros*) as the adverb 'here' in 'Thiddir the heir with mony thousand gan hy' (v.vi.8). Another sign of a word's growing archaism is when Douglas seems, according to the evidence of *O.E.D.* and *D.O.S.T.*, to be its last recorded user. An example of this is 'stithly' in the strongly alliterative 'Syne stythly in the sand vpstandis he' (v.vii.109). I do not think that in choosing such words

Douglas consciously set out to make his style unusual or old-fashioned. Such words were considered appropriate for the subject he was treating; they belonged to the heightened 'poetic' vocabulary, and he shared them with other writers in the same tradition. A last illustration is supplied by the word 'byrne' in

> He clethis hym with his scheld, and semis bald;
> He claspis hys gilt habirgyon and thrynfald;
> He, in his breistplait strang and his byrne,
> A sover swerd beltis law down by his the.
>
> (VII.x.93–6)

'Byrne' was no longer an everyday Scottish word;[56] it does not occur regularly in contemporary prose or in inventories of armour, as does 'breistplait' or 'habirgyon'. But it had been used before Douglas in the same heroic and alliterative context by romance-writers, and by Barbour and Hary:

> The blud owt at thar byrnys brest
>
> (*Bruce*, 11.352)
>
> In-to the byrneis the formast can he ber
>
> (*Wallace*, 11.106)

After Douglas this tradition of writing still lingered in William Stewart's *Croniclis of Scotland* (*c.* 1531):[57]

> With breistplait, birny, as the buriall bricht.

Douglas's liking for alliteration was clearly rooted in the traditions of native verse, yet it is important to realize that its presence in the *Eneados* can often be related to Virgil's own masterly use of alliteration and assonance. This was one aspect of Virgil's 'craft' that Douglas, not surprisingly, noticed and responded to in a variety of ways.

Sometimes Douglas attempts to copy Virgil's sound-effects very closely. The *s*-alliteration in

> With rochys set forgane the streym ful stay,
> To brek the salt fame of the seys stour
>
> (III.viii.56–7)

seems to me modelled on that in Virgil's

> obiectae salsa spumant aspergine cautes
>
> (III.534)

Douglas's line on Polyphemus, 'A monstre horribyll, onmesurabill and myschaip' (III.x.5), also attempts to convey something of the sound of its original, a line from a passage notable for its ponderous rhythm and assonance on *m*, *-um*, *-em*, etc:

> monstrum horrendum, informe, ingens, cui lumen ademptum
>
> (III.658)

Douglas follows Virgil in the description of an arrow's flight:

> The sovir schaft flaw quhisland with a quhir,
> Thar as it slydis scherand throw the ayr,
> Oneschewabill, bath certane, lang and squar.
> (XII.v.114–16)

The first two lines well translate both the sound and the sense of

> sonitum dat stridula cornus et auras
> certa secat.
> (XII.267–8)

It seems unfortunate that Douglas felt it necessary to complete the couplet by the rather wordy expansion of *certa*. Later Douglas provides a striking description of the monstrous creature that torments Turnus in the shape of an owl:

> That sum tyme into gravis, or stokkis of tre,
> Or on the waist thak, or hows rufis hie,
> Sittand by nycht syngis a sorowfull toyn,
> In the dyrk skowgis, with scrykis inoportoyn.
> This vengeabill wraik, in sik form changit thus,
> Evyn in the face and vissage of Turnus
> Can fle and flaf, and maid hym forto grow,
> Scho soundis so with mony hys and how . . .
> (XII.xiii.169–76)

The alliteration here, particularly on *s* and *f*, seems related to that in Virgil's

> quae quondam in bustis aut culminibus desertis
> nocte sedens serum canit importuna per umbras —
> hanc uersa in faciem Turni se pestis ob ora
> fertque refertque sonans clipeumque euerberat alis.[58]
> (XII.863–6)

I think, however, that Douglas's most characteristic response to Virgil's alliteration or assonance is not to adopt precisely the same sound-effects but to search for a native equivalent. A phrase like 'with mony hys and how' shows how Douglas often follows Virgil not by closely imitating him but by introducing a sound-effect of his own. Thus Virgil's *saetigerique sues* (VII.17) is rendered as 'byrsit baris' (VI.xvi.35), and, with even greater exuberance, as 'bustuus bowkis of the byrsyt swyne' (XI.v.37 = XI.198). Douglas renders Virgil's

> at tuba terribilem sonitum procul aere canoro
> increpuit
> (IX.503–4)

by

> Bot than the trumpettis weirly blastis abundis,
> With terribill brag of brasyn bludy soundis.
> (IX.viii.105–6)

Douglas had perhaps read Servius's comment on IX.503: *bene tamen hic electis verbis imitatur sonum tubarum.* It seems to me that he re-creates Virgil's effect very successfully, using plosive consonants like Virgil, but giving great prominence to *b*. A fuller illustration is provided by the account of Ascanius's killing of the hart:

> With nokkyt bow ybent all reddy bown ...
> The flane flaw fast with a spang fra the stryng;
> Throw owt the wame and entrellis all, but stynt,
> The scharp hedit schaft duschit with the dynt.
> (VII.viii.46 ff.)

Douglas's 'nokkyt bow ybent' corresponds to Virgil's *curuo . . . cornu* (VII.497); this was the starting point for a strikingly alliterative passage.[59]

Virgil provided a stimulus to Douglas in another respect. Almost invariably, when Virgil used words such as *stridor* or *stridens* or *sonitus*, Douglas responded with a burst of alliteration. Thus Virgil's

> insequitur clamorque uirum stridorque rudentum
> (1.87)

becomes in Douglas:

> Sone efter this, of men the clamour rays,
> The takillis graslis, cabillis can fret and frays.
> (1.ii.59–60)

Douglas translates the first half of Virgil's line literally, but renders *stridor* freely and vividly. Virgil's

> Talia iactanti stridens Aquilone procella
> uelum aduersa ferit
> (1.102–3)

appears as

> A blastrand bub out from the north brayng
> Gan our the forschip in the baksaill dyng.
> (1.iii.15–16)

In these and other passages describing storm on land or sea (e.g. II.vii.96–7 or III.viii.95–100) Douglas regularly uses a similar technique—heavy alliteration, more particularly on the plosive *b*. He tends to associate fricatives, for example, *s* and *quh*, with the *stridula* sound of an arrow ('with a spang fra the stryng' or 'quhisland with a quhir') or the sound made by a snake:

> Hyssyt and quhislyt with sa feill eddir sondis
> (VII.vii.91 = *sibilat*, VII.447)

He commonly, and indeed conventionally, uses *s*-alliteration in the description of snakes (see, for instance, II.viii.57–62; VII.vi.12–22; and XI.xiv.67–74). Douglas's interest in sound effects of a slightly different kind is evident in the sea scenes of book III, where he introduces the actual cries and shouts of the sailors: 'with mony heys and how' (III.ii.120), 'with hey and haill' (III.viii.36), and 'with mony heys and hayll' (III.viii.111). These either have no equivalent in Virgil or correspond to an abstract noun like *clamor* (III.524).

Douglas's use of alliteration in the *Eneados* was influenced partly by Virgil, partly by native poetic traditions. Yet it seems also to reveal a genuine interest in the limited and to some extent arbitrary power possessed by certain words not only to signify sounds and noises but also to mimic them. That Douglas was sensitive to this echoic or onomatopoeic aspect of his own language is suggested by his effective characterization of different bird-calls in Prologues VII and XII.[60] In XII Prologue 241, for instance, the quail 'quytteris'. No other user of this verb is recorded apart from Douglas, and he seems here trying to mimic the bird's distinctive cry, which is sometimes rendered by naturalists as 'quic-ic-ic' or, more jocularly, as 'wet-mi-lips'.[61] Many of the harsh monosyllabic words that Douglas uses in storm or battle scenes—*dunt, dint, swak, crak, rak, dusch, bub*—were not, of course, invented by him but were current both in popular speech and alliterative poetry. Other words, such as *thud* or *spang*, may have been equally common in the speech of his time, yet, according to the evidence of *D.O.S.T.* and *O.E.D.*, Douglas was their first recorded user. Douglas was the first and indeed sometimes the only writer recorded as using other onomatopoeic words, many of which sound highly colloquial, such as *bys*, 'buzz, hiss', and *fuf*, 'huff, puff':

> The irne lumpys in tha cavys blak
> Can bys and quhissil, and the hait fyre
> Doith fuf and blaw in blesys byrnand schire.
>   (VIII.vii.118–20)

Other examples are *flaf*, 'flap, flutter' (XII.xiii.175; X.vii.63); *geig*, 'creak, squeak' (VI.vi.62); *crowp*, 'cry hoarsely' (VII.xi.156); and *jawp*, which Douglas uses often both as noun (III.viii.97) and verb (VII.ix.101) of the splashing rebound of water. We cannot say definitely that Douglas coined these and similar words. What seems clear is that he was innovating in using them in poetry. The contexts in which they are found are dignified, not 'low' or comic or colloquial. Douglas thus seems to be extending the range of the accepted 'poetic' vocabulary.

Some of the most striking features of Douglas's style thus have a varied and complex ancestry. His archaisms are inherited from poetic tradition, but the grammatical ones seem particularly characteristic of Chaucer and the modes of writing associated with his name; the heroic terms and other archaisms of diction seem more characteristic of the northern and alliterative tradition. A further dimension is added by the practice of Virgil; his use of archaic forms had been noted by Servius and Quintilian,[62] and may therefore have been known to Douglas. Douglas's diffuseness, which has been observed by most critics,[63] springs not from one but a variety of causes. It can be traced not only to Douglas's desire to extract the fullest possible 'sentence' from Virgil but to the leisurely and ample style of much medieval poetry. Douglas's taste for piling up words in groups of two, three and even four (as in 'haldis, howsis, hyrnys and beildis', IV.iv.72) is rooted both in the commentator's practice of multiple glossing and in the fondness of the medieval poet, and particularly the alliterative poet, for such balanced phrasing. It is possible that Douglas's legal experience had a further influence on this aspect of his style. The legal documents that concern him, both in Scots and Latin, abound in such phrases as 'caus nor counsall', 'statut and ordanit', and 'consale, help, supportacion and assistance'.[64] It is less easy than it may seem at first to distinguish between explanatory phrases in the *Eneados* and rhyme-fillers, or between the pedagogic and the poetic expansions of Virgil. Ascensius is the source not only of Douglas's polysyllabic abstractions, but of concrete and vivid details. When Douglas speaks of a battle being 'thik as ony schour of scharp hailstanys' (XII.v.158), he is using a stock poetic simile, yet the stimulus comes from Ascensius's comment on Virgil's *tempestas* (XII.284): *grandinis aut niuis similis.* Douglas has a striking description of a chariot race:

> nevir sa thyk, with mony lasch and dusch,
> The cartaris smate thar horssis fast in teyn,
> With renȝeys slakkyt, and swete drepand bedeyn.
> (V.iii.82–4)

The last line is a vivid expansion of Virgil's *undantia lora* (V.146), yet it originates in one of Ascensius's double interpretations — *undantia: aut spumis abundantia, sed melius effusa, idest laxa.*

Critics have sometimes emphasized one aspect of Douglas's style at the expense of others. H. A. Mason says 'the impression of Virgil we gain from Douglas is more Chaucerian than modern'.[65] John Speirs stresses Douglas's Scottishness, and his distance from Virgil: 'it is not to Virgil's *Aeneid* but to the body of medieval Scots poetry that Douglas's *Aeneid* is immediately and organically related'.[66] Douglas himself is more ready to acknowledge the part that Virgil played in shaping his own work:

> Gyf ocht be weill, thank Virgil and nocht me
> (IX Prol 69)

Some scholars have placed an undue emphasis on the 'rustic' or 'homely' aspects of the *Eneados*.[67] These terms are ill-suited to characterize the style of a translator, who in his use of language is sometimes more learned and abstract than Virgil himself,[68] and who, long before Milton, coins such sonorous lines as:

> Placis of silence and perpetuall nycht
>   (VI.iv.60)

or

> Lyke as the comete stern sanguynolent
>   (X.v.141)

Douglas's own references to his 'bad, harsk spech' (1 Prol 21) and 'haymly playn termys famyliar' (Directioun, 94) should not be misinterpreted. They are a gesture of humility towards Virgil and the Latin language; they do not adequately describe the full range of Douglas as a translator. Prologue IX reveals indeed that he had some aspiration to follow Virgil in 'the ryall style, clepyt heroycall' (IX Prol 21). The *Eneados* must thus be related to an anonymous 'body' of English as well as Scots poets, to Chaucer, to Ascensius and other Latin commentators, and, not least, to Virgil himself.

Douglas says that he lacks 'fowth of langage' (1 Prol 120), yet this phrase best describes his stylistic variety and copiousness. The eclectism of Douglas's vocabulary has already been illustrated: the old and the conventional mix with the new and experimental; 'sudron' with 'Scottis'; apparent colloquialisms with the learned neologisms for which he seems to have had a personal predilection. Douglas can also be precise and technical in his choice of words. When he speaks of ships, he sometimes uses a formal alliterative phrase, such as 'ballyngar and barge' (v.xiv.88), yet elsewhere he is more specific: 'baksaill', 'bawbord', 'bolm', 'hechis', and 'helmstok'. He even draws on the vocabulary of ship-building, when he describes the storm raised by Aeolus as splitting 'rovis and syde semmys' (I.iii.49); *rovis*, which means 'the metal plates on to which rivets are first beaten down',[69] is a highly technical nautical term.

Douglas's syntax is also more varied than is always recognized. His sentence-structure, as noted earlier, can be extremely simple and sometimes verges on the paratactic constructions favoured by alliterative poets. Yet at other times Douglas follows the syntax of the *Aeneid* closely. He takes over some phrases which sound alien in Scots: 'so the fame is' (XII.xii.98) = *fama est* (XII.735), or 'gif myn endyt or stile may ony thing' (IX.vii.170) = *si quid mea carmina possunt* (IX.446). He uses participial constructions modelled on the Latin: 'sche sperand this' (I.vi.114 = I.370), or 'thus wepand said' (v.xiv.87 = VI.1). Douglas often follows Virgil's word order, postponing verb and subject in a way that sometimes sounds unidio-

matic: 'the sey thus trublyt . . . Felt Neptune' (1.iii.53-4 = 1.125),
and at other times is ambiguous: 'His agit frend Anchises knew thys
kyng' (111.ii.27 = 111.82). Douglas also often follows Virgil in
beginning sentences with relative pronouns: 'Quham Turnus . . .'
(ix.ix.74) = *quem Turnus* (ix.559); 'Quham ane Hysbon . . .' (x.
vii.56); 'Quham tho . . .' (xii.vi.167).[70] But such relative constructions do not always have an equivalent in Virgil. They seem to betray
Douglas's own fondness for linking sentences into larger, loosely
organized structures. To show the extent to which Douglas's syntax
was affected by Virgil's would require a close and detailed study. It
is important, however, to be aware that not all Douglas's apparent
Latinisms, in syntax as in vocabulary, derive from Virgil himself.

Douglas is not always felicitous. Sometimes he sounds as if he had
swallowed Roget's *Thesaurus*; sometimes there are jarring discrep-
ancies of tone or of diction; sometimes he sounds hurried and mech-
anical; sometimes he is clumsy or the sense is not clear. At his best,
however, there is an energy and richness in Douglas's use of language, a willingness to experiment, and a sensitivity not only to
Virgil's 'sentence' but to some aspects of his 'eloquence'. This is
apparent, it seems to me, in Douglas's handling of Virgil's similes,
an aspect of the *Aeneid* that he particularly admired. Douglas deals
skilfully with many of the varied subjects chosen by Virgil: the
snake in book 11—

> Hir slydry body in hankis rownd al run,
> Heich vp hir nek strekand forgane the son,
> With forkit tong intyll hir mouth quytterand.
> (11.viii.61-3 = 11.473-5)

or the cut flower to which Pallas is compared—

> Newly pullyt vp from hys stalkis smaill
> With tendyr fyngeris of the damysaill . . .
> (xi.ii.27-8 = xi.68 ff.)

or the splendid picture of the warrior Mezentius—

> Lyke to the strenthy sangler or the bor,
> Quham hundis quest with mony quhryne and ror . . .
> Or than the bustuus swyne weil fed, that bredis
> Amang the buskis rank of ryspe and redis,
> Besyde the layk of Lawrens, mony ʒheris,
> Quhen[71] that he is betrappyt fra his feris
> Amyd the huntyng ralys and the nettis,
> Standis at the bay, and vp his byrsys settis,
> Grasland hys tuskis with astern fyry eyn,
> With spaldis hard and harsk, awfull and teyn,
> That nane of all the huntmen thar present

Hym to engreif has strenth or hardyment.

(x.xii.47 ff. = x.707–11)

But Douglas is most responsive to Virgil's imagery of 'spayt or dyluge of watyr' (1.iii.92n):

Not sa fersly the fomy ryver or flude
Brekkis our the bankis on spait quhen it is wode,
And, with hys brusch and fard of watir brown,
The dykis and the schoris bettis doun,
Ourspredand croftis and flattis with his spait,
Our al the feildis that thai may row a bayt,
Quhil howsys and the flokkis flyttis away,
The corn grangis and standand stakkis of hay.

(11.viii.101–8 = 11.496–9)

Lyke as the swyft watir stremys cleir
Sum tyme rowtand men on far may heir,
Quhar it is stoppit with thir stanys round,
That of the ryveris brute and brokkyn sound,
Brystand on skelleis our thir demmyt lynnys,
The bankis endlang all the fludis dynnys.

(x1.vii.5–10 = x1.297–9)[72]

I end with these passages because they seem highly characteristic of Douglas: they illustrate his weaknesses as well as his strengths. There are small omissions and inaccuracies. Virgil's *aper*, for instance, is divided into two separate animals—'bor', and then 'bustuus swyne'—probably because Servius had done so in his note on x.709. Douglas also introduces several details that have no strict equivalent in Virgil: the hounds quest 'with mony quhryne and ror'; the flood rises so that 'our al the feildis . . . thai may row a bait'. Yet these are clearly visualized, and seem in harmony with Virgil's own images. The powerful line about the boar—'Grasland hys tuskis with astern fyry eyn'—is an addition; yet it seems to anticipate Virgil's own later phrase, *dentibus infrendens* (x.718), applied not to the boar but to Mezentius himself. Douglas is characteristically diffuse; he has the usual proportion of roughly two lines for Virgil's one. There are the familiar doublets: 'sangler or the bor', 'ryver or flude'; there are stock epithets, some rhyme-fillers: 'quhen it is wode'; and the traditional alliterative pairs: 'ryspe and redis', 'hard and harsk'. Yet Douglas's language transcends the conventional and the formulaic. Sometimes he selects simple but apt words to translate Virgil: 'hankis rownd', 'on spait', 'corn grangis and standand stakkis of hay'; sometimes he may well be introducing coinages of his own, like the onomatopoeic 'quytterand' and 'grasland'.[73] In the last passage Douglas seems to try to convey the sound of the dammed-up stream, but perhaps makes it more violent than Virgil's *murmur* and *crepitantibus* imply. Douglas uses forceful verbs—'rowtand', 'dynnys'—and emphatic alliteration on plosives—'brute and brokkyn', 'brystand'. Even the syntax is 'stoppit' until the last word. Here as in many other passages of the *Eneados* Douglas has remained reasonably faithful to his original, yet has re-created Virgil's images in terms of his own language, poetic traditions, and experience of the world around him.

The Prologues

Each book of Douglas's *Eneados* is provided, as the 1553 edition puts it, with 'hys perticular prologe'. Other sixteenth-century translators furnished their work with Prefaces or Prologues, but it was rare to attach them in this way to individual books. (We may regret the absence of anything similar in Surrey's translation of Virgil.) Douglas's Prologues are often thought, rightly or wrongly, to contain his most original poetry. For this reason, although much drawn upon already, they merit a chapter to themselves. The Prologues are the best known and probably the most popular of Douglas's writings. They have been the most widely anthologized, and are more easily available to the general reader than complete editions of the *Eneados*. There is a tendency therefore to read them on their own, as separate poems, quite detached from the translation of Virgil. This is no new thing: it started in the very century in which they were written, when one of the first and greatest of Scottish anthologizers, George Bannatyne, represented Douglas in his collection by Prologues IV, IX, and X. The practice continued in the eighteenth century, although Douglas's admirers then chose mainly to edit, excerpt and paraphrase the so-called 'nature' Prologues (VII, XII, and XIII)—a preference that has persisted to the present day.[1]

There is remarkable variety of subject, tone and metrical form in the Prologues. Some, such as II or VI, are logically connected with the books they introduce; others, such as VIII or X, at first sight seem very remote from the *Aeneid*. Gregory Smith noted that some Prologues lacked pertinence, and called them 'academic exercises', possibly introduced for pictorial relief.[2] Coldwell suggested that some represented poems already written, which Douglas thought too good to waste and therefore 'draped' on the *Eneados*.[3] This contains an element of truth. There are signs of earlier work being used in Prologue IX, where the first eighteen lines form a separate moralizing section in a different metre from the rest of the Prologue. Line 19, with its humorous 'Eneuch of this, ws nedis prech na mor', effects the transition to a critical passage related to the book that follows. Denton Fox has gone furthest in treating the Prologues as independent poems. He stresses their experimental character, and calls them 'a series of set pieces intended to demonstrate Douglas's competence at writing in various styles on various subjects'.[4] I think it important to read the Prologues not only as self-contained pieces of writing—which to some extent they are—but in the context within which Douglas himself placed them. Not all the Prologues may be directly related to the *Aeneid*, but all, by echoing or alluding to 'our author', are within the Virgilian ambience.

The Prologues combine two functions: they are, in part, critical and expository; in part, literary and creative. In earlier chapters I have discussed the more didactic aspects of the Prologues. But the impulse behind the *Eneados* was not simply that of the teacher. The desire of the poet to make a work of his own led Douglas away from the self-effacement of many commentators and translators towards a projection of himself as creator, and the act of translation as a great and creative enterprise. The Prologues are his chief mode of doing this. In them he suggests that he himself—not only Virgil—is at work on something momentous. Douglas drew on the long tradition of Prologue-writing, but I think he may have been stimulated by the example of writers whom he knew at firsthand: more particularly, Chaucer, Lydgate, and Boccaccio. In the *Canterbury Tales* Chaucer used Prologues and Epilogues to provide a dramatic if unfinished framework for the conventional tale-collection; so too he furnished several books of *Troilus and Criseyde* with Prologues, which employ some of the topoi used also by Douglas. Lydgate prefaced many books of his *Fall of Princes* with Prologues which treat of moral and literary issues in a way that anticipates Douglas, though more diffusely. As to Boccaccio, there are affinities less with the vernacular poems (which Douglas may not have known) than with the *Genealogy of the Gods* (which he clearly knew well). Each book of the *Genealogy of the Gods* has its own *prohemium*. Through these Boccaccio gave his work of scholarship an imaginative framework. He sustained and embroidered with much ingenious detail the common figure of the literary voyage or *navigatio*. The perils of a sea journey suggest the difficulties of the writer's task; its length suggests the magnitude of the work (see, for instance, IV and VII). Douglas used similar imagery:

> By strange channellis, fronteris and forlandis,
> Onkouth costis and mony wilsum strandis
> Now goith our barge, for nowder howk nor craik
> May heir bruke sail, for schald bankis and sandis.
> (III Prol 37–40)

There is no sign of definite indebtedness to Boccaccio here. The figure was inherited from classical poets and was popular with medieval ones—Douglas might as well be recalling its use by Dante or Chaucer (in *Troilus and Criseyde* 11.1–6).[5] But Douglas is using this image and the Prologue in which it occurs in essentially the same way as Boccaccio—to embellish his own work and also to enhance its significance in the eyes of the reader. This was no piece of hack-work, like Caxton's. Douglas's predicament resembled that of Boccaccio in another respect. Both were handling pagan subject matter, and felt the need to defend and justify themselves to Christian readers. They coped with the problem in various ways, but one solution chosen by Boccaccio was to end with a prayer: 'it has long been a wise and fitting custom, as Plato advises, in entering upon even the least of ventures, to invoke God's help, and set out in His name' (*Prohemium* 1).[6] Douglas, like Boccaccio, often concludes with a strong affirmation of his faith (e.g. Prologues I, III, V, VI, X and XI).

Douglas's framework is not as systematic or imaginatively coherent as Boccaccio's, but the result is similar. It adds an extra dimension to his *Eneados*. We are involved in the composition, and given a sense of the work in progress. There are fleeting but consistent references to the passage of the seasons—December (VII), 'Lent' (VIII), May (XII), June (XIII)—and we are told the 'tyme, space and dait' of the translation, including the day in July on which it was finished. We have brief glimpses of the poet at work, rising from bed and turning to his 'lettron' (VII Prol 143), taking out his pen and 'scriptour' (XII Prol 305), or exclaiming at the huge size of his Virgil (Exclamatioun, 22). In some of the Prologues Douglas shows his mastery of *talking* in verse, whether to himself or to his readers; yet the casual, low-pitched, conversational manner is often based on a firm rhetorical structure:

> Stra for thys ignorant blabryng imperfyte
> Besyde thy polyst termys redymyte.
> And netheles with support and correctioun,
> For naturall lufe and frendely affectioun
> Quhilkis I beir to thy warkis and endyte—
> All thocht God wait tharin I knaw full lyte—
> And that thy facund sentence mycht be song
> In our langage alsweill as Latyne tong—
> Alsweill? na, na, impossibill war, per de—
> ȝit with thy leif, Virgile, to follow the,
> I wald into my rurall wlgar gros
> Wryte sum savoryng of thyne Eneados.
> But sair I dreid forto disteyn the quyte
> Throu my corruppit cadens imperfyte—

Disteyn the? nay forsuyth, that may I nocht;
Weill may I schaw my burall bustuus thocht...
    (1 Prol 33-48)

Douglas's repeated use of *correctio* (*Alsweill?*, *Disteyn the?*) suggests a man in the act of thinking aloud, and striving for precision. His choice of words can sometimes be sensitive and exact: 'blabryng' conveys his self-contempt, 'savoryng' the difficulty of catching in a translation more than a faint glimmering of the effect of one's original. From this Prologue and others (particularly v, vii, ix, xiii and the Directioun) emerges a sense of the poet's personality: tough, humorous and argumentative. The degree to which this portrait conforms to a stock *persona*, and the precise blend of fact and fiction in the Prologues do not matter. The Prologues are imaginatively successful. They make one aware of the perennial anxieties of a writer, and bring one close to the particular problems and discomforts faced by a poet in sixteenth-century Scotland.

In the Prologues we meet themes traditionally employed in the long poem, many deriving ultimately from classical epic. The most familiar of these is the Invocation. Douglas's immediate model was no doubt Virgil himself (as in *Aeneid* 1.8 or vii.37ff.), but the Invocation was well known to medieval writers, and Douglas's practice resembles that of the Italian poets (such as Boccaccio and Dante) and Chaucer in *Troilus and Criseyde*. Each of the first six Prologues invokes or apostrophizes different deities. There is literary tact in their choice. Prologue ii links Melpomene with the 'tragedy' of the fall of Troy. The Prologue to book iii (largely concerned with the sea wanderings of Aeneas) addresses Cynthia as

    Rewlare of passage and ways mony one,
    Maistres of stremys, and glaidar of the nycht,
    Schipmen and pilgrymys hallowis thi mycht...
        (iii Prol 3-5)

The Prologue to book iv addresses with obvious appropriateness Cytherea and Cupid. Prologue v invokes Bacchus and Proserpina. The Prologue to book vi, the book of the Underworld, opens

    Pluto, thou patron of the deip Achiron,
    Fader of tormentis in thyne infernal see,
    Amyd the fludis, Stix and Flagiton,
    Lethie, Cochite, the watyris of oblivie,
    With dolorus quhirling of furyus sistyris thre,
    Thyne now salbe my muse and drery sang:
        (vi Prol 1-6)

Prologue vi ends characteristically, however, with a rejection of such inspiration, or rather a Christian re-application of it:

Thou art our Sibill, Crystis moder deir,
Prechit by prophetis and Sibilla Cumane;

. . . .

Sathan the clepe I, Pluto infernall,
Prynce in that dolorus den of wo and pane.
(vi Prol 145 ff.)

This rejection of the pagan muses and deities had itself become an important topos among Christian writers from as early as the fourth century:

Negant Camenis nec patent Apollini
Dicata Christo pectora.[7]

Douglas ends other Prologues (such as ii, v, and x) with a similar turn in the thought. It forms an important concluding theme of Prologue i:

Thou prynce of poetis, I the mercy cry,
I meyn thou Kyng of Kyngis, Lord Etern,
Thou be my muse, my gydar and laid stern . . .
On the I call, and Mary, Virgyn myld—
Calliope nor payane goddis wild
May do to me na thing bot harm, I weyn:
In Criste is all my traste, and hevynnys queyn.
(i Prol 452 ff.)

Douglas here picks up a phrase from the opening lines of this Prologue, in which he addressed not a muse but Virgil himself—'of Latyn poetis prynce'.[8] Douglas is not so much contradicting himself as modifying his former thought, reminding us that Virgil was 'bot ane mortal man sum tyme' (474). For the Christian poet Virgil and his pagan inspiration are ultimately transcended by Christ, 'that hevynly Orpheus' (469).[9]

The Invocation is essentially a feature of beginnings. It occurs near the opening of a poem, or it introduces new and demanding subject matter: *maius opus moueo* (*Aeneid* vii.44). Medieval poets also employed what might be called *continuing* devices to indicate the arduousness of their task or the need for a renewal of the poet's energies. It was common for the poet towards the middle or end of a long poem to express his weariness (as does Douglas in vii Prol 155), a sense of longing to have his book finished (viii Prol 142), or his determination to start again by symbolically sharpening his pen (ix Prol 92–3). Lydgate too resolves:

And riȝt anon to scharp[e] my poyntel
I wil me dresse, þis story to entrete.
(*Troy Book* ii.5064–5)

In Prologue viii of the *Fall of Princes* Lydgate represents Boccaccio

in debate with Lady Sloth, who advises him to stop his work;
Petrarch appears and speaks 'in rebukyng of vicious idilnesse'.
Douglas expresses this 'weariness' or 'persistence' topos most vividly
in VII Prol 149 ff.:

> And to my self I said: 'In gud effect
> Thou mon draw furth, the ȝok lyis on thy nek.'
> Within my mynde compasyng thocht I so,
> Na thing is done quhil ocht remanys ado . . .
> And, thocht I wery was, me list not tyre,
> Full laith to leif our wark swa in the myre,
> Or ȝit to stynt for bitter storm or rane.
> Heir I assayt to ȝok our pleuch agane,
> And, as I couth, with afald diligens,
> This nixt buke following of profond sentens
> Has thus begun in the chil wyntir cald,
> Quhen frostis doith ourfret baith firth and fald.

A century earlier Lydgate had written:

> For almost wery, feint & waike I-now
> Be the bestes & oxes of my plow,
> þe longe day ageyn þe hil to wende.
> But almost now at þe londes ende
> Of Troye boke, ficche I wil a stake.
>
>   (*Troy Book* v.2927–31)

Later Spenser drew on the same imagery to provide a temporary end
to the first edition of the *Faerie Queene*:

> But now my teme begins to faint and fayle,
> All woxen weary of their iournall toyle:
> Therefore I will their sweatie yokes assoyle
> At this same furrowes end, till a new day:
>
>   (III.xii.47)

The plough image was clearly traditional in such contexts: it indicated the sheer hard work—the *labor improbus*—of bringing a long
poem to completion. [10]

Douglas's translation of the *Aeneid* is followed not only by book
XIII and its Prologue, but by six different pieces of verse in which
Douglas—among other things—bids farewell to Venus and Aeneas,
to Virgil himself, to his patron, to his readers, and even to his critics
—those 'detractouris and oncurtas redaris that beyn our studyus, but
occasioun, to note and spy owt faltis or offencis in this volum'
(IV.p.192). Curtius implies that most medieval writers preferred to
end their works abruptly, and says that 'only one antique concluding
topos passed over into the Middle Ages'. [11] Yet Douglas's prolonged
and ceremonious leave-taking can be paralleled in Chaucer and

Lydgate,[12] and some of his themes were traditionally used at the conclusion of a work by classical or medieval writers.

One instance of this is Douglas's envoi:

> Go, wlgar Virgill, to euery churlych wight,
> Say, I avow thou art translatit rycht,
> Beseyk all nobillys the corect and amend,
> Beys not afferyt tocum in prysaris sycht;
> The nedis nocht to aschame of the lycht,
> For I haue brocht thy purpos to gud end:
> Now salt thou with euery gentill Scot be kend,
> And to onletterit folk be red on hight,
> That erst was bot with clerkis comprehend.
>
> (Exclamatioun, 37–45)

The address to one's book was a poetic theme of great antiquity—parallels exist in Ovid, Martial, and Statius;[13] but the most famous and touching example in English is Chaucer's

> Go, litel bok, go, litel myn tragedye,
> Ther God thi makere yet, er that he dye,
> So sende myght to make in som comedye!
> But litel book, no makyng thow n'envie,
> But subgit be to alle poesye.
>
> (*Troilus and Criseyde*, v.1786–90)

The phrase 'Go, litel bok' appears again and again in the envois of fifteenth-century Chaucerians, even being applied by Lydgate to the voluminous *Troy Book*.[14] The tone is customarily apologetic: the poet of the *Kingis Quair* (stanza 194) exclaims 'Go litill tretise, nakit of eloquence'; and at the end of *La Belle Dame Sans Merci* Ros links the one formula with another—the rather abject appeal to his readers 'Thee to correcte in any part or al'.[15] In the *Palice of Honour* (2161–9) Douglas had similarly—and conventionally—rejected his 'breif buriall quair of Eloquence all quite' and prayed 'ilk man til amend the'. Here, however, he tailors the theme to his own ends. He speaks not of any 'litel bok' but more exactly of his 'wlgar Virgill'. He discriminates as to who has the right to 'correct and amend', and his tone is bold and confident, assured of the value of what he has written.

The Exclamatioun that contains this envoi picks up the nautical image that Douglas had already used in Prologue III, and brings it to an appropriate conclusion:

> Now throw the deip fast to the port I mark,
> For heir is endyt the lang disparyt wark,
> And Virgill hes hys volum to me lent:
> In sovir raid now ankyrrit is our bark;

We dowt na storm, our cabillys ar sa stark.

(Exclamatioun, 1–5)

In his *Conclusio* to the *Genealogy of the Gods* Boccaccio fastens his 'craft to the shore with anchors and cables of my own invention'.[16] In the *Faerie Queene* VI.xii.1 Spenser uses similar imagery to express his sense of relief at the completion of a long and laborious enterprise. Possibly all three writers recalled the usage of classical poets, such as Statius (*Silvae* IV.4.89; *Thebaid* XII.809) or Virgil's

> ni iam sub fine laborum
> uela traham et terris festinem aduertere proram
> (*Georgic* IV.116–17)

Such imagery at such a position in the work was deeply traditional.

Perhaps the boldest and most interesting of these Epilogues is the Conclusio (IV. p. 187):

> Now is my wark all fynyst and compleit,
> Quham Iovis ire, nor fyris byrnand heit,
> Nor trynschand swerd sal defas ne doun thryng,
> Nor lang proces of age, consumys al thyng.
> Quhen that onknawyn day sal hym addres,
> Quhilk not bot on this body power hes,
> And endis the dait of myn oncertan eld,
> The bettir part of me salbe vpheld
> Abufe the starnys perpetualy to ryng,
> And heir my naym remane, but enparyng;
> Throw owt the ile yclepit Albyon
> Red sall I be, and sung with mony one.
> (1–12)

Douglas seems to have been one of the first to express in English what by the end of the sixteenth century had become a poetic commonplace: the assertion that a work of art can confer immortality.[17] Douglas may have known Horace's *Exegi monumentum aere perennius* (Odes, III.30), but it is the conclusion to the *Metamorphoses* (XV.871–9) that he has here paraphrased and audaciously appended to a translation not of Ovid but of Virgil.[18] He continues:

> Thus vp my pen and instrumentis full 3or
> On Virgillis post I fix for evirmor,
> Nevir, from thens, syk materis to discryve:
> My muse sal now be cleyn contemplatyve.
> (13–16)

Douglas here alludes to a votive offering: when a man took leave of his life's work he might offer tools or weapons connected with it to the appropriate deity. Curtius notes that the poets of the Greek Anthology 'are fond of putting on this mask . . . an old scribe, for example, dedicates his pencil, rule, inkwell, reed pens, and penknife to Hermes'.[19] Horace, too, humorously dedicated to Venus *arma defunctumque bello | barbiton* (Odes, III.26). Douglas has drawn much of his imagery from pagan antiquity, yet the sense of mutability that he expresses would be congenial to most medieval readers. Douglas seems — half-humorously, half-mournfully — to be saying farewell not just to the *Eneados* but to poetry itself and youth:

> Adew, gallandis, I geif ӡou all gud nycht.
>
> (23)

What, though, is the 'strategy'[20] of the separate Prologues? How closely are they articulated with the different books of the *Aeneid*? Few would question the relevance of the first six Prologues. Prologue I clearly combines the functions of Dedication and general Preface. The following five Prologues — and Prologue IX also — contain a similar mixture of literary criticism and moral reflections. All are concerned partly to defend Virgil, partly to interpret him. Each attempts to characterize briefly the subject or mood of the book it introduces. Prologue II, for instance, speaks of the 'dedly tragedy' of Troy's fall; Prologue III of the 'wild auentouris, monstreis and quent effrayis' that are to follow; Prologue V of the 'sportis, myrthis and myrry plays' that occur at the funeral games; Prologue VI expounds the 'hyd sentence' of book VI. The moralizing of Prologue IV might seem remote from the dramatic sympathy with which Virgil portrays Dido and Aeneas. Nonetheless, the Prologue fits logically into its context; a reading of book IV might well prompt such reflections in a pious reader. The question of relevance is posed most acutely by some of the last Prologues. It is these that critics seem particularly ready to 'hive off' as sermons or nature poems. Douglas does indeed range far from the *Aeneid* at times, yet even here he shows an awareness of the need for relevance and literary propriety. He himself attempts to justify the placing of his winter Prologue between books VI and VII:

> Thys proloug smellis new cum furth of hell,
> And, as our buk begouth hys weirfar tell,
> So weill according dewly bene annext
> Thou drery preambill, with a bludy text.
>
> (VII Prol 163–6)

Whether we find this valid or not, Douglas shows here a sensitivity to poetic decorum that recalls — perhaps consciously — Henryson's

> Ane doolie sessoun to ane cairfull dyte
> Suld correspond, and be equivalent.
>
> (*Testament of Cresseid*, 1–2)

Prologue xiii has often been regarded chiefly as a nature poem, yet of all the Prologues it is perhaps the one most closely integrated with the book that follows. So too other Prologues have closer links with their respective books than is always realized.

Prologue viii might appear the most remote from the *Aeneid* both in form and content, with its elaborate alliterative stanza and its satirical complaint on the evils of the times. L. M. Watt called it a 'most alien interpolation'.[21] Coldwell, however, explained it as representing 'the distortion of the true *polis* . . . a foil to the idealized state of the noble Evander'.[22] This is ingenious but not convincing. I think Douglas is here indulging in a joke, a piece of comic relief to the heroic subject matter of the *Aeneid*. But the shape of the joke has an unexpected relevance to the book that follows. At the beginning of book viii Aeneas falls asleep beside the Tiber, and has a vision of the river-god, who admonishes him and prophesies the founding of the city Alba. In this Prologue Douglas, too, falls asleep and is admonished by 'a selcouth seg' (4), but instead of the dignified speech of Tiberinus he hears ranting and 'ravyng' (177). Virgil's stress on the truth of Aeneas's vision—*ne uana putes haec fingere somnum* (viii.42)—is replaced by an attack on the deceptiveness of dreams:

> For swevynnys ar for swengeouris that slummyrris nocht weill;
> Mony mervellus mater nevir merkit nor ment
> Will seggis se in thar sleip, and sentens but seill:
> War all sic sawys suythfast, with schame we war schent.
> (viii Prol 171–4)

And whereas Aeneas finds that his dream comes true, Douglas finds that the hoard of pennies has vanished:

> Bot, quhen I walknyt, all that welth was wiskyt away,
> I fand nocht in all that feild, in faith, a be byke.
> (viii Prol 163–4)

Prologue viii thus forms a grotesque parody of the opening lines of book viii; it is a 'foil' but of a different kind from that suggested by Coldwell.

Prologue x has a pattern found also in Prologues iv and xi: a substantial moral section, then a briefer passage linking it with the book that follows. It seems probable that this meditative and highly devout Prologue, unlike Prologue iv, was not prompted by a reading of Virgil, but may have pre-existed as a devotional poem on the paradoxes of the Creation and the Incarnation. Nonetheless Prologue x is linked very ingeniously with *Aeneid* x. The bridging passage (151–75) continues to praise God—the central theme of the whole Prologue—but now employs terms which have highly Virgilian associations. (There is perhaps a humorous double meaning in Douglas's 'furth I write so as myne autour dois' at line 155.) Douglas says

> Is nane bot thou the Fader of goddis and men,
> Omnipotent eternal Ioue I ken;
> Only the, helply Fader, thar is nane other.
>
> (x Prol 156–8)

Douglas is here re-applying to the Christian God phrases and epithets which Virgil had used of Jupiter: the solemn formula *diuum pater atque hominum rex* (x.2 and 743), *pater . . . aeterna potestas* (x.18) and *pater omnipotens* (x.100). The etymology that lies behind 'helply fader' may best be explained by Douglas himself:

> Ioue or Iupiter by the gentillis was clepit the mast soueran god, fader of goddis and men, and all the otheris war bot haldyn as poweris dyuers of this Iupiter, callit 'iuuans pater',[23] the helply fader.
>
> (I.v.2n)

Douglas says of the Christian God

> Thou haldis court our cristall hevynnis cleir,
> With angellis, sanctis and hevynly spretis seir,
> That, but cessyng, thy glor and lovyng syngis:
> Manifest to the, and patent bene all thyngis.
>
> (x Prol 166–9)

At the opening of book x Jupiter too presides over a *concilium* (2)— Douglas's chapter heading terms it 'the court of goddis'—and he too surveys all things:

> terras unde arduus omnis
> castraque Dardanidum aspectat populosque Latinos.
>
> (x.3–4)

Yet by contrast with the *discordia* (9) that Virgil notes among both gods and men, Douglas stresses the 'Concord for ever, myrth, rest and endles blys' (171) that exists in the realm of his God, and prays 'Mak ws thy sonnys in cherite, but discord' (165). The queen of this heaven is not Juno but Mary; the 'sistir and spows' of Jupiter (1.i.82n) is replaced by the Christian paradox of 'spows . . . maid and moder deir' (170). In so re-applying the phrases of Virgil Douglas is drawing on a tradition of great antiquity[24] to effect a neat and apposite transition between apparently disparate themes.

Prologue xi does more than couple 'the praise of true knighthood . . . to Vergil's fiercest fighting'.[25] In its praise of fortitude and admonitions against 'sleutht and cowardyce' (193) it furnishes a Christian equivalent to Aeneas's exhortations to his followers in the opening lines of book xi:

maxima res effecta, uiri; timor omnis abesto,
quod superest; . . .
arma parate, animis et spe praesumite bellum
ne qua mora ignaros, ubi primum uellere signa
adnuerint superi pubemque educere castris,
impediat segnisue metu sententia tardet.
    (XI.14 ff.)

In Prologue XI Douglas delivers a forceful sermon on the spiritual conflict that faces every Christian, a sermon whose phrasing and imagery may seem to owe more to St Paul[26] than to Virgil. Yet the bridge passage (177–200) makes quite explicit the analogy between Aeneas's efforts to gain his 'fatale cuntre of behest' and the Christian's endeavours to attain the realm that he too has been promised: 'the quhilk was hecht till Abraham and hys seyd' (199). At the same time it drives home the contrast between the eternal kingdom that should be the Christian's goal and the temporal one sought by Aeneas:

Exempill takis of this prynce Ene,
That, for hys fatale cuntre of behest,
Sa feill dangeris sustenyt on land and see,
Syk stryfe in stour sa oft with speir in rest,
Quhill he hys realm conquest bath west and est:
Sen all this dyd he for a temporall ryng,
Pres ws to wyn the kynryk ay lestyng,
Addres ws fast fortill opteyn that fest.
    (XI Prol 177–84)

I have reserved for more detailed discussion three Prologues—VII, XII, and XIII—which have been much praised, and commonly linked together as 'nature poems'[27] or 'portraits of the seasons'.[28] These Prologues indeed resemble one another in subject and descriptive technique, and within the framework of the whole *Eneados* each functions similarly, as a much expanded *chronographia*. Such ornate and ceremonial descriptions of the time of day or season were popular with both medieval and classical poets, and Virgil himself may have supplied a model to Douglas in his many descriptions of the dawn. Yet each Prologue has its distinctive structure and significance which may be obscured by over-insistence on such group labels.

Prologue XII has provoked strikingly different reactions from modern readers. L. M. Watt found its description of May 'vibrant with the freshness of the living air,'[29] whereas Coldwell said dismissively that 'convention to a large extent dictated what Douglas was to see . . . the poem might as well have been written in his stall at St Giles' as in the fields of Midlothian'.[30] Douglas's contemporaries had a different approach to the Prologue, stressing its learning and its 'craft'. The 1553 side note terms it 'ane singular lernit Prologue', perhaps following a manuscript comment such as the Cambridge manuscript's *explicit scitus prologus*. Douglas himself calls it a 'lusty crafty preambill' (307). No one can fail to observe the learned, Latinate character of much of the diction: *purpurat, nocturnall, diurnall, obumbrat, rubicund, venust*. Such words are used not because Douglas has particularly recondite ideas to express but in the interest of rhyme, rhythm, and verbal aureation. The natural world is often presented in terms of myth. We meet familiar personifications: Nature, Flora, Priapus and Ceres. We read not of the owl but 'Nycthemyne' (11), not of the cock but 'Phebus red fowle' (155), not of the spider but 'Aragne' (170). We are in the ambiguous world of the *Metamorphoses*, where

> Progne had or than sung hir complaynt,
> And eik hir dreidfull systir Philomeyn
> Hyr lays endyt, and in woddis greyn
> Hyd hir selvyn, eschamyt of hir chance;
> And Esacus completis hys pennance
> In ryveris, fludis, and on euery laik.
>
> (282–7)

The opening lines of this Prologue abound in Ovidian echoes. The stars are put to flight; Aurora opens

> the wyndois of hir large hall,
> Spred all with rosys, and full of balm ryall,
> And eik the hevynly portis cristallyne
> Vpwarpis braid, the warld till illumyn.
>
> (17–20)

The sun has a golden chariot, drawn by 'Eous the steid' (25) and flames burst from his nostrils (29). The face of Phoebus and his bright throne are dazzling: 'For quhais hew mycht nane behald hys face' (38). All these find parallels in Ovid's account of the sun and his palace in *Metamorphoses*, 11:

> ecce vigil rutilo patefecit ab ortu
> purpureas Aurora fores et plena rosarum
> atria: diffugiunt stellae, quarum agmina cogit
> Lucifer
>
> (112–15)
>
> aureus axis erat, temo aureus, aurea summae
> curvatura rotae
>
> (107–8)

> quadripedes animosos ignibus illis,
> quos in pectore habent, quos ore et naribus efflant.
> (84–5)
> neque enim propiora ferebat
> lumina.
> (22–3)

The artifice of this Prologue is as striking as its learning. As in the *Palice of Honour* and Dunbar's *Goldin Targe* the natural world is described in imagery that derives from man's artefacts. Nature provides a tapestry (102), and the soil is embroidered (65); Douglas speaks of 'the fertill *skyrt lappys* of the grund' (85), 'the variand *vestur* of the venust vaill' (87), and terms corn a 'glaidsum *garmont revestyng* the erd' (78). Images of jewels and other precious substances abound: silver and gold and ivory (22, 31, 36, 55, 14, etc.); Phoebus's hair is 'brycht as chrisolyte or topace' (37); and we read of 'beriall' streams (60) and emerald meadows (151). Such imagery both reinforces the sense of radiant light—the world sparkles and gleams—and suggests the idealized nature of this description. Coldwell comments incredulously on Douglas's phrase 'fervent heit' (174): 'In May? In Scotland?' But the Prologue has several other distinctly un-Scottish features, such as the trellised grapes (99–100) and the olive trees (165).[31] These clearly derive from the Mediterranean tradition of the *locus amoenus*.[32] Prologue XII was never conceived as a naturalistic description of one particular Scottish landscape—the picture is an idealized and composite one. Yet there is evidence that Douglas saw through his own eyes as well as through those of earlier poets. He describes

> The syluer scalyt fyschis on the greit
> Ourthwort cleir stremys sprynkland for the heyt,
> With fynnys schynand brovn as synopar,
> And chyssell talys, stowrand heir and thar.
> (55–8)

Fishes' silver scales had been noted by many earlier poets,[33] but Douglas draws our attention to other features: the distinctive colour (cinnabar is a reddish-brown mineral), the chisel-shaped tail, and above all their quick, wriggly movement. Here and elsewhere in the Prologue Douglas revivifies traditional themes through vivid and minute observation.

Convention by no means 'dictated' everything that Douglas saw, but it prescribed to him many features of his style, above all the poetic technique that dominates the Prologue:

> The dasy dyd onbreid hir crownell smaill,
> And euery flour onlappyt in the daill;

In battill gyrs burgionys the banwart wild,
The clavyr, catcluke, and the cammamyld;
The flour delys furthspred hys hevynly hew,
Flour dammes, and columby blank and blew;
Seir downys smaill on dent de lyon sprang,
The ʒyng greyn blomyt straberry levys amang;
Gymp gerraflouris thar royn levys onschet,
Fresch prymros, and the purpour violet;
The roys knoppys, tutand furth thar hed,
Gan chyp, and kyth thar vermel lippys red.

(113–24)

James Russell Lowell denounced this *'item* kind of description':

It is a mere bill of parcels, a *post-mortem* inventory of nature, where imagination is not merely not called for but would be out of place. Why, a recipe in the cookery book is as much like a good dinner as this kind of stuff is like true word-painting.[34]

One answer to Lowell is that catalogues have had a perennial appeal to poets; we find them as early as Homer and as recently as Auden. Douglas is using a descriptive technique that was popular not only with medieval poets but with many classical ones, such as Ovid, Statius and Lucan.[35] It is perhaps more important to note that Douglas does not give us a *post-mortem* of the natural world. He describes movement, change, and growth — 'onlappyt', 'furthspred', 'sprang', 'tutand furth thar hed'; his nature is living, not static or inanimate. Where Douglas is most open to criticism is in his lack of selectivity. His catalogues are often long—this list of flowers runs to over thirty lines, three times the length of a similar list in the *Culex* (398–407)—and there are so many of them that they form not a decorative set-piece, not even a 'purple patch', but the whole fabric of the poem.

It is perhaps this aspect of his style, together with Douglas's allusiveness and the occasional unfamiliarity of his vocabulary, that has obscured for many readers the structure of this Prologue, and consequently its meaning. Even appreciative critics, such as John Veitch, speak of its 'lack of unity'.[36] A brief analysis of its structure may therefore be helpful. I do not think that Douglas intended primarily to describe 'a day lived through in every detail'[37] or 'the fields of Midlothian' or even the *locus amoenus*. Prologue XII is, above all, a hymn of praise to the sun, and implicitly to the sun's Creator. God is not named in the Prologue, but there are frequent references to God's vicegerent, Nature (e.g. 84, 102, 154, 230, 248). The Prologue celebrates first the glory of the sun-rise—Douglas later

revealingly speaks of it as a 'tryumphe' (275)—and then of the
month in which the revitalizing power of the sun is most apparent
(Douglas dates the Prologue as written on the 9 May).[38]

The splendid ceremonial opening shows the sun rising, emerging
like a monarch from his palace. The planets flee from his presence,
and Aurora casts open before him the 'hevynly portis cristalline'.
The first rays of light

> Persand the sabill barmkyn nocturnall,
> Bet doun the skyis clowdy mantill wall.
>
> (23–4)

The regal imagery is sustained by allusions to the sun's 'palyce
ryall', crown, and throne (35, 36, 47). Later in the Prologue it is
recalled in allusions to 'the cummyng of this king . . . Newly aryssyn
in hys estait ryall' (273 ff.; see also 141).

Douglas then turns to the sun's influence upon the earth. We
move from light itself—'twynklyng', 'lemand', 'glytrand', 'illu-
minat', reflected in streams and casting shadows (60 ff.)—to its
effects upon flowers and plant life (73–148); upon birds and animals
(151–86); and upon man (187–230). Plants respond to the 'ȝong
sonnys' warmth (96) by fresh growth and unbudding:

> The dasy dyd onbreid hir crownell smaill,
> And euery flour onlappyt in the daill . . .
>
> (122 ff.)

Birds and animals respond by procreating: swans are pictured 'seir-
sand by kynd a place quhar thai suld lay' (154). In Douglas's be-
guiling account of the animals each is accompanied by its young:

> The sprutlyt calvys sowkand the red hyndis,
> The ȝong fownys followand the dun days,
> Kyddis skippand throu ronnys efter rays;
> In lyssouris and on leys litill lammys
> Full tayt and tryg socht bletand to thar dammys,
> Tydy ky lowys, veilys by thame rynnys;
> All snog and slekit worth thir bestis skynnys.
>
> (180–86)

Here there are no barren or diseased animals; instead the calves are
'sowkand', the cows 'tydy', that is, 'giving milk', and their coats are
'snog and slekit'. Up to this point the picture is highly idealized.
Nature is plentiful, joyful, and harmonious. Only from man is the
response to the season discordant. Side by side with the Maytime
courtship and 'caralyng' of young people is practised 'bawdry and
onlesum meyn' (210). To Douglas this appears

> schamefull play,
> Na thyng accordyng to our hailsum May,

Bot rather contagius and infective,
And repugnant that sesson nutrytyve
   (225–8)

The climax of the Prologue comes when the birds sing a hymn
of praise to the sun, a skilful rhetorical summing-up of earlier themes:

Welcum the lord of lycht and lamp of day,
Welcum fostyr of tendir herbys grene,
Welcum quyknar of floryst flowris scheyn ...
Welcum the byrdis beild apon the brer,
Welcum master and rewlar of the ʒer,
Welcum weilfar of husbandis at the plewys,
Welcum reparar of woddis, treis and bewys,
Welcum depayntar of the blomyt medis,
Welcum the lyfe of euery thyng that spredis ...
   (252 ff.)

The last section (267–310) is in a different key; personal, conversational, and humorous, it forms the transition to book XII. The bird-
song rouses Douglas—as it rouses other sleeping poets[39]—and
fills him with the desire to see the dawn (273). Their last word,
'sluggardy', pricks his conscience and calls him back to his 'lang-
sum wark / Twichand the lattyr buke of Dan Virgill' (270–1).

In this Prologue Douglas clearly owes much to other poets. There
are echoes not only of Ovid but also of Chaucer and Henryson, and
the central section of the Prologue seems highly Virgilian.[40] Several
details—above all the conception of an almost sentient universe in
'The sulʒe spred hir braid bosum on breid' (74)—were inspired by
the *laus veris* in *Georgic* II. Much else in the shape and subject matter
of the Prologue is highly traditional. Many poets before Douglas had
celebrated the revivifying power of the sun, the rebirth of the world
in spring, and the fecundity of Nature, 'Seand throu kynd ilk thyng
spryngis and revertis' (230). The most famous example is perhaps
Chaucer's opening to the *Canterbury Tales*. Yet Douglas uses his
inheritance to good effect. He conveys in a way of his own both the
cosmic grandeur of the season and its many tiny consequences:
'seir downys smaill on dent de lyon sprang'. Prologue XII is impressive as a whole, not simply for scattered details; it is in the best sense
what Douglas himself calls it: 'a lusty crafty preambill'.

Many critics have praised Prologue VII. They find it 'the most
original of the three',[41] the most realistic,[42] and the most genuinely
Scottish.[43] Prologue VII seems to me indeed original both in conception and execution, yet I feel that the nature of Douglas's achievement here needs to be more precisely defined. It does not consist
solely in his descriptive realism, nor in his first-hand observation of

a Scottish winter. Douglas could be a remarkably accurate and vivid observer, alert not only to visual images but to very small movements and sounds:

Ryveris ran reid on spait with watir brovne
(19)
The wynd maid waif the red wed on the dyke
(59)
    scharp hailstanys mortfundeit of kynd
Hoppand on the thak and on the causay by.
(136–7)

Yet I think there has been a critical over-emphasis on this aspect of the Prologue. Here, as in the other Prologues, Douglas's inspiration was partly literary in kind. His imagination was fired by the writings of others, not just by looking directly at the natural world. There are several passages in this Prologue which are clearly indebted to other writers. It is quite false to say of it that 'apart from a passing reference to Boreas and Eolus the whole . . . is founded solely on Scottish experience'.[44]

The very first lines of the Prologue illustrate this:

As bryght Phebus, scheyn souerane hevynnys e,
The opposit held of hys chymmys hie,
Cleir schynand bemys, and goldyn symmyris hew,
In laton cullour alteryng haill of new,
Kythyng no syng of heyt be hys vissage,
So neir approchit he his wyntir stage;
Reddy he was to entyr the thrid morn
In clowdy skyis vndre Capricorn:
(1–8)

Douglas is adhering to tradition both in his syntax—the suspended temporal clause, with 'as' or 'when'—and in his dating of the poem by a reference to the sun's position in the Zodiac. Lydgate had opened his Prologue to the *Siege of Thebes* similarly:

Whan briȝt Phebus passed was þe ram
Myd of Aprille & in to bole cam
And Satourn old wt his frosty face
In virgyne taken had his place . . .
(1–4)[45]

Lydgate is recalling still more famous opening lines: 'Whan that Aprill with his shoures soote . . .'. Spring openings were clearly the most popular, yet other medieval poems, such as the *Kingis Quair* and Lydgate's *Temple of Glas*, purport to start in winter, and Chaucer dated his *House of Fame* on 10 December. Douglas seems here, however, to be echoing another poem of Chaucer's. The striking image of the sun's change from gold to 'laton' (i.e. copper) derives from Chaucer's

> Phebus wax old, and hewed lyk laton,
> That in his hoote declynacion
> Shoon as the burned gold with stremes brighte.
>> (*Franklin's Tale*, v.1245–7)[46]

Another poet also contributed to Douglas's opening. His lines on the constellation Orion

> Rany Oryon with his stormy face
> Bewavit oft the schipman by hys race.
>> (27–8)

allude to Orion's shattering of Aeneas's fleet (*Aeneid* 1.535). Douglas certainly recalls Virgil's epithets for Orion—*nimbosus* (1.535), *aquosus* (IV.52) and *saeuus* (VII.719). In such a Virgilian context Douglas's mention of 'Frawart Saturn, chill of complexioun' (29), though highly traditional,[47] may also echo Virgil's *frigida Saturni . . . stella* (*Georgic* 1.336).

Such allusiveness is not confined to the opening of the Prologue. When Douglas describes the birds that he hears as he lies awake in bed (105–25), he is giving new life to an ancient literary genre, the bird-catalogue.[48] He recalls and seems to challenge comparison with well-known lists of birds in Chaucer's *Parliament of Fowls* and Virgil's *Georgic* I. There are clear echoes of Chaucer in Douglas's reference to the cock as the 'nyghtis orlager' (113—cf. *Parliament of Fowls*, 350), and to the 'trumpat' voice of the crane (121—cf. *Parliament of Fowls*, 344). In *Georgic* 1.360 ff. the birds figure in the guise of weather prophets. So too for Douglas the cry of the cranes

> bene pronosticatioun
> Of wyndy blastis and ventositeis.
>> (122–3)

Nonetheless, here—and also in Prologue XII—Douglas makes his contribution to the genre memorable and distinctive. He puts it into a realistic-seeming context: the birds are heard 'on the ruyf aboyn' (118) or 'by my chalmyr in heich wysnyt treis' (124). Although he notes some visual details—the owl has a 'crukyt camscho beke' (107), and cranes fly 'on randon, schapyn like ane Y' (120)—Douglas concentrates on one particular aspect of the birds: their cries. For the most part he characterizes them effectively and accurately through their distinctive calls: the 'claking' of the wild geese, the 'crowpyng' of the cranes, the 'pew' of the kite, and the 'wild elrich screke' of the owl. A modern naturalist speaks similarly of the barn owl's 'prolonged, strangled, eldritch screech',[49] and Douglas is clearly attempt-

ing to suggest the sound made by these birds in his choice of onomatopoeic words.

Henryson had devoted two stanzas to winter in an account of the
Seasons (*Fables*, 1692–1705), and supplied a bleak, wintry Prologue
to his *Testament of Cresseid*. A generation after Douglas, Lindsay
described winter in the Prologue to his *Dreme*. From this it has been
inferred that 'a welcome and refreshing realism' was a mark of the
Scottish descriptive tradition.[50] I think, however, that the native
tradition to which Douglas owed most in this Prologue was less
Scottish than alliterative. When we read his

> Scharp soppys of sleit and of the snypand snaw
>
> (50)

we may be reminded of a line from *Sir Gawain* (2003):

> þe snawe snitered ful snart, þat snayped þe wylde.

The comparison highlights the greater economy and verbal energy
of the *Gawain*-poet; yet it also illustrates that Douglas was familiar
not necessarily with a specific poem such as *Sir Gawain* but with the
traditional collocations of alliterative poetry. In the *Awntyrs of
Arthure* (stanza vii) we read similarly of 'þe slete and þe snawe, þat
snayppede þame so snelle'. Alliteration contributes many stock
epithets and collocations to Prologue VII: 'raggit rolkis', 'schouris
snell', 'firth and fald'; but it is far more than an ornament. The rhyth-
mical structure of many lines is emphatically alliterative:

> So bustuusly Boreas his bugill blew,
> The deyr full dern doun in the dalis drew;
> Smale byrdis, flokkand throu thik ronys thrang,
> In chyrmyng and with chepyng changit thar sang,
> Sekand hidlis and hyrnys thame to hyde . . .
>
> (67–71)

From poems such as *Sir Gawain* or the *Morte Arthur* or *The Destruction of Troy* Douglas may have acquired a greater sensitivity to
stormy weather and wild and remote scenery, and a greater readiness
to describe them. He certainly shared with the authors of these
alliterative poems a much wider vocabulary than Chaucer or Lydgate
possessed for describing natural phenomena.

Yet Douglas was unusual in devoting such a long, sustained piece
of writing to the subject of winter. There are hundreds of medieval
descriptions of May or spring, but no poet writing in English before
Douglas seems to have made the experience of winter the centre of
his poem. Earlier English poets refer to winter, it is true, but usually
briefly and in long poems chiefly as a means of dating the action.
Often, as in Dunbar's 'In to thir dirk and drublie dayis' or the Harley
lyric 'Wynter wakeneth al my care', the season serves as a symbolic

starting point for a meditation on death or mutability. There are traces of both these functions in Douglas: the Prologue marks a stage in the composition of the whole *Eneados*, and to the poet who had just translated *Aeneid* vi winter appears

> a symylitude of hell,
> Reducyng to our mynd, in euery sted,
> Gousty schaddois of eild and grisly ded.
> (44–6)

Nonetheless, the chief object of the Prologue seems to be to characterize the complexity and multifariousness of winter. Douglas's originality consists partly in this, and partly in his revitalization of ancient poetic themes and images. He draws on many diverse traditions, and successfully blends material from earlier poets with material from his own experience. In this as in other Prologues first-hand observation co-exists with tradition; the one does not necessarily exclude the other.

Prologue vii has been subject to the same criticisms as Prologue xii—a lack of unity and too much of the '*item* kind of description'.[51] Yet if it is read attentively this Prologue consists of far more than a mere collection of vivid but haphazard details. It has a structure, and conveys a distinct sense of progression. Its movement might be compared to that of a film, which ranges over a wide panoramic landscape and gradually moves in to a close-up. The subject is the winter solstice—'tha schort days that clerkis clepe brumaill' (14). Douglas purports to be writing on the third morning after the sun had entered Capricorn, that is, not on Christmas Eve[52] but on 15 December. The time of year and even the mood resemble the opening of Donne's *Nocturnall upon St Lucies Day*: "Tis the yeares midnight and it is the dayes'. The first thirty-four lines of the Prologue are learned and abstract. The season is characterized chiefly in astronomical and mythological terms: Phebus, Neptunus, 'Mars occident', 'Rany Oryon'—

> Frawart Saturn, chill of complexioun,
> Throu quhais aspect darth and infectioun
> Beyn causyt oft, and mortal pestilens,
> Went progressyve the greis of his ascens;
> And lusty Hebe, Iunoys douchtir gay,
> Stude spulʒeit of hir office and array.
> (29–34)

The last two lines clearly refer to the cupbearer of the gods, who slipped and was disgraced, and succeeded by Ganymede. But what is Hebe doing in this Prologue? It is worth explaining her presence, not only because it illustrates Douglas's highly allusive technique but because it clears him from the charge of irrelevance. Douglas seems to have in mind the symbolic interpretation of the myth, such as he would find it in Boccaccio. Hebe primarily signifies youth (cf. the note to 1.i.52) and the renewal of life associated with spring, but her nakedness and loss of 'array' is linked with the fall of leaves in autumn. Ganymede, who took over her 'office', is identified with the sign Aquarius into which the sun moves on leaving Capricorn:

> Tandem adveniente tempore partus, id est vere novo, Hebem parit [Iuno], id est iuventutem et rerum omnium renovationem, frondes, flores, et germina omnia ea emittuntur tempestate. . . . Tandem adveniente autumno, in quo Sol incipit versus solstitium hyemale tendere . . . virentia omnia cessare, et frondes arborum cadere incipiunt, et sic Hebes, dum deteguntur que occultaverunt frondes nudari dicitur, et obscena monstrare, et a pincernatu etiam removetur, et Ganimedes substituitur, qui Aquarii signum dicitur, eo quod eo tempore pluviosa sit hyemps.[53]

Douglas then moves from this grand, cosmic picture of the season quite literally 'down to earth'. The symbolic image of Hebe, 'spulȝeit of hir office and array', foreshadows the wintry landscape that follows, studded with 'epithets coldly expressive of privation':[54]

> The grond stud barrant, widderit, dosk or gray,
> Herbis, flowris and gersis wallowyt away.
> Woddis, forrestis, with nakyt bewis blowt,
> Stude stripyt of thar weid in euery howt.
>   (63–6)

Yet this is still a composite picture of many aspects of winter. We move from mountain to plain, from snow and ice to muddy roads, 'full of floschis, dubbis, myre and clay' (54). With line 68 occurs an important shift of focus. Living creatures had hardly been mentioned in the first section of the Prologue, but now they come into the foreground and their response to winter is sympathetically described. Animals and men are linked together in a shared endurance of the elements:

> The deyr full dern doun in the dalis drew . . .
> Puyr lauboraris and bissy husband men
> Went wait and wery draglit in the fen.
> The silly scheip and thair litil hyrd gromys
> Lurkis vndre le of bankis, woddis and bromys.
>   (68 ff.)

Finally we move to the poet himself—from man in general to one individual. Both the place and the time are more precisely indicated, and the scene has the vividness of a Flemish genre painting:

The callour ayr, penetratyve and puyr,
Dasyng the blude in euery creatur,
Maid seik warm stovis and beyn fyris hoyt,
In dowbill garmont cled and wily coyt,
With mychty drink and metis confortyve,
Agane the stern wyntir forto stryve.
Repatyrrit weil, and by the chymnay bekyt,
At evin be tyme dovne a bed I me strekyt,
Warpit my hed, kest on clathis thrynfald,
Fortil expell the peralus persand cald.
        (87–96)

In his search for warmth and shelter Douglas is at one with the other living creatures he had described earlier. He describes how he opens the window to look out, and is repelled by what he sees:

The schot I closit, and drew inwart in hy,
Chyvirrand for cald, the sesson was so snell,
Schupe with hayt flambe to fleym the fresyng fell.
        (138–40)

In this Prologue there is no sense of delight in a snowy landscape, such as is found in one of the poems ascribed to the medieval Welsh poet, Dafydd ap Gwilym.[55] The mood is rather one of 'shivering repugnance';[56] this is indeed a *tristis prologus*.

The bridge passage (141–62) is managed skilfully. Douglas awakes, and the day's labours recommence—the theme, in part, of Prologues XII and XIII. He employs the traditional plough-imagery to express his weariness, but the images arise appropriately from what has preceded. Like the 'dantit grettar bestiall' (79) and the 'puyr lauboraris and bissy husband men' already described, the poet must pick up the work he has started despite his own reluctance and the inclement weather.

It is something of a misnomer to call Prologue XIII a 'nature' Prologue. The description of a June evening is not the centre of the poem, but a beautiful and symbolic setting for the poet's dream-dialogue with Maphaeus Vegius. The Prologue is one of Douglas's most accomplished pieces of writing, and makes one regret that he abandoned poetry—as he seems to have done—shortly after composing it. It has an ease and fluidity of style. There is no straining after extreme aureation. By contrast with Prologue XII, far less space is devoted to astronomy, and there are fewer mythological allusions and jewel images. Yet Douglas still cannot refrain from a three-fold description of dew as 'beryall droppis' and 'cristall knoppis or smal siluer bedis' (26–8). The tone is largely conversational, and often humorous. Douglas makes fun both of himself and Maphaeus, and

is jocular in his use of number symbolism. He undertakes to translate Maphaeus's book as well as the twelve books of the *Aeneid*

> in honour of God
> And hys Apostolis twelf, in the number od.
> (151–2)

There is a skilful modulation of tone, from the near-slapstick of the
dream to the sense of awe that dawn provokes:

> ʒondyr dovn dwynys the evyn sky away,
> And vpspryngis the brycht dawyng of day
> Intill ane other place nocht far in sundir
> That tobehald was plesans, and half wondir.
> (159–62)

Yet the Prologue is unified by a prevailing serenity, even cheerful-
ness of mood: June is 'the ioyus moneth' (3), the birds and beasts
are tranquil, 'at thar soft quyet' (48), and the planets—Venus and
Jupiter—are auspicious (70–2).

Douglas's sense of form is apparent in this Prologue: its structure
is simpler and more dramatic. The Prologue begins at twilight and
ends at dawn, and there is much patterning of contrasted images:
the setting and the rising sun; the evening star and the morning star;
bat and lark (symbolic creatures of dusk and dawn). Verbal antitheses sometimes reinforce these oppositions: Phoebus declines, but
Esperus 'vpspryngis' (20); and

> Vpgois the bak with hir pelit ledderyn flycht,
> The lark discendis from the skyis hycht . . .
> (33–4)

Yet Douglas is not blind to the similarity between these periods of
half light. In the evening, as later in the dawn, he notes how

> Owt our the swyre swymmys the soppis of myst.
> (37)

I take this patterning to be intentional, and to serve as more than
ornament. The contrasts enforce a sense of natural rhythm, the
repeated cycle of night and day. This in turn has a symbolic correspondence to the poet's own changing mood. The opening lays stress
on the night's function—'eftir laubour to tak the nychtis rest' (10)
—and

> Still war the fowlis fleis in the air,
> All stoir and catall seysit in thar lair,
> And euery thing, quharso thame lykis best,
> Bownys to tak the hailsum nychtis rest.[57]
> (43–6)

Douglas, too, thinks that he has completed his labours on the *Aeneid*.
But the Prologue ends with a new beginning. Dawn—*referens opera*

atque labores (*Aeneid* XI.183)—brings the resumption of activity by
bird, beast, man and the poet himself:

> Belyve on weyng the bissy lark vpsprang,
> To salus the blyth morrow with hir sang;
> Sone our the feildis schynys the lycht cleir,
> Welcum to pilgrym baith and lauborer;
> Tyte on hys hynys gaif the greif a cry,
> 'Awaik, on fut, go till our husbandry' . . .
> Tharto thir byrdis syngis in the schawys,
> As menstralis playng 'The ioly day now dawys.'
> Than thocht I thus: 'I will my cunnand kepe,
> I will not be a daw, I will not slepe,
> I wil compleit my promys schortly, thus
> Maid to the poet master Mapheus.'
>   (167 ff.)

The Prologue is thus far from static; there is a sense of change and
progression both in the outside world and in the poet's mind.

At the centre of Prologue XIII are two stock medieval forms: the
dream and the interview. The *Palice of Honour* indicates very clearly
Douglas's familiarity with the many and varied uses to which the
dream form had been put by medieval poets. In this Prologue, however, Douglas says quite explicitly that one particular dream was in
his mind:

> I wait the story of Iherom is to ʒou kend,
> Quhou he was dung and beft intill hys sleip,
> For he to gentilis bukis gaif sik keip.
>   (122–4)

Maphaeus replies contemptuously:

> 'ʒa, smy,' quod he, 'wald thou eschape me swa?
> In faith we sall nocht thus part or we ga!
> Quhou think we he essonʒeis hym to astart,
> As all for consciens and devoit hart,
> Fenʒeand hym Iherom forto contyrfeit,
> Quhar as he lyggis bedovyn, lo, in sweit!
> I lat the wyt I am nane hethyn wight,
> And gif thou has afortyme gayn onrycht,
> Followand sa lang Virgill, a gentile clerk,
> Quhy schrynkis thou with my schort Cristyn wark?'
>   (131–40)

Jerome's dream was famous and influential. It was sometimes re-
presented in art—as we may see from Botticini's painting in the
National Gallery—and memories of it shaped the dreams of other
Christians besides Douglas. The twelfth-century bishop, Herbert of

Norwich, had a vision in which he was told that 'the same mouth should not preach Christ and recite Ovid.'[58] Douglas is thus giving a new and humorous slant to what was clearly a well-known story. In so doing Douglas lets his readers know that he is aware of a classic discussion of the Christian's attitude to pagan literature. At the same time he is associating himself with a great saint and scholar, and what is more significant, the translator of the Vulgate. The pretension is at once ridiculed by Maphaeus—'Fenȝeand hym Iherom forto contyrfeit'—yet the link has been made.

The poet's interview with someone who commands him to write was a popular theme, and often linked with the dream. It perhaps originated partly as a humorous development of the humility topos: the poet writes not out of 'vane presumptioun' but at the request of another. Chaucer experienced a vision in which Cupid commanded him to write poems in praise of love and women; the *Legend of Good Women* followed. Douglas recalls this situation in his own *Palice of Honour*, and humorously tells us that the *Eneados* was prompted by the request of Venus (Directioun, 120–27; *Palice of Honour*, 1749–57). Other writers well known to Douglas had put the form to many and different uses. In Lydgate's *Fall of Princes* (II.3844–4212) Thyestes and Atreus demand that the poet put their stories into verse; later in the *Fall of Princes* (Prologue VIII) Lydgate has an imaginary conversation with Boccaccio and Petrarch. In *Prohemium* III of the *Genealogy of the Gods* Boccaccio describes an interview of a different kind, in which an attempt is made to dissuade him from writing; an old man, Numenius, chides him for harming the *numen* of the gods.

The closest parallel to Prologue XIII, however, is provided by Henryson. In his Prologue to the Fable of the Lion and the Mouse Henryson takes a walk on a June day, falls asleep beneath a hawthorn, and has a vision of the poet Aesop. Douglas clearly recalled Henryson when writing this Prologue. He describes Maphaeus as 'lyke to sum poet of the ald fasson' (88)—a line which in slightly different form Henryson used twice, of Aesop (*Fables*, 1353), and of Mercury (*Testament of Cresseid*, 245). Yet the differences are as striking as the resemblances. The hawthorn is replaced by the laurel (64, and cf. 87), traditionally associated with epic poetry.[59] And instead of the grave dialogue between Henryson and Aesop Douglas gives us something more like a 'flyting'. At first he addresses Maphaeus 'with reuerens' (89), but Maphaeus's tone towards Douglas is consistently contemptuous—his use of the slighting 'thou' and 'thee' should be noted. Douglas uses the form for his own ends, to dramatize a conflict within his own mind. Maphaeus is Douglas's *alter ego*, and voices some of Douglas's own views. The dialogue embodies a kind of literary criticism. It puts forward Douglas's defence for translating book XIII, yet shows that he is aware of its inferiority and the impropriety of adding it to Virgil. Yet this is all a humorous ploy; Douglas is making a show of being forced into something that he really wants to undertake. Prologue XIII is thus a successful piece of writing in itself, yet closely linked with the book that it precedes.

It will be clear that I depart from some earlier critics in my interpretation of these three Prologues. I do not think that in any of them 'landscape is depicted solely for its own sake',[60] or that Douglas was 'the first poet in our language to take landscape in itself and for itself as a subject'.[61] This seems no more true of Douglas than of Virgil in the *Georgics* or Milton in *L'Allegro* or *Il Penseroso*. Nonetheless, I think Douglas is a figure of some importance in the writing of descriptive poetry. Nature is still celebrated in moral or philosophical terms, or designed in part as a setting or correlative to the poet's mood, but it is given enormously increased prominence in these Prologues. No other poet writing in English before Douglas devotes so much space to the continuous description of the natural world. Again, for accuracy and close observation of detail Douglas seems unrivalled at this time. The presence of conventional features cannot detract from this. Douglas not only imitated Virgil but learnt from him, and seems to have been the first to introduce the *Georgics* into the English poetic tradition. In this he anticipates Thomson, but does not seem to have influenced him.

The Prologues are still, as they have long been, the best way of approaching Douglas. They form an excellent introduction not only to the *Eneados*, but to the *Palice of Honour*. From them we learn something of his critical preconceptions as well as his aims and difficulties as a translator. The Prologues are also extremely enjoyable; in them Douglas speaks to us across the centuries, rather as Dryden does in his later Prefaces. Douglas sometimes argues rationally with his readers, sometimes chats familiarly, and sometimes harangues them as if he were in the pulpit. His tone ranges from the humorous to the devout, from the intimate to the public and hortatory. This skilful modulation of tone and style can be observed within a single Prologue. Prologue I opens with a fanfare: Virgil's perfection is symbolized in a series of striking and quite unnaturalistic images. But when Douglas turns to Caxton, his mood of disgust is expressed in highly physical and colloquial language: 'I spittit for dispyte', or 'I hald my tung for schame, bytand my lyp' (150, 252). Douglas's Prologues reveal a mixture of emotions familiar to most writers: pride, anxiety, concern as to the reception his work will receive from the public. They also display a fundamental good sense; the reader is asked to consider the work as a whole—to 'grape the mater cleyn' (1 Prol 497)—and to read attentively:

> Consider it warly, reid oftar than anys;
> Weill at a blenk sle poetry nocht tayn is.
>   (1 Prol 107–8)

Above all, they convey a sense of delight, both in the reading of Virgil and even, burdensome though it may have sometimes seemed, in the act of translation.

[8]

Conclusion

Throw owt the ile yclepit Albyon
Red sall I be, and sung with mony one.
(Conclusio, 11–12)

Douglas's prediction may be greeted sceptically today, yet it is true
that within the sixteenth century his poetry was read and admired in
England as well as in Scotland. Douglas was too learned a poet to
have the wide-ranging popularity of sir David Lindsay, yet he was
never, like some Middle Scots poets, completely forgotten. An
interest in him persisted through the centuries, even though he
seems sometimes to have been remembered less for his intrinsic
poetic merits than for his association with Virgil or for the usefulness
of his language to antiquaries and lexicographers. Indeed there are
tell-tale signs that occasionally his name was praised, while his works
were unread. The history of Douglas's reputation is of great interest,
and has been admirably charted by several scholars.[1] Here I wish to
concentrate primarily on the contemporary response to Douglas, on
what is known of his first readers and their evaluation of his poetry.

The early popularity of Douglas's *Eneados* is suggested by the
number of manuscripts that survive: five complete ones, and the
fragments of a sixth. These belong to the period between the completion of the translation in 1513 and the appearance of the first
printed edition at London in 1553. Scholars have concluded, from
the evidence of variant readings, that there must also have existed
other intermediate texts now lost—J. A. W. Bennett estimates that
'at least ten copies of this long work . . . were made in less than forty
years'.[2] The *Palice of Honour* was also in sufficient demand to be published several times. An edition was printed in London (*c.*1553) by
William Copland, the printer of the *Eneados*; and in 1579 it was
printed at Edinburgh by John Ross for Henry Charteris. Of this
edition only two copies are now extant, yet 280 'Palices of Honor,
vnbund' were in the possession of John Ross at the time of his death
in 1580.[3] In his Address to the Reader, Charteris speaks critically of
'the diuers Impressiones befoir Imprentit of this Notabill werk'; he
mentions 'not onlie that quhilk hes bene Imprentit at London, bot
also the Copyis set furth of auld amangis our selfis'. Unfortunately
there survive only fragments of this early Scottish edition, ascribed

to the press of Thomas Davidson and tentatively dated *c.* 1530–40.[4]

Douglas recognized that his translation would be useful to students of Virgil, and hoped that they would read it not from compulsion but from their own thirst for the subject (cf. Directioun, 88). He seems to have envisaged an audience composed chiefly of youthful aristocrats, such as the 'gentil barroun and knycht' (ix Prol 88) to whom he dedicated the *Eneados*.[5] Lord Sinclair is unlikely to have seen the completed work, but one manuscript at least was owned by a Scottish nobleman, William Ruthven, first earl of Gowrie; and another was available to Henry Howard, earl of Surrey, even if not in his possession. What little we know of the ownership and transmission of Douglas's poems suggests that they were of interest, not surprisingly, to other poets—Drummond of Hawthornden owned copies of the 1579 *Palice of Honour* and the 1553 *Eneados*;[6] to burgesses, such as George Bannatyne and David Anderson of Aberdeen, who was the second owner of the Elphinstoun manuscript of the *Eneados*; to lawyers, such as 'Henry Aytoun notare publict', who in 1547 copied out the Bath manuscript; and also to churchmen: the Cambridge manuscript belonged to John Danielston, 'rector a Dysert', and in 1527 William Hay, canon of Aberdeen and 'person of Turreff' recorded his ownership of the Elphinstoun manuscript. Douglas may not have expected deeply learned 'clerkis' to be among his readers, yet his translation of the *Aeneid* found a place on the shelves of these two churchmen, along with works by Polydore Vergil, Cassiodorus, Erasmus, St Ambrose, and other theologians.[7] The evidence is clearly fragmentary, yet—rather like the tip of an iceberg—it suggests that Douglas's readership was more extensive and more varied than we might at first suspect today.

If we can judge from the choice of Prologues in his anthology (iv, ix.1–18, and x), George Bannatyne esteemed Douglas most highly as a moral and devotional poet. The comments of other sixteenth-century Scotsmen tell us that Douglas was also admired for his learning and his rhetoric. John Leslie spoke of his *ingenii acumen acerrimum, ac eruditionem singularem*.[8] Henry Charteris praised Douglas for his 'ornate meter',[9] and the poet John Rolland called him 'an honest Oratour, Profound Poet, and perfite Philosophour' (*Court of Venus*, iii.112–13).[10] In a brief survey of Scottish poets, written less than ten years after Douglas's death, Lindsay makes no mention of Henryson, devotes two lines to Dunbar, and fifteen to Douglas:

> Allace for one, quhilk lampe wes of this land,
> Off Eloquence the flowand balmy strand,
> And, in our Inglis rethorick, the rose,
> As of Rubeis the Charbunckle bene chose:

> And, as Phebus dois Synthia presell,
> So Gawane Dowglas, Byschope of Dunkell,

> Had, quhen he wes in to this land on lyue,
> Abufe vulgare Poetis prerogatyue,
> Boith in pratick and speculatioun ...
>   (*Testament of the Papyngo*, 22 ff.)

This eulogy of Douglas's 'eloquence' follows traditional lines. It recalls Dunbar's praise of Chaucer, and Douglas's own praises of Virgil and Chaucer. Lindsay himself, although best known today as a polemicist and satirist, sometimes wrote in the ceremonious, high style, of which Douglas was considered to be a master. There are several signs that Lindsay had read Douglas attentively, as in his lines on James I:

> Gem of Ingyne, and peirll of polycie,
> Well of Iustice, and flude of Eloquence
>   (*Testament of the Papyngo*, 431–2)[11]

His description of a spring garden in the Prologue to the *Monarche* has many affinities with Prologue XII of the *Eneados* and the opening of the *Palice of Honour*. There is the same abundance of learned, semi-scientific language—'holsum herbis medicinall' (134) or 'donke impurpurit vestiment nocturnall' (146)—and a periphrasis, used also in the *Palice of Honour* (49–52) and Dunbar's *Goldin Targe*, to indicate fine weather: 'Neptune that day and Eoll held thame coye' (185). The *Palice of Honour* and the *Goldin Targe* were outstanding Scottish examples of this rhetorical style of writing; it is perhaps for this reason that they are juxtaposed in the *Complaynt of Scotlande* (usually dated *c.* 1549).[12] Yet the mention of both poems in this long list of romances and marvellous tales may simply indicate that they were then valued more highly than today for their sheer story-content.

Douglas was admired also by John Bellenden, a younger contemporary of Lindsay's, who was in the service of James V, and later archdeacon of Moray. He may perhaps have known Douglas personally; a man of the same name was secretary to the earl of Angus in 1528, and his writings are said to show a conspicuous 'devotion to the Douglas cause'.[13] Bellenden clearly imitated the *Palice of Honour* in a piece of writing, commonly known as the 'Proheme of the Cosmographie', which precedes his prose translation of Hector Boece's *History* (*c.* 1531):

> Me thocht I wes in to ane plesand meid
> Quhair flora maid the tendir blewmis spreid
> Throw kyndlie dew and humouris nutrative.
> Quhen goldin titan wt his flammis reid
> Aboif the seis rasit vp hir [sic] heid

Diffounding down his heit restoretive
To every frute that natur maid on lyve.
Quhilk wes afoir in to the wintir deid
For stormis cawld and froistis penetryve.
 (55-63)[14]

Several of the images here and much of the diction—the 'kyndlie'
dew, 'nutrative', 'diffounding', and 'heit restoretive'—can be traced
to the Prologue of the *Palice of Honour*. There are other resemblances
also, such as the run-on syntax, the elaborate stanza (which Douglas
employed in the first two sections of his poem), and the use of the
dream form as a vehicle for an allegorical debate between Virtue and
Delight. Bellenden is remembered today chiefly as a translator, and
it is possible—though there is no definite proof—that the example
of the *Eneados* spurred him to make his own translation of the first
five books of Livy.

 Another Scottish admirer of the *Palice of Honour* was John Rolland,
a notary public at Dalkeith, who flourished in the mid-sixteenth
century. Only two works of his survive: a version of the *Sevin Sages*,
and the *Court of Venus*, a poem which clearly reveals Rolland to be a
follower of Douglas. Although not printed till 1575, it was composed before the *Sevin Sages* (dated 1560), and apparently in the lifetime of Lindsay and Bellenden. The very title of the poem suggests
the allegorical and courtly tradition to which it belongs. Much in the
poem is so conventional that it has many medieval parallels, yet it is
clear that its peculiar 'blend of gallantry, satire, fantasy and pedantry'[15] was shaped by one work in particular, Douglas's *Palice of
Honour*. Rolland does not attempt to disguise his interest in Douglas.
At the opening of book III is a list of 'Nymphs', and as authority for
the correctness of their names Rolland mentions Virgil, Ovid, and
also

   the palice of honour,
Maid be Gawine dowglas of Dunkell ...
Weill put in vers in gude still and ordour,
Thir Nimphis names, thair he dois trewlie [tell].
 (*Court of Venus*, III.110 ff.)

Stylistically, the two poems have much in common. Rolland uses the
nine-line stanza that Bellenden and Douglas had also used. He has the
same taste for catalogues and classical allusions, and he carries his
fondness for what he calls 'clerklie termis' (such as 'morigerate' or
'obnubilate') to far greater lengths than Douglas. Numerous small
details and phrases recall the *Palice of Honour*: 'font caballine' (III.
899), or 'my honour war degraid' (IV.237), or 'beggit termes', used
by Rolland, as by Douglas, in a piece of self-depreciation:

> Now pas thy wayis, thou barrant buik new breuit,
> With beggit termes, & barbar toung mischeuit.
> (Prol 319–20)[16]

Structurally, too, Douglas's influence is clear. The kernel of the plot, slight as it is, comes from the *Palice of Honour*—the 'blasphematioun' (1.748) against Venus, the trial of the blasphemer, and his defence by Vesta. Rolland does not follow Douglas in every respect, however. He exploits the comic potentialities of the legal framework in ways not used by Douglas: Vesta objects that the jury are biased in Venus's favour and therefore 'all suspicious' (111.190). Rolland's work is less complex than Douglas's: it is essentially a debate on the nature and value of human love.

Apart from its mention in Bale's *Catalogus* (1559), the only early references to the *Palice of Honour* are Scottish. Despite the existence of the London edition it seems to have been better known—or better appreciated—in Scotland than in England. Perhaps this is because the taste for aureate diction and the dream-poem lingered far longer in Scotland than in England, although the taste was becoming increasingly old-fashioned in the second half of the sixteenth century. James VI and the group of poets associated with his court admired new verse-forms and styles of writing, and sought to pattern their own poetry on English and continental models. Yet some of the new poets were clearly familiar with older Scottish writers; there are echoes of Dunbar, and possibly of Douglas also, in Alexander Montgomerie's allegorical *Cherrie and the Slae*.[17] First published in 1597 and re-printed again and again in the seventeenth century, this poem is a witness to the surprisingly long life of the allegorical tradition in Scotland.

The *Eneados*, unlike the *Palice of Honour*, does not seem to have been imitated by Scottish poets. Yet there are signs that it was read attentively by those who possessed copies, or by the scribes themselves. Marginal comments on some of the manuscripts, such as those already mentioned (p.108), indicate that the *Eneados* was a living work for a generation or two after Douglas wrote it, and that it sometimes evoked a response similar to that aroused by the *Aeneid* itself. The most rudimentary type is a *Nota*, such as is often found in books of this period, usually drawing attention to a moral or sententious passage (as at x.viii.73 in the Cambridge manuscript, or xi. vii.23 in the Ruthven manuscript). In the Elphinstoun manuscript there are a few attempts at rhetorical guidance: *loquitur Aeneas in propria persona* (1.ii.14), or *Oratio Didonis* (1v.vi.49). Similar annotations are printed in the edition of 1553. Here passages are often classified—as 'a piteous exclamation' (11.vii.1), 'a consolation' (xi.i.124), or an 'inuectif oracion' (xi.viii.1). (Virgil was frequently praised at this time for his 'oraisons' or his 'tragicall exclamations'.)[18] Other marginal notes emphasize the princely virtues of Aeneas: 'Eneas lyk a wys and constant prynce ouercummis his affectyons with reson' (iv.vii.63); or 'A good prynce is euer vigilant and cairful for hys subiectys' (x.v.3). This latter type of comment is not found in any manuscript of the *Eneados*, and must, I think, be ascribed not to Douglas himself but to Douglas's editor. The same preoccupation with reading the *Aeneid* as a mirror for princes seems to have led him to alter Douglas's text; he adds six lines to Prologue I and a prose passage between book vi and book vii.[19] A similar readiness to tamper with Douglas's text can be seen in the removal of references to the Virgin and Purgatory—the Protestantism for which this edition is best known. A passage of sixty-eight lines (iv.iv.65 – iv.v.42) dealing with Dido's love for Aeneas is omitted, as is the whole of Douglas's Directioun. Douglas's humour is often toned down, as in the re-writing of the last four lines of the Conclusio, where his light-hearted 'gallandis' is replaced by 'gud readeris'. Such 'editing' stresses some aspects of the *Aeneid* more than did Douglas himself, and often mutilates Douglas's own writing. The side-notes and the alterations to the text betray a serious but rather simple-minded approach both to Virgil and to Douglas. Yet their very number suggests what an impact the *Eneados* made on the particular reader responsible for them. Whether this was Copland himself is far from clear. The annotations have many traces of Scots both in their spelling and syntax (as in 'Tratouris that betrasis . . .' at vi.ix.195), and the translation itself is only partially anglicized.

Interest in the *Eneados* was far from being confined to Scotland. Douglas's eulogy of Chaucer in Prologue I is quoted by Thomas Speght in the 1602 edition of his *Chaucer*, and there are other English references to Douglas, most if not all complimentary. Thomas Twyne, however, adopts a rather censorious tone in his explanation of why he translated Maphaeus Vegius:

> I haue not done it vpon occasion of any dreame as Gawin Dowglas did it into the Scottish, but mooued with the worthines of the worke and the neerenes of the argument, verse and stile vnto Virgil.[20]

Perhaps the most convincing proof of English interest in Douglas comes from two poets who betray his influence, even though they make no mention of his name. The better known of these is the earl of Surrey, whose use of Douglas in his own translation of *Aeneid* II and IV was first suggested by G. F. Nott,[21] and has since been discussed by several scholars, the most recent and exhaustive of whom is Miss F. H. Ridley.[22] Surrey's relationship to Douglas is not easy to assess. It is complicated less by the uncertainty over dating his translation than by its textual problems. Book II exists only in Tottel's print of 1557, but book IV exists in three versions: Tottel, 1557; the Day-Owen print of 1554; and manuscript Hargrave 205. It is possible to over-estimate Surrey's indebtedness to Douglas: some similarities may well be explained as coincidental, deriving from their common original, their common use of the Latin commentators, and the very genius of the language into which they translated. Nonetheless Surrey's debts to Douglas are many and pervasive; he takes over words, phrases, single lines, and, on one occasion, the greater part of a rhyming couplet (IV.540–1).

The most interesting question, which can here be only briefly discussed, is what it was in the *Eneados* that Surrey admired. I think that Surrey consulted Douglas in the first place as an aid to understand the *Aeneid*. Coldwell says that 'Surrey's familiarity with Latin would make vernacular help unnecessary'.[23] Yet the very frequency with which he turned to Douglas's translation points to the opposite conclusion: the *Eneados* was a supplement to the Latin commentaries upon Virgil that Surrey undoubtedly also used. Surrey's aims as a translator were very different from Douglas's. He sought both to match Virgil's compression and to 'imitate' many of the more striking formal qualities of the *Aeneid*.[24] Despite this, Surrey seems to have recognized the poetic merits of the *Eneados*. When Douglas is unusually concise—and thus in accord with Surrey himself—whole lines are incorporated in his translation:

> Upsprang the crye of men and trompettes blast
> (II.399)
> Fell on the bed, and these last words she said
> (IV.870)

These derive, almost verbatim, from Douglas (II.vi.31; IV.xii.14); they also correspond exactly to single Virgilian lines (II.313; IV.650). At other times Surrey pruned Douglas, choosing one out of his piled up synonyms: 'wilis' (II.247), for instance, instead of 'wilis and slychtis' (II.iii.97). Surrey clearly found much in Douglas's use of language attractive. He imitated his rhythms again and again, as in

> Their grisly backes were linked manifold
> (II.263; cf. II.iv.15)

He often adopted into his own translation words that still seem apt and expressive. He took over Douglas's 'lukkit' (II.vii.43) in 'Our first labor thus lucked well with us' (II.494) and Douglas's 'strykkyn hynd' (IV.ii.40) in IV.88. He preserved the most striking elements in Douglas's

Now fletis the mekil holk with tallonyt keyll
(IV.vii.74)

as 'Now fleetes the talowed kele' (IV.525).

Surrey sometimes adopted from Douglas an archaism like 'scathe-full' (II.42; cf. II.i.34), or distinctively Scottish words like 'bing' (IV.529; cf. IV.vii.80) and 'ugsome' (II.1002; cf. II.xi.124). This aspect of Surrey's interest in Douglas has been obscured by Tottel; in his print of Surrey's book IV he or his editor often seem to replace unusual words derived from Douglas by more commonplace ones. Thus Douglas's 'grekyng' (IV.xi.4), an archaic and poetic term for the grey light of dawn, lies behind Surrey's 'crekyng', recorded in both the Hargrave manuscript and the Day print; Tottel, however, reads 'the peping day' (IV.782). Emrys Jones says that 'regarded as a translation, Tottel's version is the fullest and most accurate of the three'.[25] Yet this is not invariably so. In rejecting words that he either did not like or understand, Tottel sometimes makes Surrey appear less accurate as a translator than I think he was. Thus Surrey is made to mistranslate Virgil's *umentem . . . umbram* (IV.7) in Tottel's 'shadowes dark' (IV.10); Hargrave's 'dank' is far closer not only to Douglas ('donk . . . clowd', IV.i.13) but to Virgil. So too with Virgil's *feruere litora flammis* (IV.567), which Douglas translates accurately as 'al the cost belyue of flambys scald' (IV. x.89). Surrey, I think, adopted *scald*, which still survives in Hargrave's 'skalt', and is misprinted in Day as 'stald'; Tottel, how-ever, enfeebles Surrey in his version: 'the shore all *spred* with flame' (IV.759).

Surrey must have seen a manuscript of the *Eneados*, since he was executed in 1547. The 1553 edition was available, however, to a later English poet, Thomas Sackville. His Induction to the *Mirror for Magistrates* (which first appeared in the 1563 edition of that work) shows that he had read some parts of the *Eneados* attentively. The first nine stanzas of the Induction have a striking winter-setting; according to Paul Bacquet, Douglas's Prologue VII 'a fourni à Sack-ville la plupart des éléments de son tableau'.[26] This is something of an exaggeration. There is indeed a thematic resemblance, but most of the points at which Sackville recalls Prologue VII—such as Sack-ville's reference to Saturn's 'frosty face' or the blasts of Boreas—are highly conventional. The closest verbal similarity is perhaps between Douglas's

Smale byrdis, flokkand throu thik ronys thrang,
In chyrmyng and with cheping changit thair sang
(69–70)

and Sackville's

And small fowles flocking, in theyr song did rewe
The winters wrath ...
   (12–13)[27]

Later in the Induction there is stronger proof that Sackville had read not only the *Aeneid* but Douglas's translation of it, more particularly books II and VI. Sackville's

I can no more but tell howe ther is sene
Fayer Ilium fal in burning red gledes downe
And from the soyle great Troy, Neptunus towne.
   (474–6)

is a truncated and rather clumsy copy of Douglas's

And tho beheld I al the cite myschevit,
Fayr Illion all fall in gledis down,
And fra the soyll, gret Troy, Neptunus town,
Ourtumlyt to the grond ...
   (II.X.112–15)[28]

So too Sackville's lines on

Blacke Cerberus the hydeous hound of hell,
With bristles reard, and with a three mouthed Iawe,
Foredinning the ayer with his horrible yel
   (499–501)

recall Douglas's

Cerberus, the hydduus hund, that regioun
Fordynnys, barkand with thre mowthis soun.
   (VI.VI.69–70)

Fordin is common in Douglas. It is a distinctively Scottish verb, and *O.E.D.* records no other English user apart from Sackville.[29] Sackville shared Douglas's fondness for alliteration and archaisms of diction and grammar. He evidently knew and imitated Lydgate also, and the shape and style of his Induction owed much to medieval poetic traditions.

Douglas's translation clearly met a need in the sixteenth century. It was useful to those who wanted to know more of the *Aeneid*, but could not cope unaided with Virgil's Latin. It may perhaps have been used side by side with the text of Virgil, fulfilling a function similar to the Loeb editions of the classics today. For more than half a century Douglas's *Eneados* was the only complete translation available to English readers as well as to Scottish. Selections only from the *Aeneid* were offered by Surrey and Stanyhurst. The first serious rival to Douglas's *Eneados* was the translation started by Thomas Phaer: the first seven books of this appeared in 1558, and it was completed by Thomas Twyne in 1573, book XIII being added in 1584. Writing in 1563, Barnabe Googe praised Surrey, who

did bryng a pece
of *Virgils* worke in frame,
And *Grimaold* gaue the lyke attempt,
and *Douglas* wan the Ball,
Whose famouse wyt in Scottysh ryme
had made an ende of all.
But all these same did *Phayre* excell ...
(*Epytaphe of Maister Thomas Phayre*)[30]

Googe is over-complimentary to Phaer's fourteeners, but he seems to have assessed the taste of his time correctly. The Phaer-Twyne translation of the *Aeneid* was a success, and by 1620 had been re-printed at least four times. It seems indeed to have virtually superseded Douglas's translation at the end of the century. No further edition of the *Eneados* appeared until Thomas Ruddiman produced his influential *Virgil's Aeneis Translated into Scottish Verse* (Edinburgh 1710).[31]

Some of Douglas's first readers found his translation not only useful but attractive. The *Eneados* seems to have appealed to both Surrey and Sackville for its language—the distinctively Scottish words, the archaisms, the sheer strangeness of its diction. Yet their occasional misinterpretation of Douglas's meaning helps to explain why the *Eneados* did not retain its popularity with English readers. Surrey, for instance, seems to have taken Douglas's *hy* (11.i.4), 'haste', as meaning 'high' (11.21). He also misunderstood Douglas's description of Dido's nurse, who

Hychit on furth with slaw pays lyke a trat.
(IV.xi.114)

Trat means 'old woman', but in his translation of the same passage Surrey took it over in quite a different sense:

redouble gan her nurse
Her steppes, forth on an aged womans trot.
(IV.857–8)

Sackville, too, adopted unusual words from Douglas that he did not fully understand, such as *swelth* or its variant *swelch*, which Douglas commonly uses in the sense "whirlpool'. It translates *vertex* at 1.iii.42, and is applied to Acheron's 'holl bysme and hydduus swelch onrude' (VI.v.3). Sackville follows Douglas in applying the word to the rivers of hell, but seems to give it a more concrete sense:

Rude Acheron, a lothsome lake to tell,
That boyls and bubs vp swelth as blacke as hell.[32]   (480–1)

Even in Scotland at this time there are signs that Douglas's vocabulary was, for various reasons, not always understood. The copyists sometimes mangled his Latinisms, turning 'eliphantyne' (VI.xv.114) into 'elephantis'; 'inhibitioun' (x.i.22) into 'inhabitatioun'; 'invincible' (x.v.68) into 'invisible'; 'inundacioun' (xII.iv.113) into 'invadatioun'; and 'panaces' (i.e. panacea, xII.vii.91) into 'penates'.[33] They sometimes, as I have already illustrated (p.154), substituted more commonplace words for his archaisms. There is some evidence also that the *Palice of Honour* was not always understood. The National Library of Scotland possesses a copy of the 1579 edition, which contains emendations made by a late sixteenth-century reader; some of these indicate that Douglas's language was growing increasingly archaic and unfamiliar.[34] In 1614 John Norden substituted Douglas for Lydgate in the traditional triad of poets:

Chawcer, Gowre, the *bishop of dunkell,*
In ages farre remote were eloquent.[35]

Norden complained that the most praised poems of his time were 'beset with Chaucers wordes and phrases ancient'; the same aura of antiquity was beginning to surround Douglas.

In the course of the centuries, Douglas, like Chaucer, has evoked very different responses from his readers. In the sixteenth century he was praised for his learning; at the end of the seventeenth century, Francis Junius remarked on the 'monkish ignorance' that infected his translation.[36] Thomas Warton makes some of his Prologues sound like an anticipation of the *Lyrical Ballads*:

they are the effusion of a mind not overlaid by the descriptions of other poets, but operating, by its own force and bias, in the delineation of a vernal landscape, on such objects as really occurred.[37]

Yet the twentieth-century editor of the *Eneados* finds little but convention and rhetoric in these same Prologues. Different ages have viewed Douglas from different standpoints: sometimes they criticized him because of their higher standard of classical scholarship; sometimes they singled out for praise what was most acceptable to contemporary canons of taste. Such partial judgments, from which no critic, of course, is immune, have sometimes failed to take account of Douglas's own objectives and the circumstances in which he wrote. It would be undesirable, even if it were possible, to view Douglas's poetry solely through sixteenth-century eyes. Yet some historical perspective is necessary, if we are to make an evaluation of Douglas that is both just and sympathetic.

The *Palice of Honour* well illustrates the vicissitudes in Douglas's reputation. To David Irving it was a 'Gothic structure'.[38] To Gregory Smith it possessed 'nothing in *motif* or in style to cause us to suspect the humanist'.[39] Yet some recent scholars have referred to the

'Renaissance' aspects of the poem, and termed it 'a manifesto of Renaissance and humanistic ideals'.[40] They apparently assume that it is self-explanatory to attach to the *Palice of Honour* so elusive, emotive and Protean a label. The term 'Renaissance' is notoriously difficult to define, and has very different meanings when applied to the art of fifteenth-century Florence, or to the drama of late sixteenth-century England. Does the *Palice of Honour* qualify as a 'Renaissance' poem simply because it refers to some Italian humanists ? Perhaps the poem's strongest claim to such a description is the plea that it seems to contain for a more humane and literary kind of education, such as was advocated by many humanists and most eloquently of all by Leonardo Bruni:

> Poet, Orator, Historian and the rest, all must be studied, each must contribute a share. Our learning thus becomes full, ready, varied and elegant . . . But to enable us to make effectual use of what we know we must add to our knowledge the power of expression . . . Where, however, this double capacity exists — breadth of learning and grace of style—we allow the highest title to distinction and to abiding fame.[41]

Douglas's sympathy with such ideals is latent in the central section of the *Palice of Honour*, yet it is not so clear and explicit as to form a 'manifesto'. Douglas's pre-occupation with literary fame, his love of classical mythology, and his echoes from Ovid and Virgil were no doubt congenial to the humanists among his readers. But they form one strand among many in a complex poem. I do not find the term 'Renaissance' particularly helpful in defining the nature of a poem that in form and content is so deeply rooted in the literature of the preceding centuries.

Yet the *Palice of Honour* is far from being merely 'a periphrastic study in a worn-out poetical fashion'. I cannot agree with the unsympathetic critics who stress its conventionality and represent it as the dead-end of a tradition.[42] To understand the *Palice of Honour* we must know something of its antecedents, such as Chaucer's dream-poems; but Douglas is saying something quite different from Chaucer, and his poem is more than a pale shadow of the *House of Fame*. It has an originality which consists not in striking innovations of form and subject-matter but in small shifts of emphasis, re-workings of old themes, a modification rather than a rejection of the past. It displays, intermittently, a vitality in the handling of language, which emerges more fully in the *Eneados* and its Prologues.

The claim for Douglas as a 'Renaissance' figure might be more securely based upon his *Eneados*. This is the work where he shows himself most responsive to new ideals and currents of thought. The

Eneados was the first translation of a great classical poem into any form of English, yet the pioneering aspect of Douglas's translation is still not always recognized. H. B. Lathrop, in his valuable survey of early translations from the classics, considers the age in which Douglas wrote 'an essentially medieval period', when Ovid and Virgil were 'represented by summaries and *rifacimenti*'; for him, as for many readers, the great period of translation, characterized by 'large undertakings of permanently important books' is the second half of the sixteenth century.[43] Yet as early as 1513 Douglas gave his readers not a re-telling of the *Aeneid* or a translation at second- or third-hand; not a sample of one or two books only; but the whole work, something that no translator into English succeeded in completing single-handed until over a century later. Douglas's achievement is impressive when we consider the paucity of his scholarly tools, and the absence of many reference-works that we now take for granted. The length and arduousness of an undertaking does not guarantee its greatness, yet there is something monumental about Douglas's *Eneados*. To paraphrase Dryden: it is one thing to take pains on a fragment and translate it perfectly; and another thing to have the weight of a whole poem on one's shoulders.[44]

Our attitude to Douglas's *Eneados* must inevitably differ from that of its first readers. Every century, if not every generation, needs to make its own translation of foreign masterpieces—only the very greatest, such as Dryden's *Aeneid* or the Authorized Version of the Bible, long outlive their original audiences. This is particularly true of verse translations. Yet both as a poem and as a translation Douglas's *Eneados* has had discerning admirers in the twentieth century. Ezra Pound thought that Douglas 'gets more poetry out of Virgil than any other translator'.[45] Tillyard, with more caution, called the *Eneados* 'probably the best translation of one of the great epics till Dryden and Pope'.[46] But the best tribute both to Douglas's readability and his insight as a translator comes from a classical scholar. Contrasting him with Dryden, R. G. Austin says:

> He makes one want to keep turning on and on to see how he has handled this or that passage . . . each interpretation has seen something of the essential Virgil; and because of his more direct approach, Douglas often has things to tell the professional scholar that cannot be learnt from Dryden.[47]

Praise of this kind must not raise our expectations too high. Like most translators, Douglas is better at rendering some aspects of his original than others. Some passages he may have found difficult; others he may have hurried over; he may have responded more deeply to others, and thus expended more care upon their translation.

Most crucial of all was the adequacy of his own style and poetic traditions to the rendering of Virgil. Douglas's verse cannot match the variety and power of Virgil's; only rarely, as in some alliterative passages, does he even attempt to catch some of Virgil's sound effects. He loses the compression of his original, and often simplifies much that is daring and unusual in Virgil's handling of language. Douglas is rarely successful in rendering the *Aeneid*'s great set speeches. He fails, for instance, to convey the sophistry and irony in Juno's rhetorical speeches (VII.v.24 ff.; or x.ii.3–96). He is far better with short snatches of dialogue, and, not surprisingly, with invective (as at IX.x.17 ff.). Douglas seems to have found particularly intractible those passages in the *Aeneid* which are close packed with mythological allusion or heavy with the weight of Roman history (such as Anchises' speech to Aeneas at the end of book VI). He is far better with straight narrative: with portraits, descriptive passages, and scenes of action, such as the hunt in book IV, or many of the battle scenes. Here the experience that Virgil describes is not remote from his own time. Yet where Douglas excels is at rendering the more universal and timeless parts of the *Aeneid*—descriptions of the natural world, as in the similes and the storm scenes of books I and III; or descriptions of the supernatural, as in the portraits of Charon and Polyphemus. The opening sections of book VI are devoted to the 'dern skuggis dyrk' and the 'waist dongion of Pluto kyng' (VI. iv.57, 69); this is not Virgil's underworld, yet it conveys a powerful sense of a mysterious and melancholy 'otherworld'. Douglas is always responsive to the latent pathos or tenderness of a scene: to 'the ȝong babbys sawlys weping' at the threshold of the underworld, to the grief of Dido, or the deaths of Pallas, and Nisus and Euryalus. Douglas clearly has weaknesses—chief among them diffuseness and occasional pedantry—yet at his best he is a responsible and sensitive translator, transmitting to us much of Virgil's 'sentence' and 'eloquence'.

Douglas clearly has a cultural and historical importance. From him we can learn much of the literary tastes and attitudes not only of Scotsmen in the reign of James IV but of many educated men at his time. Scholars have made surmises, not always well-founded, about the nature of Henryson's reading; but we can be precise and definite about many of the books that Douglas read and admired. Douglas gives us an insight into the way in which readers of the early sixteenth century approached a great Latin poet. He illustrates very vividly what they valued in Virgil, and also how they read and studied the text of his poems. In the *Eneados* we can sometimes get close to Douglas as a translator, and examine the degree of consistency between his theories and his actual practice. This is possible, partly because he voices some of his ideas in the Prologues, partly because we know, fairly definitely, what edition of Virgil he used. Douglas's *Eneados* sometimes sheds light on the practice of later sixteenth-century translators, such as Surrey, Golding, or Chapman. The explanatory technique that he adopted (termed by H. B. Lathrop 'the expanded method of translation')[48] had its critics, such as Nicholas Grimald;[49] but it continued to be used long after Douglas's time, in Colville's Boethius (1556), Phaer's Virgil, and Marlowe's First Book of Lucan.[50] Even Dryden in the late seventeenth century did not disdain to incorporate notes and explanatory glosses in his translation of Virgil.[51]

Douglas's first claim on our attention, however, must be as a poet. He has often been termed, along with Henryson and Dunbar, a 'Scottish Chaucerian'. Yet labels of this kind—attempts to 'formulate' him upon a pin—only make one aware of how much he differs both from Chaucer and from other Scottish poets of his age. Douglas is not profoundly original, yet he has an individual voice; a distinctive personality, sometimes eccentric and pedantic, sometimes lively and humorous, emerges from his writings. This may be seen even in the *Palice of Honour*, and is revealed most clearly in the Prologues. In the *Eneados* itself Douglas displays not only honesty as a translator but a zest and verbal energy that have kept his poem alive for more than its first readers, something that is far from true of all translations of the *Aeneid*.

The chief obstacle to the enjoyment of Douglas's poetry is not peculiar to the twentieth century: it is the difficulty of his language, especially to English readers. Middle Scots requires an effort of the modern reader, a readiness to extend his vocabulary and adjust to unfamiliar spelling conventions; above all, it requires him to rid his mind of an erroneous notion that goes back to Trevisa (and even earlier, to William of Malmesbury) that the tongue of northerners is barbarous, and sounds 'scharp, slytting and frotyng'. Middle Scots is not uniformly rustic or 'quaint and crabbed', but a language employed by poets and courtiers as well as peasants, a language in which—as Dunbar, Henryson and Douglas demonstrate—fine gradations of tone and style are possible. Where Douglas offers a difficulty of his own is in the idiosyncrasy of his vocabulary; here he is sometimes difficult in the manner not of Chaucer but of the *Gawain*-poet. Yet, paradoxically, what may repel the casual reader constitutes part of his strength as a poet: his willingness to invent and experiment and use the full range of the vocabulary, his sheer 'fouth' of language.

Notes and References

CHAPTER ONE
Gavin Douglas's Life
1. Small, I, p. xxxvi.
2. Small, I, p. xcix.
3. Small, I, p. civ.
4. See below, p. 12, and note 77.
5. From Dacre, Magnus and William-son: 27 January, 1515. *Letters and Papers Foreign and Domestic of the Reign of Henry VIII*, catalogued by J. S. Brewer, vol. II (1864) no. 63.
6. *Diurnal*, ed. T. Thomson, Banna-tyne Club (Edinburgh 1833) p. 5.
7. I, p. 19.
8. G. Donaldson *Scotland: James V to James VII* (Edinburgh 1965) p. 12; cf. T. I. Rae *The Administration of the Scottish Frontier* (Edinburgh 1966) pp. 4–8.
9. Small, I, p. xlii.
10. *Early Records of the University of St Andrews*, ed. J. M. Anderson, SHS, series 3, vol. 8 (Edinburgh 1926) p. 187.
11. *Acta Facultatis Artium Universi-tatis Sanctiandree 1413–1588*, ed. A. I. Dunlop, SHS, series 3, vols. 54–5 (Edinburgh 1964) vol. II, p. 245.
12. Dunlop *Acta*, vol. I, pp. lxxxi–lxxxii.
13. *Acts of the Lords of Council in Public Affairs 1501–1554: Selections from Acta Dominorum Concilii*, ed. R. K. Hannay (Edinburgh 1932) p. 41.
14. J. R. Hale *Renaissance Europe 1480–1520* (1971) pp. 15–16.
15. See the *Dialogus inter duos famatos viros*, prefixed to his Commentary on the First Book of Sentences (1510); and the Dedication to the Commen-tary on the Fourth Book of Sen-tences (1516). These are reprinted in *A History of Greater Britain by John Major*, trans. and ed. A. Constable,

SHS 10 (Edinburgh 1892) pp. 428 and 437. See also Small, I, p. iii.
16. Dunlop *Acta*, vol. II, pp. 241 and 245.
17. Dunlop *Acta*, vol. I, p. cxiv.
18. Alexander Myln 'Lives of the Bishops' (= *Vitae Episcoporum Dunkeldensium*) in *Rentale Dunkel-dense*, trans. and ed. R. K. Hannay, SHS, series 2, vol. 10 (Edinburgh 1915) p. 332.
19. Dunlop *Acta*, vol. I, p. cli.
20. Dunlop *Acta*, vol. I, p. clii.
21. *Protocol Book of James Young 1485–1515*, ed. H. M. Paton and G. Donaldson, SRS (Edinburgh 1941, 1952) no. 790.
22. *History of the Houses of Douglas and Angus* (1644) p. 220. Douglas's will, now in the Register House, Edinburgh, makes a bequest to *Margarete Douglas, consanguinee*. See Small, I, p. cxxiv; W. Fraser *The Douglas Book* (Edinburgh 1885) vol. II, p. 139.
23. Small, I, pp. cxix–cxxiv.
24. cf. R. L. Mackie *King James IV of Scotland* (Edinburgh 1958) p. 156, discussing the practice of bishops Brown and Elphinstone.
25. M. Mahoney 'The Scottish Hierarchy, 1513–1565' in *Essays on the Scottish Reformation 1513–1625*, ed. D. McRoberts (Glasgow 1962) p. 45.
26. See W. Croft Dickinson *Scotland from the Earliest Times to 1603* (1961) pp. 125–7.
27. See D. E. Easson *Medieval Religious Houses: Scotland* (1957) pp. 20–1; and A. Ross 'Some Notes on the Religious Orders in Pre-Reformation Scotland' in McRoberts *Scottish Reformation*, pp. 213–14, 218–27.

28. See *A Source Book of Scottish History*, vol. 11, 1424–1567, ed. W. Croft Dickinson, G. Donaldson, and I. A. Milne (1958) pp. 83–93; and R. K. Hannay *The Scottish Crown and the Papacy, 1424–1560* (Historical Association of Scotland) 1931.

29. Fraser *Douglas Book*, vol. 111, p. 164 (no. 148). A co-witness was James Young, notary public.

30. *Acts of the Lords of Council in Civil Causes 1496–1501*, ed. G. Neilson and H. Paton (Edinburgh 1918) pp. 81–2. See also Introduction, p. liii.

31. op. cit., pp. 241 and 284.

32. 28 February 1527. See *Fasti Ecclesiae Scoticanae Medii Aevi*, 2nd draft by D. E. R. Watt (Edinburgh 1969) p. 105.

33. Dunlop *Acta*, vol. 11, pp. 231 and 245.

34. More details are given below, p. 9.

35. 'Lives' *Rentale Dunkeldense*, pp. 320–2. Hepburn, unlike Douglas, 'does not leave the church of Dunkeld'.

36. *The Register of the Privy Seal of Scotland*, vol. 1, ed. M. Livingstone (Edinburgh 1908) no. 139.

37. *Privy Seal*, vol. 1, no. 199. It is said to pertain 'to our soverane lordis presentatioun'.

38. Six months earlier the same formula had been used to assign Glenholm to a different man (*Privy Seal*, vol. 1, no. 156). On Glenholm, see I. B. Cowan *The Parishes of Medieval Scotland*, SRS, vol. 93 (Edinburgh 1967) p. 75.

39. Coldwell, 11, p. 1. He is styled similarly in the Lambeth and Bath manuscripts of the *Eneados*.

40. See D. E. Easson 'Foundation Charter of the Collegiate Church of Dunbar, A.D. 1342' *Miscellany of the Scottish History Society*, series 3, vol. 6 (1939) pp. 81–109. Douglas's early biographers misread or misinterpreted 'Hauch' as Heriot or Hawick (Small, 1, pp. vi–vii).

41. 'Lives' *Rentale Dunkeldense*, p. 332.

42. Dated 1513–14. *The Letters of James V*, calendared by R. K. Hannay and ed. D. Hay (Edinburgh 1954) p. 6. See also the letter from Turnbull, in Small, 1, p. lv.

43. Easson, loc. cit., p. 103.

44. *Privy Seal*, vol. 1, no. 1020.

45. Gavin Douglas is also called dean of Brechin in the *Protocol Book of John Foular 1501–28*, ed. W. Macleod and M. Wood, SRS, vols. 1–3 (Edinburgh 1930–53) vol. 1, no. 640 (26 April 1510). I do not know of other evidence that he held this office, and there may be confusion with *Hugh* Douglas, apparently dean of Brechin 1487–1512 (Watt *Fasti*, p. 44).

46. *Accounts of the Lord High Treasurer of Scotland*, ed. T. Dickson and sir J. Balfour Paul (Edinburgh 1877–1916) vol. 11, p. 360.

47. *Registrum Cartarum Ecclesie Sancti Egidii de Edinburgh*, ed. D. Laing, Bannatyne Club (Edinburgh 1859) pp. 203–7, 224–6. I am indebted to Dr John Durkan for additional information about these and other extensions to St Giles'.

48. Printed in J. Leland *De Rebus Britannicis Collectanea* (1770) vol. IV, p. 289.

49. *King James IV of Scotland*, p. 109.

50. *Protocol Book of John Foular*, no. 691.

51. op. cit., no. 633.

52. *The Fetternear Banner: a Scottish Medieval Religious Banner* (Glasgow, n.d.) pp. 21–7.

53. Douglas was succeeded by Robert Crichton, who was in occupation by 1 September 1517 (Watt *Fasti*, p. 357).

54. Laing *Registrum*, p. xxxiv.

55. *Acta Rectorum*, vol. 1, pp. 59 and 61. (Unpublished MS in St Andrews University Archives.)

56. *Register of the Great Seal of Scotland*, ed. J. M. Thomson and sir J. Balfour Paul (Edinburgh 1882–

1914) vol. I, no. 3389; vol. I, no. 3413; vol. II, no. 2988.

57. Fraser *Douglas Book*, vol. III, pp. 180–1 (no. 158).

58. Fraser *Douglas Book*, vol. III, p. 191 (footnote).

59. Fraser *Douglas Book*, vol. III, p. 198 (footnote).

60. Fraser *Douglas Book*, vol. III, pp. 438–9 (no. 447).

61. Fraser *Douglas Book*, vol. III, pp. 210–13 (no. 182).

62. I, p. ix. The legal evidence is printed in R. Pitcairn *Ancient Criminal Trials in Scotland*, Maitland Club (Edinburgh 1833) vol. I, pp. *78–9.

63. I. D. Willock *The Origins and Development of the Jury in Scotland*, Stair Society 23 (Edinburgh 1966) p. 169.

64. *Extracts from the Records of the Burgh of Edinburgh 1403–1528*, ed. J. D. Marwick, Scottish Burgh Records Society (Edinburgh 1869) vol. I, p. 144.

65. Hannay *Acts of Council*, p. 1.

66. Hannay *Acts of Council*, p. 4. In the first half of 1514 Douglas attended meetings regularly (op. cit., pp. 11, 13, 14, 17 and 18).

67. Hannay *Acts of Council*, p. 19.

68. Hannay *Acts of Council*, p. 20.

69. Hannay *Acts of Council*, pp. 23 and 25.

70. Hannay *Acts of Council*, p. 26.

71. Small, I, p. xxiv.

72. Small, I, pp. xxxvi–xli.

73. *Letters of James V*, p. 14. Hannay dates this in September–October 1514. For earlier letters, see pp. 6, 12–13.

74. *Leonis X Pontificis Maximi Regesta*, ed. J. S. R. E. Hergenroether (Freiburg 1884) vol. I, nos. 12931 and 13140.

75. Hannay *Acts of Council*, p. 11.

76. Brewer, I, no. 3468.

77. For a translation of the whole letter, see Small, I, pp. xxviii–xxix.

78. Leo x informed Margaret of this on 8 December 1514 (*Letters of James V*, pp. 15–17). For further discussion, see Hannay *Acts of*

Council, p. xliv; J. Herkless and R. K. Hannay *The Archbishops of St Andrews* (1907–1915) vol. II, pp. 91 and 105. On the struggle between Hepburn and Douglas's followers for the castle of St Andrews, see Margaret's letter of 23 November, and John Leslie *The History of Scotland*, Bannatyne Club (Edinburgh 1830) p. 101.

79. Small, I, p. xxxvi. R. K. Hannay suggested that Douglas's visit to bishop Brown at Clony a year earlier might have been made 'with an eye to obtaining a resignation of the bishopric in his favour'. *Rentale Dunkeldense*, p. xxiii.

80. Hannay *Acts of Council*, p. 49.

81. One letter to Leo (17 January 1515) is printed by Small, I, p. xxxv; for another, see *Letters of James V*, p. 17. For Margaret's letter to Henry, see Brewer, II, no. 47 (22 January 1515).

82. *Letters of James V*, pp. 17–18; text in Small, I, pp. xliii–xliv.

83. Small, I, pp. lv and lvii. On 29 June 1515 Douglas's proctor paid at Rome a papal tax of 450 gold florins. See J. Dowden *The Bishops of Scotland* (Glasgow 1912) p. 83.

84. Hannay *Acts of Council*, pp. 40–50.

85. *Archbishops of St Andrews*, vol. II, pp. 136–9.

86. Hannay *Acts of Council*, p. 59; see G. Donaldson 'Crown rights in episcopal vacancies' *Scottish Historical Review* 45 (1966) 331.

87. This phrase comes from the 'Memorial' attributed to Douglas (Small, I, p. cvii). For references to Douglas's imprisonment, see Myln 'Lives' *Rentale Dunkeldense*, p. 332; Dacre's letters to the Privy Council (Brewer, II, nos. 705 and 779).

88. Small, I, pp. lxx–lxxiii.

89. Small, I, p. lxxv.

90. Small, I, p. lxxvii (corrected). The date of this is uncertain. Brewer (II, no. 1672) assigns it to March 1516.

91. Hannay *Acts of Council*, p. 69.

92. *Privy Seal*, vol. 1, no. 2807.
93. 'Lives' *Rentale Dunkeldense*, p. 331.
94. Small, 1, p. lv.
95. 'Lives' *Rentale Dunkeldense*, pp. 333–4.
96. Small, 1, p. lxxviii; *Letters of James V*, p. 32.
97. 'Lives' *Rentale Dunkeldense*, p. 334.
98. 'Lives' *Rentale Dunkeldense*, p. 304.
99. 'Lives' *Rentale Dunkeldense*, pp. 305–6.
100. *Letters of James V*, p. 17.
101. Myln 'Lives' *Rentale Dunkeldense*, p. 314.
102. *Rentale Dunkeldense*, pp. 151 and 152.
103. The *St Andrews Formulare 1514–46* (ed. G. Donaldson and C. Macrae, Stair Society, 1942–4) is a style book, but is thought to contain copies of actual writs. Dates are not given and initials are often used instead of names, but in many instances they can be interpreted.
104. *Formulare*, vol. 1, no. 57.
105. *Formulare*, vol. 1, no. 86.
106. *Formulare*, vol. 1, no. 96.
107. *Acts of Council*, p. 121. See also p. 122 (30 June).
108. *Formulare*, vol. 1, no. 98.
109. *Formulare*, vol. 1, no. 164.
110. Hannay *Rentale Dunkeldense*, p. 339.
111. Small, 1, p. lix.
112. Small, 1, pp. lvii–lviii.
113. The will calls him *vicarium de Tibbirmure* (Small, 1, p. cxxiv).
114. *Privy Seal*, vol. 1, nos. 3031, 3088, and 3068. The mention of vicars general suggests Douglas's absence from his see.
115. *Treasurer's Accounts*, vol. v, pp. 118–19, and 152; see also p. 151.
116. Hannay *Acts of Council*, pp. 93–4.
117. Hannay *Acts of Council*, p. 105.
118. *Skipper from Leith: the History of Robert Barnton of Over Barnton* (Philadelphia 1962) p. 135.

119. *Flodden Papers: Diplomatic Correspondence between the Courts of France and Scotland 1507–1517*, ed. M. Wood, SHS, series 3, vol. 20 (Edinburgh 1933) pp. 123–40.
120. *Privy Seal*, vol. 1, no. 2900.
121. Small, 1, pp. lxxxiv–lxxxv.
122. Brewer, 11, no. 3583.
123. Leslie called her a 'gentle woman' of Douglasdale (*History*, p. 112). Small identified her as lady Janet Stuart, daughter of lord Traquair (1, p. lxxxix).
124. The letter is undated, but Brewer places it in April 1519 (111, no. 166). Margaret says that her husband has not come near her for the last six months, and that she will part with him if she may by God's law and with honour to herself.
125. Hannay *Acts of Council*, p. 134.
126. *Acts of Council*, p. 137. The citations from the *Regiam Majestatem* that follow are the earliest to be recorded. See Rt. Hon. T. M. Cooper 'Regiam Majestatem and the Auld Lawes' *An Introductory Survey of the Sources and Literature of Scots Law*, Stair Society 1 (Edinburgh 1936) p. 80.
127. In Margaret's letter to Henry (note 124) she says that Dunkeld and his other kinsmen caused Angus to deal sharply with her.
128. Dacre mentions this in a letter of July 1519 (Brewer, 111, no. 373).
129. Hannay *Acts of Council*, p. 132.
130. Marwick *Edinburgh Burgh Records*, vol. 1, pp. 278–80.
131. Hannay *Acts of Council*, pp. 146–7.
132. Hannay *Acts of Council*, p. 149.
133. Hannay *Acts of Council*, p. 150.
134. Marwick *Edinburgh Burgh Records*, vol. 1, p. 194.
135. Buchanan *The History of Scotland*, trans. J. Aikman (Glasgow 1827–9) vol. 11, p. 278; Pitscottie *The Historie and Croniclis of Scotland*, ed. A. G. Mackay, STS (1899–1911) vol. 1, p. 281.
136. Pitscottie, vol. 1, pp. 281–2.

137. Buchanan, vol. II, p. 279.
138. Pitscottie, vol. I, p. 283. The square brackets and the words they enclose are in the STS edition. Buchanan, vol. II, p. 279, says 'many fled to the convent of the Dominicans for shelter'.
139. Fraser *Douglas Book*, vol. III, p. 220.
140. In a letter to Wolsey (February 1521) Douglas expressed forebodings as to what would happen on Albany's return (Small, I, p. xc).
141. Small, I, p. xci.
142. Small, I, p. xciv (corrected).
143. Small, I, p. xcviii.
144. Brewer, vol. III, no. 1857.
145. Small, I, p. xcvi; Buchanan supports this (vol. II, p. 280).
146. Small, I, p. cii (corrected).
147. *Letters of James V*, p. 88; also in Small, I, p. cxiv.
148. Small, I, p. ci.
149. Small, I, p. civ (corrected).
150. Small, I, p. cxviii.
151. Small, I, p. cxxiv.
152. Small, I, p. cxvi (corrected).
153. *Letters of James V*, p. 90.

CHAPTER TWO
The Cultural Background
1. See J. Durkan 'The Cultural Background in Sixteenth-Century Scotland' in McRoberts *Scottish Reformation*, pp. 274–331; and J. MacQueen 'Some aspects of the early Renaissance in Scotland' *Forum for Modern Language Studies* 3 (1967) 201–22.
2. *Privy Seal*, vol. I, nos. 1059, 1251 and 1425.
3. *Privy Seal*, vol. I, no. 1606.
4. See A. I. Dunlop *Scots Abroad in the Fifteenth Century*, Historical Association Pamphlet, no. 124 (1942).
5. cf. L. J. Macfarlane 'William Elphinstone, founder of the University of Aberdeen' *Aberdeen University Review* 39 (1961) 1–18.
6. *The Meroure of Wysdome*, vol. II, ed. F. Quinn, STS, series 4, no. 2

(1965) p. xiii.
7. Hannay *Acts of Council*, p. 41.
8. Silvester was Wolsey's agent at Rome, and seems to have acted on Douglas's behalf. See Turnbull's letter to Douglas in Small, I, p. liv; and *Letters of James V*, p. 23. On the Friscobaldi, see Turnbull's letter to Angus, in Small, I, pp. lxx–lxxii.
9. Small, I, p. xl.
10. Small, I, p. lv.
11. Dunlop *Acta*, vol. I, p. lxxxv and vol. II, p. 282; *Formulare*, vol. I, no. 102; Durkan 'Cultural Background', p. 285.
12. So much has been destroyed that it is difficult to generalize about the visual arts at this time. My impression is that Flemish influence was strong, but that evidence for Italian influence is scanty. James III's groat of *c.* 1485 is regarded as the earliest Renaissance coin portrait outside Italy, yet there was a return to medieval style in the coinage of James IV. For Flemish influence and contacts, see D. McRoberts 'Notes on Scoto-Flemish artistic contacts' *Innes Review* 10 (1959) 91–6; and 'Material Destruction caused by the Scottish Reformation' in *Scottish Reformation*, pp. 456–7; also L. J. Macfarlane 'The Book of Hours of James IV and Margaret Tudor' *Innes Review* 11 (1960) 3–21.
13. Glasgow 1961; first printed in *Innes Review* 9 (1958) 1–167.
14. Master Thomas Bellenden was one of the witnesses to Douglas's contract with Elizabeth Auchinleck in 1520 (Fraser *Douglas Book*, vol. III, p. 220). The Lambeth MS was 'writtin be the hand of Iohanne mudy with master thomas bellenden of auchinoull Iustis Clerke' in 1544.
15. Durkan 'Cultural Background', p. 276.
16. On Ascensius, see P. Renouard *Bibliographie des Impressions et des Oeuvres de Josse Badius Ascensius* (Paris 1908); for some of his

Scottish connections, see entries in the index under Boece, Caubraith, Lauxius, Lokert, and Vaus.

17. See L. Delisle 'L'imprimeur parisien Josse Bade et le professeur écossais Jean Vaus' *L'Ecole de Chartes* 57 (1896) 205–16.

18. Dunlop *Acta*, vol. I, p. lxxxiv: translating the entry for 5 December 1471.

19. The source is not known. Douglas refers to the authority of 'clerkis', but he may have owed the idea for such a digression to Chaucer's 'Soun ys noght but eyr ybroken . . .' (*House of Fame*, 765 ff.).

20. Douglas's argument here and in the accompanying marginal commentary resembles a passage in the Prologue to Nicholas Oresme's *Livre de Ethiques*, translated *c.* 1370 from Grosseteste's Latin version of Aristotle, at the request of Charles V of France. See further my 'The Complaynt of Scotlande: a French debt' *Notes and Queries* (October 1957).

21. H.L.R. Edwards *Skelton* (1949) p. 21.

22. *The History of English Poetry* (1824) vol. III, p. 111.

23. I, p. 6.

24. Douglas's name does not seem to occur in the volumes so far printed of *Auctarium Chartularii Universitatis Parisiensis*, ed. H. Denifle, A. Chatelain and others (Paris 1894–1964). This is not surprising since they cover a period no later than 1494. Dr John Durkan tells me that he has found no reference to Douglas in the unprinted 'Livre du Receveur de la Nation d'Allemagne 1494–1530'.

25. Dedication to the Fourth Book of Sentences; reprinted in Major *History*, p. 437.

26. See A. Renaudet *Préréforme et Humanisme à Paris pendant les Premières Guerres d'Italie (1490–1517)* 2nd edn (Paris 1953) pp. 268–9.

27. Not the George Hepburn who

litigated with Douglas; abbot of Arbroath.

28. See J. Durkan 'John Major: after 400 years' *Innes Review* I (1950) 131–57; J. H. Burns 'New light on John Major' *Innes Review* 5 (1954) 83–100.

29. *Privy Seal*, vol. I, no. 1977.

30. Paris 1519, folio a i (v); the *Dialogus* is reprinted in Major *History*, pp. 425–8.

31. Major *History*, I, 2 (p. 10).

32. On Cranston, see J. Durkan 'John Major after 400 years' *Innes Review* I (1950) 138, 146–9.

33. Folio a ii.

34. From the Preface to his *Introduction to Logic* (1496); quoted in Renaudet *Préréforme*, p. 275.

35. *Erasmi Epistolae*, ed. P. S. Allen (Oxford 1906–58) vol. I, no. 64; cf. M. Mann Phillips *Erasmus and the Northern Renaissance* (1949) pp. 21 ff.

36. Folio a ii (v). On Valla and the response to him, see Renaudet *Préréforme*, p. 81.

37. cf. his reference to the 'Psalmyst', St Paul, 'the Apostyll' (= St Paul), and St Augustine (XI Prol 29, 62, 74 and 185). St Paul to the Ephesians, 2.3, lies behind *Palice of Honour*, 1386 ff.

38. *The Meroure of Wysdome*, vol. I, ed. C. Macpherson, STS, series 2, no. 19 (1926) II. 4 (p. 81).

39. cf. *The Scottish Tradition in Literature* (1958) pp. 82–3.

40. See Renaudet *Préréforme*, pp. 274–5; Durkan 'Cultural Background', p. 285, notes that Ascensius dedicated to him his editions of Sulpizio and Filelfo.

41. Renaudet *Préréforme*, p. 271.

42. In the *Adagia;* for a translation, see M. M. Phillips *Erasmus on his Times: a Shortened Version of the Adages* (Cambridge 1967) pp. 104–6.

43. See Durkan 'Cultural Background', p. 286.

44. *Letters of James IV 1505–13*, ed. R. K. Hannay and R. L. Mackie, SHS (1953) pp. 160–1.

45. *Vergil's English History*, ed. sir H. Ellis, Camden Society 36 (1846) vol. I, p. 105. This anonymous mid-sixteenth century translation is based on the 1546 edition of the *Historia*. See D. Hay *Polydore Vergil* (Oxford 1952) p. 84.

46. *History*, I, 9 (p. 51).

47. T. D. Kendrick *British Antiquity* (1950) pp. 78–9.

48. *Acta*, vol. I, pp. lxxxv–lxxxvi.

49. J. Durkan 'The beginnings of humanism in Scotland' *Innes Review* 4 (1953) p. 1.

50. These were owned respectively by Robert Cockburn; David Abercromby, principal of Glasgow University; Archibald Whitelaw, secretary to James III; John Sinclair, bishop of Brechin; William Scheves; Walter Ogilvie; Hector Boece; and John Vaus. See Durkan and Ross *Early Scottish Libraries*.

51. cf. Renaudet *Préréforme*, p. 255; P. O. Kristeller *Renaissance Thought: Papers on Humanism and the Arts*, Torchbook edition (1965) p. 42.

52. Durkan and Ross *Early Scottish Libraries*, pp. 32, 122.

53. cf. E. R. Curtius *European Literature and the Latin Middle Ages*, trans. W. R. Trask (1952) p. 431.

54. On the twin Venuses, see E. Panofsky *Studies in Iconology* (1962) pp. 142 ff.

55. See Renaudet *Préréforme*, pp. 122 ff. and W. P. Mustard *Eclogues of Faustus Andrelinus and Ioannes Arnolletus* (Baltimore 1918).

56. On Scotsmen's knowledge of Greek, see Durkan 'Cultural Background', pp. 288–9.

57. See note 20 above.

58. Douglas refers also to the 'quent philosophy' of metempsychosis associated with the name of Pythagoras: I Prol 185–6 and VI Prol 130.

59. References are to *Genealogie Deorum Gentilium Libri*, ed. V. Romano, 2 vols. (Bari 1951). For other quotations at secondhand, see below in chapter 5.

60. *Oratio animum auditoris idonee comparans ad reliquam dictionem; quod eveniet si eum benivolum, attentum, docilem confecerit.*

61. For allusions to Sallust or his work, see *Palice of Honour*, 252, 1688 and 1775. For an allusion to Suetonius, see I, v. 102 n.

62. See J. Crosland 'Lucan in the Middle Ages' *Modern Language Review* 25 (1930) 32–51.

63. Reviewing Coldwell's *Selections from Gavin Douglas* in *Medium Aevum* 34 (1965) p. 161.

64. P. O. Kristeller *Renaissance Thought: the Classic, Scholastic and Humanist Strains*, Torchbook edition (1961) pp. 8–10. R. Weiss discerns in Scotland 'no real outside humanist influence during the early decades of the century': 'Italian Humanism in Western Europe' in *Italian Renaissance Studies*, ed. E. F. Jacob (1960) p. 82.

65. See Durkan 'Beginnings of humanism' *Innes Review* 4 (1953) 8.

66. J. W. L. Adams 'The Renaissance poets: Latin' in *Scottish Poetry: a Critical Survey*, ed. J. Kinsley (1955) p. 72.

67. On the diversity of Scottish poetry at this time, see C. S. Lewis 'The Close of the Middle Ages in Scotland' in *English Literature in the Sixteenth Century* (Oxford 1954); and J. M. Smith *The French Background of Middle Scots Literature* (1934).

68. See J. A. H. Murray *The Dialect of the Southern Counties of Scotland* (1873); and G. Gregory Smith *Specimens of Middle Scots* (1902).

69. See Caxton's *Book of the Ordre of Chyvalry*, ed. A. T. P. Byles, EETS. OS. 168 (1926) pp. xxvi–xxx; and D. Bornstein 'The Scottish prose version of Vegetius's *De Re Militari*' *Studies in Scottish Literature* 8 (January 1971) 174–83.

70. See *Lydgate's Troy Book*, ed. H. Bergen, EETS. ES, 97, 103, 106 and 126 (1906–35) vol. IV, pp. 46–50.

71. *The Meroure of Wysdome*, vol. 1, pp. 166–70.

72. See R. F. Jones *The Triumph of the English Language* (Stanford 1953) pp. 7 ff.

73. *Meroure*, vol. 1, p. 74.

74. D. Fox 'The Scottish Chaucerians' in *Chaucer and Chaucerians*, ed. D. S. Brewer (1966) p. 169.

75. I have discussed this more fully in 'Gavin Douglas and Chaucer' *Review of English Studies* n.s. 21 (1970) 401–21.

76. cf. D. Pearsall *John Lydgate* (1970) pp. 51–8.

77. See 1 Prol 341: 'balmy cundyt'; 1 Prol 9: 'sweit sours and spryngand well'. Pearsall, op. cit., pp. 99–100, quotes several instances of the latter. But they were probably panegyrical commonplaces—cf. 'Condute of comforte and well most souerayne' in Skelton's *Knowledge, Acquaintance, Resort, Favour with Grace*.

78. cf. *Troy Book*, I.1214 and 2736; III.18. For Lydgate's use of the plough-image to express weariness, see below, p. 169.

79. It was still popular in the fifteenth century. See D. Allen Wright 'Henryson's *Orpheus and Eurydice* and the tradition of the muses' *Medium Aevum* 40 (1971) 41–7.

80. For another instance, in Prologue XIII, see below, p. 189.

81. 'The Scottish alliterative poems' *Proceedings of the British Academy* 28 (1942) 217–36. He points out that in Scotland the alliterative poems were still sufficiently popular in the sixteenth century to be printed. In England, apart from the special case of *Piers Plowman*, 'not a single piece has survived except in manuscript'.

82. 'To knaw the naym of the translatour': IV, p. 139.

83. See *Scottish Alliterative Poems*, ed. F. J. Amours, STS, series 1, nos. 27 and 38 (1897).

84. J. P. Oakden estimates that in this Prologue '76 per cent of the lines have 4 or 5 alliterating syllables'; he notes that Douglas often (as in 27–9) links consecutive lines by identical alliteration. (*Alliterative Poetry in Middle English: the Dialectal and Metrical Survey* (Manchester 1930) pp. 226 and 222.) Amours, op. cit., p. lxxxv, says of the poems in his collection: 'the last line of the stanza is often without alliteration, or sometimes runs on the same letter as the preceding line'.

85. *Reulis and Cautelis . . . in Scottis Poesie*, in *Elizabethan Critical Essays*, ed. G. Gregory Smith (1904) vol. 1, pp. 218 and 223.

86. To Dr John Moore, 2 August 1787: *Selected Letters of Robert Burns*, ed. D. Ferguson (Oxford 1953) p. 55.

87. Small, 1, p. cxii.

88. Small, 1, p. cvi; Donaldson *Scotland: James V to James VII*, p. 36.

89. *History*, IV, 15 (p. 205).

90. *Hary's Wallace*, ed. M. P. McDiarmid, STS, series 4, nos. 4–5 (1968–9) vol. 1, p. ix.

CHAPTER THREE
The Palice of Honour

1. *Treasurer's Accounts*, vol. 1, p. 188.

2. See the discussion of James's character in R. L. Mackie *King James IV*, pp. 118 ff.

3. See entries in *Treasurer's Accounts*, vol. 1, p. 133; and vol. II, pp. 112, 120 and 152.

4. p. 218. Bale is the source of the later lists in Simlerus, Thynne, Vossius, and Dempster, which have no independent value. For full references and citations, see W. Geddie *A Bibliography of Middle Scots Poets*, STS (1912) pp. 235–9.

5. D. Irving *History of Scotish Poetry* (Edinburgh 1861) p. 289.

6. 'Did Gavin Douglas write *King Hart?*' *Medium Aevum* 28 (1959) 31–47; and *Shorter Poems*, pp. lxxii–lxxviii. See also F. H. Ridley 'Did Gawin Douglas write *King Hart?*' *Speculum* (1 34959) 402–12.

7. Douglas uses the verb *iowke* in VIII.iv.120 and x.ix.38; and *went* or *war* + *adew* in I.vi.174 and IV Prol 255. On the currency of these expressions, see *D.O.S.T.*, under IOWKE, ADEW.

8. On the differences between these editions, see *Shorter Poems*, pp. xv–xxvii.

9. Small, I, p. viii.

10. *Virgil's Aeneis, Translated into Scottish Verse* (Edinburgh 1710) p. 448. *Lundeys* perhaps derives from Scots *loun*, a contemptuous term meaning variously 'rascal', 'lecher', 'whore'. *D.O.S.T.* records various spellings, including one with final *d*—'A lound is a name of reproch'. The phrase *lundeys lufe* might then be interpreted as 'love of a lecherous kind', or, more specifically, 'love directed towards whores'. Such an interpretation would not rule out an allusion to Ovid. For further discussion of the 'Mensioun', see below, p. 88.

11. See *Shorter Poems*, pp. xxix–xxxvii; also J. M. Smith *The French Background of Middle Scots Literature*, pp. 109–17, and W. A. Neilson *The Origins and Sources of the Court of Love* (Boston 1899).

12. *The Italian Influence on Scottish Literature* (Edinburgh 1972) pp. 24–7.

13. See *Parliament of Fowls*, 283–94; *House of Fame*, 388–426; *Confessio Amantis* VIII.2500 ff.; *Temple of Glas*, 55–144; for parallels in French poetry, see *Shorter Poems*, p. xxxii.

14. See Matteo de' Pasti's description of his design for the Triumph of Fame—'there are to be four elephants pulling her chariot'. E. H. Gombrich 'The Early Medici as Patrons of Art' in *Italian Renaissance Studies*, ed. E. F. Jacob, p. 298; for an illustration, see plate VI in the same work. See also R. van Marle *Iconographie de l'Art Profane au Moyen-Age et à la Renaissance* (La Haye 1932) vol. II, pp. 110–30; and

A. Fowler *Triumphal Forms* (Cambridge 1970) pp. 23–61.

15. A fuller account of these works is given, with details of editions, in *Shorter Poems*, pp. xxxv–xxxvii. See also R. J. Lyall 'Tradition and innovation in Alexander Barclay's "Towre of Vertue and Honoure"' *Review of English Studies* n.s. 23 (1972) 1–18.

16. See C. R. Post *Mediaeval Spanish Allegory* (Cambridge, Mass. 1915) p. 74. Another allegorical poem about Honour, Cámara's *Cadira del Honor*, is summarized by Post, pp. 254–6.

17. C. S. Lewis *English Literature in the Sixteenth Century*, p. 77.

18. Lewis, op. cit., pp. 77–8; K. Wittig *The Scottish Tradition in Literature* (1958) p. 81; Coldwell, I, pp. 81–7.

19. C. S. Lewis *The Allegory of Love*, rev. edn (Oxford 1938) p. 290.

20. D. Fox, in *Chaucer and Chaucerians*, p. 196.

21. *Acts of Council*, pp. 48–9.

22. For other instances, see lines 82–4, 128 ff., 174–81, 403–10, and passim.

23. See I Prol 339–43, quoted above, p. 39.

24. See *Shorter Poems*, pp. xxxiii–xxxv; and D. Fox, in *Chaucer and Chaucerians*, pp. 193–6.

25. *Materiam superabat opus* (*Metamorphoses*, II.5). The picture of the sea-nymphs (1849–54) similarly derives from *Metamorphoses*, II.11–14. For other reminiscences of Ovid, see *Shorter Poems*, p. xxix.

26. See below, pp. 167–8.

27. See lines 545, 410–11, 788–9; for discussion, see Curtius *European Literature and the Latin Middle Ages*, pp. 159–62.

28. C. Butler *Western Mysticism*, reprint of 2nd edn (1960) p. 126.

29. *Honour in his Perfection* (1624) p. 4. For a useful survey of attitudes to honour, see C. B. Watson *Shakespeare and the Renaissance Concept of Honor* (Princeton 1960) pp. 1–75.

30. Cicero *Brutus*, lxxxi.281.
31. See M. P. Tilley *A Dictionary of the Proverbs in England in the Sixteenth and Seventeenth Centuries* (Ann Arbor 1950) H 571.
32. *Factorum Dictorumque Memorabilium Libri Novem*, I.I.
33. Douglas all des here to Virgil, Eclogue IV.3; much of Prologue IX expounds the medieval rhetorical scheme, sometimes known as the *Rota Virgilii*. Three styles were distinguished, *humilis, mediocris*, and *gravis*, corresponding respectively to the *Eclogues, Georgics*, and *Aeneid*. For Douglas, as for most other writers, the opposition between *humilis* and *gravis* seems the most important. He mentions some of the traditional attributes of the latter style, such as 'lawrer' and 'cedyr'; and

> Stra forto spek of gayt to
> gentill wight;
> A hund, a steid, mar langis for a
> knyght.
> (41–2)

See further A. T. Langesen 'La Roue de Virgile' *Classica et Medievalia* 23 (1962) 248 ff.
34. See below, p. 144.
35. See Curtius, op. cit., pp. 162–6.
36. *The Complaynt of Scotlande*, ed. J. A. H. Murray, EETS.ES.17 (1872) p. 16. On the connection between 'eloquence' and learned neologisms, see R. F. Jones *The Triumph of the English Language*, pp. 6–31.
37. Lewis *English Literature in the Sixteenth Century*, p. 79.
38. It is an equal exaggeration to say that 'it is the quality of the diction that distinguishes Douglas's poetic summer from his winter' (J. Speirs *The Scots Literary Tradition*, 2nd edn (1962) p. 74). In Prologue VII the diction is far from being exclusively 'native'; words like 'symylitude', 'reducyng', 'congelit', 'penetratyve', 'pronosticatioun' and 'ventositeis' contribute much to its distinctive tone.

39. G. Saintsbury *A History of Criticism and Literary Taste in Europe* (1900) vol. I, p. 464.
40. In *Chaucer and Chaucerians*, p. 198.
41. *The Allegory of Love*, p. 291.
42. cf. Chaucer, General Prologue, I.198–9.
43. See also *Shorter Poems*, p. xxviii.

CHAPTER FOUR
Douglas's Virgil
1. 'The Scottish Chaucerians' in *The Cambridge History of English Literature*, ed. A. W. Ward and A. R. Waller (1932) vol. II, p. 264.
2. See E. Mâle 'Virgile dans l'art du moyen âge français' *Studi Medievali* 5 (1932) 325–31. The theme was a favourite with the illustrators of Petrarch's *Trionfi*; it occurs also in a late fifteenth-century birth tray (*desco da parto*) in the Victoria and Albert Museum, which shows Aristotle and Virgil in a basket among the victims of a triumphant Cupid.
3. John Rolland *The Seuin Seages*, ed. G. F. Black, STS (1932) 2625.
4. *The Asloan Manuscript*, ed. W. Craigie, STS, 2 vols. (1923 and 1924) vol. II, p. 279; cf. also another Scottish poet: 'Virgill quhilk was prudent graif and saige / Was lichtleit be his lufe without remeid / And for dispyt scho hang him in ane caige' (*The Bannatyne Manuscript*, ed. W. Tod Ritchie, STS, 4 vols. (1928–33) vol. IV, p. 29).
5. This is documented by D. Comparetti *Vergil in the Middle Ages*, trans. E. F. M. Benecke (1895) pp. 239 ff.
6. *Virgil the Necromancer* (Cambridge 1934) p. 267.
7. Comparetti, op. cit., pp. 28–33.
8. C. R. Borland *A Descriptive Catalogue of the Western Mediaeval Manuscripts in Edinburgh University Library* (Edinburgh 1916) no. 195. See also C. P. Finlayson 'A Glamis Virgil?' *Scottish Historical Review* 32 (1953) 99–100.

9. Durkan and Ross *Early Scottish Libraries*, p. 84.
10. op. cit., p. 166.
11. See ed. cit., pp. 5, 13, 37, 107, 134 and *passim*.
12. *Letters of James IV*, September 1507, p. 85.
13. Hannay *Archbishops of St Andrews*, vol. 1, p. 226.
14. Epistles 129.4, 121.10. For discussion and further illustration, see H. Hagendahl *Latin Fathers and the Classics* (Göteborg 1958) pp. 276 ff.
15. Epistle 22.29. See Hagendahl, op. cit., pp. 109 ff.
16. Comparetti, op. cit., p. 92. A similar story is told of Hugh of Cluny.
17. So V. Zabughin *Vergilio nel Rinascimento Italiano da Dante a Torquato Tasso*, 2 vols. (Bologna 1921, 1923) vol. 1, p. 4.
18. See Zabughin, op. cit., vol. 1, pp. 109 ff., and H. Baron *The Crisis of the Early Italian Renaissance* (Princeton 1966) pp. 297 ff.
19. M. M. Phillips 'Erasmus and the Classics' in *Erasmus*, ed. T. A. Dorey (1970) p. 5.
20. cf. D. C. Allen *Mysteriously Meant: the Rediscovery of Pagan Symbolism and Allegorical Interpretation in the Renaissance* (Baltimore 1970) p. 155.
21. M. M. Phillips *Erasmus on his Times: a Shortened Version of the Adages* (Cambridge 1967) p. 160.
22. Phillips 'Erasmus and the Classics', p. 4.
23. The syntax of the Cambridge manuscript reads oddly; the Bath and Lambeth manuscripts read 'so of poetis be thair crafty curis' (195), which is perhaps preferable.
24. *Commentum . . . super Sex Libros Eneidos Virgilii*, ed. G. Riedel (Greifswald 1924) p. 1. The notion derives ultimately from Macrobius; see J. R. O'Donnell 'The sources and meaning of Bernard Silvester's commentary on the Aeneid'

Mediaeval Studies 24 (1962) 233–49.
25. *Policratici sive de Nugis Curialium*, ed. C. C. J. Webb, 2 vols. (Oxford 1909) v.22.
26. Allen 'Undermeanings in Ovid's *Metamorphoses*' op. cit., pp. 163–99.
27. cf. 'For vnder a colour a truth maye aryse', Stephen Hawes *Pastime of Pleasure*, ed. W. E. Mead, EETS.OS. 173 (1928) 50 ff.
28. Latin quotations are taken from *Genealogie Deorum Gentilium Libri*, ed. V. Romano. For a translation of the last two books, see C. G. Osgood *Boccaccio on Poetry* (Princeton 1956).
29. The term derives from the romance by Euhemerus (3rd century B.C.).
30. See further J. Seznec *The Survival of the Pagan Gods,* trans. B. F. Sessions New York 1953) pp. 11 ff.
31. I have here corrected Coldwell's reading of the text.
32. cf. Seznec, op. cit., pp. 37 ff. and F. Saxl 'The Revival of Late Antique Astrology' in *A Heritage of Images* (1970) pp. 27–41.
33. I, p. 154.
34. Commentary on *Aeneid* I. 223.
35. The Harvard edition of Servius prefers a slightly different reading, but this is the wording in Ascensius's Servius.
36. See J. W. Jones 'Allegorical interpretation in Servius' *The Classical Journal* 56 (1961) 217–26.
37. The exact date of the composition and first publication of this work is obscure; there are many printed editions, and an early manuscript, dated 1476. For a detailed study, see E. Wolf 'Die allegorische Vergilerklärung des Cristoforo Landino' *Neue Jahrbücher für das Klassische Altertum Geschichte und Deutsche Literatur* 22 (1919) 453–79. See also D. C. Allen, op. cit., pp. 142–54; and Zabughin, op. cit., pp. 194–202.
38. This term is not explained by Coldwell; it seems to render *Ambitio*, or *Cupiditas*.

39. Seznec, op. cit., p. 98.

40. Many instances are to be found in D. C. Allen; see also R. Lebègue 'Christian Interpretations of Pagan Authors' in *French Humanism 1470–1600*, ed. W. L. Gundersheimer (1969) pp. 197–206.

41. Douglas means St Paul, to whom Ascensius compares Virgil in his Preface to the *Aeneid*, and occasionally in his commentary (as in his note on VI.741).

42. Filelfo is referred to in the Preface to the *Aeneid*; and Politian is quoted in the note to *Eclogue* IV.63.

43. cf. H. Hagendahl *Augustine and the Latin Classics* (Göteborg 1967) pp. 437–44.

44. B. M. Arundel Manuscript 82.

45. *Manuale Vergilianum*; see further, P. Renouard *Bibliographie des Impressions et des Oeuvres de Josse Badius Ascensius*, III (Paris 1908) pp. 365–6.

46. Chapter 33. Caxton followed his French source—'ce fut mensonge'. For details of editions, see below, note 63.

47. B. G. Koonce *Chaucer and the Tradition of Fame* (Princeton 1966) p. 121.

48. VI Prol 108–12. It was commonly believed that the Creation took place at the vernal equinox. Ascensius notes on *Georgic* II. 336 that Virgil *consentit ergo cum fide*.

49. *Quaestiones Camaldulenses*, book 3 (Venice 1505) sig. i 4(r).

50. See, for instance, the notes of Servius and Ascensius on *Eclogue* III.60; and Servius on *Georgic* IV. 221. Augustine quotes *Eclogue* III.60 five times in his own writings; see further, Hagendahl *Augustine and the Latin Classics*, pp. 394–5.

51. cf. L. P. Wilkinson *The Georgics of Virgil: a Critical Survey* (Cambridge 1969) p. 285.

52. Comparetti, op. cit., pp. 99–103.

53. See Ascensius's introduction to *Eclogue* IV.

54. For further discussion and bibliography, see R. M. Lumiansky

'Legends of Troy' in *A Manual of the Writings in Middle English 1050–1500*, ed. J. Burke Severs, I (Newhaven, Conn. 1967) pp. 114–18.

55. See M. R. Scherer *The Legends of Troy in Art and Literature* (New York 1963) p. 241.

56. John Young in Leland's *De Rebus Britannicis Collectanea* (1770) vol. IV, p. 295; quoted also in Aikman's translation of Buchanan's *History* (Glasgow 1827–9) vol. II, p. 240.

57. C. Bingham *James V King of Scots* (1971) p. 173.

58. Lumiansky (loc. cit., no. 75) finds the attribution to Barbour unconvincing; see also Bergen *Troy Book*, vol. IV, p. 46.

59. See M. R. James *A Catalogue of the Medieval Manuscripts in the University Library of Aberdeen* (Cambridge 1932) no. 214.

60. *Asloan Manuscript*, vol. I, p. 318.

61. Wyntoun *Original Chronicle*, ed. F. J. Amours, STS (1903–14) vol. II, p. 264.

62. Seznec, op. cit., p. 24.

63. The *Livre des Eneydes* was printed at Lyons by Guillaume le Roy in 1483. Caxton's *Eneydos* was edited by W. T. Culley and F. J. Furnivall, EETS.ES. 57 (1890).

64. L. B. Hall has discussed some of these changes in 'Caxton's "Eneydos" and the redactions of Vergil' *Mediaeval Studies* 22 (1960) 136–47; and 'Chaucer and the Dido and Aeneas story' *Mediaeval Studies* 25 (1963) 148–59.

65. Caxton's *The Recuyell of the Historyes of Troy* was first published *c.* 1474 (ed. H. O. Sommer, 2 vols., 1894). Douglas's use of the plural 'Recolles' (I Prol 206) suggests that he read not the French version or Caxton's first edition but the edition of 1503 by Wynkyn de Worde, whose title begins: 'The recuyles or gaderyng togyder . . .' (Sommer, vol. I, pp. xciv–xcviii).

66. There may be a pun on Caxton (cask + tun). But the image was

favoured by humanists, such as Reuchlin, who remarked 'Wine that is often drawn off the cask loses in splendour. The same applies to translations . . .' (W. Schwarz *Principles and Problems of Biblical Translation* (1955) p. 71).
67. See G. K. Galinsky *Aeneas, Sicily and Rome* (Princeton 1969) pp. 46 ff.
68. ed. N. E. Griffin (Cambridge, Mass. 1936) pp. 217–37.
69. Servius and Ascensius comment on the same question at this point (*Aeneid* 1.242), which was traditionally a focus for such discussion.
70. *Asloan Manuscript*, vol. 1, pp. 185, 310.
71. *Asloan Manuscript*, vol. 1, p. 197; cf. also vol. 1, p. 185.
72. See, for instance, Lydgate's *Complaint of the Black Knight*, 375 and *Temple of Glas*, 58; Gower's *Confessio Amantis*, VIII.2552–3; Hoccleve *Letter of Cupid*, 309–15.
73. See L. B. Hall 'Chaucer and the Dido and Aeneas story'; and E. F. Shannon *Chaucer and the Roman Poets* (Cambridge, Mass. 1929) pp. 196–208.
74. For further discussion of this note, see below, p. 108.
75. In the Prohemium to his Virgil he contrasts Aeneas with Xenophon's Cyrus: Cyrus was a model ruler, Aeneas an example to all mankind, regardless of rank. *Interpretationes in P. Vergilium* (Florence 1487) folio 1 (v); cf. D. C. Allen, op. cit., p. 149.
76. From *De Educatione Liberorum*, trans. A. Cox Brinton, in *Maphaeus Vegius and his Thirteenth Book of the Aeneid* (Stanford 1930) p. 27.
77. Ascensius's phrasing seems here to echo Landino's.
78. *An Apology for Poetry*, ed. G. Shepherd (1965) pp. 100 and 110.
79. See Coldwell, 1, pp. 101–3.
80. 1, pp. 29, 32 and 37. See also B. Dearing 'Gavin Douglas' *Eneados*: a reinterpretation' *PMLA* 67 (1952) 845–62.

81. *Bellenden's Translation of Livy*, ed. W. A. Craigie, 2 vols., STS (1901–3) vol. 1, p. 4.
82. Quoted by Ascensius in his Dedication to Louis of Flanders.
83. cf. E. R. Curtius *European Literature and the Latin Middle Ages*, p. 356 and note.
84. *Saturnalia*, ed. J. Willis (Leipzig 1963) 1.24.8. In v Prol 33–7 Douglas touches on other themes explored by Macrobius—the variety of Virgil's style, and its connection with his *eloquentia* (*Saturnalia*, v. 1.3–7); and his omniscience—*omnium disciplinarum peritus* (*Saturnalia*, 1.16.12).
85. See Comparetti, op. cit., pp. 36–7; Comparetti documents copiously the early admiration for Virgil as a rhetorician (pp. 34–49).
86. *Aeneidos Liber Primus* (Oxford 1971).
87. See Bawcutt 'The source of Gavin Douglas's "Eneados", IV Prol 92–9' *Notes and Queries* (October 1969) 366–7.
88. See J. Sparrow 'Latin Verse of the High Renaissance' in *Italian Renaissance Studies*, ed. E. F. Jacob (1960) pp. 363–5; and H. O. White *Plagiarism and Imitation during the English Renaissance* (Cambridge, Mass. 1935) pp. 19–20.
89. See *Shorter Poems*, p. xxviii.
90. See W. P. Mustard 'Virgil's *Georgics* and the British poets' *American Journal of Philology* 29 (1908) 1–31; and L. P. Wilkinson *The Georgics of Virgil*, p. 288.
91. Wilkinson, op. cit., p. 291.
92. Wilkinson, op. cit., p. 294.

CHAPTER FIVE
The Eneados: '*Text*' *and* '*Sentence*'
1. F. Tupper 'The envy theme in prologues and epilogues' *JEGP* 16 (1917) 551; cf. also E. P. Hammond *English Verse between Chaucer and Surrey* (Durham, N.C. 1927) p. 392. On the eschewal of idleness as a stock theme, see H. S. Bennett

English Books and their Readers, 1475–1552 (Cambridge 1952) p. 61.

2. T. Janson *Latin Prose Prefaces* (Stockholm 1964) p. 52.

3. Hammond *English Verse between Chaucer and Surrey*, p. 90.

4. See *Gilbert of the Haye's Prose Manuscript*, ed. J. H. Stevenson, STS, series 1, nos. 44 and 62 (1901, 1914) 1, p. 2.

5. See Durkan and Ross *Early Scottish Libraries*.

6. Preface to the first edition of the New Testament: trans. by M. Mann Phillips *Erasmus and the Northern Renaissance* (1949) p. 77.

7. See R. R. Bolgar *The Classical Heritage and its Beneficiaries* (Cambridge 1953) Appendix 11: 'Translations of the Greek and Roman Classical Authors before 1600'; also A. Hulubei 'Virgile en France au XVIe Siècle' *Revue du Seizième Siècle* 18 (1931) 1–77.

8. It is mistaken to think that Douglas mentions Saint Gelais in VI Prol 101. (See J. M. Smith *The French Background of Middle Scots Literature*, pp. 106–7.) Here, as at IX Prol 57, Douglas's 'Octauian' refers to the emperor Caesar Octavianus, later known as Augustus. Saint Gelais is not so close a translator as Douglas. A few resemblances of phrasing are pointed out by E. Schmidt *Die Schottische Aeneis-übersetzung von Gavin Douglas* (Leipzig 1910) pp. 105–12.

9. See C. F. Bühler *The Fifteenth Century Book* (Philadelphia 1960) pp. 33 and 117; also note 8, on p. 216 above.

10. For information on these editions, see Mambelli, op. cit., nos. 93, 99, and 106.

11. Aldus here reads *immortalis*; Ascensius's commentary has *si essem iam mortalis ego*.

12. 'Gavin Douglas and the text of Virgil' *Edinburgh Bibliographical Society Transactions*, vol. 4, part 6 (1973) 213–31.

13. On Aldus, see E. Goldsmid *A Bibliographical Sketch of the Aldine Press* (1887).

14. *Bibliographie des Impressions et des Oeuvres de Josse Badius Ascensius*, 3 vols (Paris 1908) vol. 1, p. 29. On Ascensius's popularity, see Renouard, vol. 1, pp. 140 ff. and E. Benoist, *Oeuvres de Virgile: Bucoliques et Georgiques* (Paris 1884) pp. xxv–xxx.

15. For further discussion see T. K. Rabb 'Sebastian Brant and the first illustrated edition of Vergil' *Princeton University Library Chronicle* 21 (1960) 187–99.

16. This was first suggested by A. Schumacher *Des Bischofs Gavin Douglas Übersetzung der Aeneis Vergils* (Strassburg 1910) pp. 88 ff., but not illustrated in any detail until Coldwell's edition.

17. See Coldwell, 1, pp. 59–60; and 'Gavin Douglas and the text of Virgil', loc. cit., pp. 227 ff.

18. *Die Schottische Aeneisübersetzung von Gavin Douglas*, pp. 12–13.

19. *Specimens of Tudor Translations from the Classics* (Heidelberg 1923) p. 3.

20. *The 'Aeneid' of Henry Howard, Earl of Surrey* (Berkeley and Los Angeles 1963) pp. 22 ff.

21. Ridley, op. cit., p. 25.

22. See below, p. 109.

23. For other examples of this practice, see 'Gavin Douglas and the text of Virgil', loc. cit., pp. 230–1.

24. Folio 1 (v). For discussion of the *argumenta*, see O. Ribbeck *Prolegomena ad Vergilium*, vol. IV, p. 369.

25. This theory is mentioned by R. G. Austin in his *Aeneidos Liber Primus*, p. 25.

26. A. Cox Brinton *Maphaeus Vegius and his Thirteenth Book of the Aeneid* (Stanford 1930) pp. 29–30.

27. Folio 288.

28. Dedicatory Epistle to Cardinal Bembo.

29. On Caxton's practice, see N. Blake *Caxton and his World* (1969)

p. 110. Lydgate terms the smaller divisions of his books 'chapitles': *Troy Book*, v.2883, 2933; *Fall of Princes*, VIII. 421.

30. This 'systematic articulation' of long works originated with the Schoolmen; editors applied it to the works of classical authors, and translators seem to have carried it into the vernacular. See A. D. Menut 'Maistre Nicole Oresme: Le Livre de Yconomique d'Aristote' *Transactions of the American Philosophical Society* n.s. 47, part 5 (1957) p. 792.

31. See Bergen, vol. IV, pp. 15, 41 and 54.

32. On this see Amours' Introduction, p. xlviii.

33. So Small, II, p. 318; L. M. Watt *Douglas's Aeneid* (Cambridge 1920) p. 132; Coldwell, I, p. 97.

34. There is another debt to Landino in I.iv.49n.

35. See E. Jacobsen *Translation: a Traditional Craft* (Copenhagen 1958).

36. St Jerome, Epistle to Pammachius, 57.5. In a note to I Prol 395, Coldwell cites Gregory's *non quidem iuxta verbum, sed iuxta sensum*.

37. Hammond *English Verse between Chaucer and Surrey*, p. 393, gives illustrations from Lydgate and Bokenham.

38. The Ruthven Manuscript is particularly bad (cf. Coldwell, I, p. 98). Sometimes its scribe seems to make deliberate changes, as in the amusing substitution of 'britanys' and 'west part' in Douglas's 'The 3ondermast pepill, clepit Bractanys, / Quhilk neir the est part of the warld remanys' (VIII.xii.31–2).

39. *The Works of Virgil*, ed. J. Conington, rev. H. Nettleship (1875–81) note on *Aeneid* XII. 64–6.

40. e.g. *Saturnalia*, I.21.15. Douglas also incorporated etymologies at VI.iv.13–14 and VII.vii.17–18. In the former case he translated a line often regarded as spurious (VI. 242); in the latter he translated an erroneous reading, *aui* instead of *auis* (VII. 412).

41. A. Denieul-Cormier *The Renaissance in France, 1488–1559*, trans. A. and C. Fremantle (1969) p. 239. Nicholas Oresme also employed 'double translation' in his rendering of the medieval Latin versions of Aristotle. See A. D. Menut *Le Livre de Ethiques* (New York 1940) pp. 69 ff.

42. On the practice of Lydgate and other poets, see E. P. Hammond *English Verse between Chaucer and Surrey*, p. 447. For its use elsewhere in Douglas, see I Prol 453.

43. Since Ascensius often includes Servius's notes in his own commentary it is not always possible to say which is Douglas's source.

44. Other possible instances are 'the fury mynd of this theif' (VIII.iv.53) = *furis / furiis* (VIII. 205); or 'all hys armour quhite' (x.ix.80) = *armis / albis* (x.539).

45. 'Gavin Douglas' Eneados: a reinterpretation' *PMLA* 67 (1952) 859.

46. I, p. 37.

47. loc. cit., p. 857.

48. Lewis *English Literature in the Sixteenth Century*, p. 86.

49. J. W. Mackail *The Aeneid* (Oxford 1930) p. 244.

50. Contrast Ascensius, who interprets *gurgite uasto* (VI. 741) as holy water!

51. *Aeneidos Liber Secundus* (Oxford 1964) note to II.804.

CHAPTER SIX
The Eneados: '*Eloquence*'

1. 'The Dedication of the Aeneis' in *The Poems of John Dryden*, ed. J. Kinsley, 4 vols. (Oxford 1958) vol. III, p. 1057.

2. 'On Translating Vergil' *The Listener* (2 August 1951) p. 171.

3. See also I Prol 491–2; IX Prol 72; Directioun, 95–6.

4. Quoted in M. Aston *The Fifteenth Century* (1968) pp. 197–8.

5. cf. J. R. Hale 'Gunpowder and the Renaissance' in *From Renaissance to Counter-Reformation,* ed. C. H. Carter (1964) p. 116.

6. cf. C. S. Lewis *English Literature in the Sixteenth Century,* p. 82.

7. See *O.E.D.,* under ARCTURUS.

8. R. G. Austin *Some English Translations of Virgil* (Liverpool 1956) pp. 15–16.

9. See below, pp. 159–60.

10. Surrey is similarly periphrastic, translating as 'thre forked mace' (11.535). As late as 1579, North speaks of 'the three piked mace, which is the figure of Neptune, called his Trident' (*Plutarch's Lives* (1898) vol. I, p. 37).

11. See Small, vol. I, p. cxlv, or Coldwell *Selections from Gavin Douglas* (Oxford 1964) p. viii.

12. See the illustrative quotations in *O.E.D.* under NUN, *sb.* North speaks similarly of 'a Nun of the temple', ed. cit., vol. I, p. 34.

13. The phrase used on the title-page of the Day-Owen print of Surrey's *Aeneid* IV (1554).

14. *A History of English Prosody* (1906) vol. I, p. 266.

15. cf. *Troilus and Criseyde,* v. 1795–6.

16. There has been little discussion of Douglas's versification. The fullest account is in Coldwell, I, pp. 70–5. Tillyard's criticism in *The English Epic and its Background* (1954) pp. 338–40, is undermined by the poor text from which he quotes. For some of the variations of pronunciation here mentioned, see G. G. Smith's Introduction to *Specimens of Middle Scots* (1902).

17. See also the rhymes in VII.iv. 205–6 and XII.vii.11–12. On the restricted distribution of these shortened forms in Scots poetry, see A. J. Aitken 'Variation and Variety in written Middle Scots' in *Edinburgh Studies in English and Scots,* ed. A. J. Aitken and others (1971) pp. 196–7.

18. cf. 'ma do incres' (1 Prol 73); and

'doyng furth sprowt' (VI.iii.97).

19. In the Cambridge MS *gan* is the most common form, but the Elphinstoun MS often reads *can* instead of *gan*. Since substitution of one form for another would be easy, it is difficult to know which of these auxiliaries Douglas (as opposed to his scribes) preferred.

20. R. Taylor 'Some notes on the use of *Can* and *Couth* as preteritive auxiliaries in Early and Middle Scottish poetry' *Journal of English and Germanic Philology* 16 (1917) p. 583.

21. I, pp. 71–2.

22. See, for example, *Eneados* I.ii.67: 'And schortly, bayth ayr, se and heuyn'. On such deficient lines in Lydgate and other writers, see E. P. Hammond *English Verse between Chaucer and Surrey* (Durham, N. C. 1927) pp. 21 and 83–4.

23. Other errors which suggest indifference to vowel-quantities are the misreading of *cŭra* as *cūra* at III. 476 (see III.vii.9–10); and the confusion of *sălum,* 'high sea', with *sāl,* 'salt' ('salt fame' in I.viii.76, II.iv.16). Douglas also confuses *lābris,* 'cauldrons', with *lăbris,* 'lips', which results in a comic mistranslation at XII.vii.85–7; Venus does not spit in Virgil (*Aeneid* XII.417). But Douglas was sometimes misled by the commentators, as in his translation of *aeripedem* (VI.802) not as 'bronze-footed' but as 'wynd swift' (VI. xiii.100), as if from *āer,* 'air'. Servius too explains it in this way.

24. See D. Attridge *Well-weighed Syllables: Elizabethan Verse in Classical Metres* (Cambridge 1974).

25. For other chapters which open in this way, see II.v; IV.x; IV.xi; v.ii; v.iii; VI.ix; VIII.v; and IX.viii.

26. The briefest example in Chaucer is 'Up roos the sonne, and up roos Emelye' (*Knight's Tale,* 1.2273); but see also *Squire's Tale,* v. 263 ff.; or *Troilus and Criseyde,* v.8 ff. The poet of *Sir Gawain* makes exceptionally skilful use of the device in the open-

ing to books II and IV; a clumsier use occurs in the openings to books III, IV, V, and VI of Hary's *Wallace*. For further discussion, see D. Pearsall *John Lydgate*, pp. 136–7; G. V. Smithers in his edition of *Kyng Alisaunder*, EETS. OS. 227 and 237 (1952 and 1957) vol. II, pp. 35–9; and E. R. Curtius *European Literature and the Latin Middle Ages*, pp. 275–6.

27. I, p. 54.

28. *The Aeneid* (Oxford 1930) pp. 208 and 297.

29. Lydgate seems particularly fond of this comparison; cf. *Troy Book,* I. 1977, where Jason's hair is 'crisped liche gold wyre'. For its use by Scottish poets, see *Kingis Quair,* 4, and *Testament of Cresseid,* 177.

30. This may have been prompted by Virgil's own imagery drawn from the chase (XII.749–57).

31. For comparison of tears to rain, cf. *Prioress's Tale,* VII.674; *Troilus and Criseyde,* IV.873; for 'thik as haill', see *Legend of Good Women,* 655; the comparison to a 'wood leon' occurs in *Knight's Tale,* I, 1656, and *Wife of Bath's* Prologue, III.429 and 794. 'Thick as haill' was a standard image in descriptions of battle.

32. For other uses in the *Eneados,* see XI.xvii.43; XII.x.130; and XIII.v.22.

33. For Chaucer, see also *Knight's Tale,* I.914 and 2878; for Lydgate, see *Troy Book,* IV.579 and 717; see also Hary's *Wallace,* I.107 or II.334.

34. cf. R. Woolf *The English Religious Lyric in the Middle Ages* (Oxford 1968) p. 28.

35. cf. 'the storie telleth us', *Troilus and Criseyde,* V. 1037; *House of Fame,* 406. Virgil himself records a tradition by *fertur* or *ut fama est.*

36. This was a common tag—cf. *Wallace,* II.314; or *Knight's Tale,* I. 1358 and 1895.

37. cf. 'What nedeth wordes mo?', General Prologue, I.849, and *Knight's Tale,* I.1029; 'What wole ye more?', *Legend of Good Women,* 1284; also *House of Fame,* 883.

38. Very common in Chaucer; cf. *Man of Law's Tale,* II.170; *Merchant's Tale,* IV.2132, and *passim.*

39. Similar phrases occur in Hary's *Wallace;* cf. 'quhar thai stud' (VI. 566).

40. E. P. Hammond *English Verse between Chaucer and Surrey,* p. 88.

41. Some of the material in this section first appeared, in a fuller form, in two articles: 'Did Gavin Douglas write *King Hart?*' *Medium Aevum* 28 (1959) 31–47; and 'Gavin Douglas and Chaucer' *Review of English Studies* n.s. 21 (1970) 401–21.

42. cf. 'fere of hym Arcite', *Knight's Tale,* I.1333; or 'Of him Mercurie', Lydgate *Temple of Glas,* 130.

43. *The Dialect of the Southern Counties of Scotland,* Transactions of the Philological Society (1873) p. 47.

44. E. K.'s gloss to 'yblent' in *The Shepheardes Calender,* April, 155.

45. Many other instances can be found in Coldwell's Glossary.

46. In the *Palice of Honour* Douglas uses English words like 'tho' (121) instead of 'than', and English spellings for the rhyme (as at 1295); he uses *bene* as a plural form of 'be' (236, 240 and *passim*); past participles like 'ichangit' (753); and infinitives in –(*e*)*n*, such as 'endyten' (1399) or 'gone' (1297).

47. *Discoveries* in *Works,* ed. C. H. Herford and P. and E. Simpson, vol. VIII (Oxford 1947) p. 618.

48. Translating *dolis* (I.673); cf. 'If Love hath caught hym in his las' *Romaunt of the Rose,* 3533; also *Knight's Tale,* I.1817.

49. The fullest treatment is to be found in Coldwell, I, pp. 69–70.

50. See *Knight's Tale,* I.2605–16; and *Legend of Good Women,* 635–48.

51. See E. Nitchie *Vergil and the English Poets* (New York 1919) p. 84; H. B. Lathrop *Translations from the Classics into English,* p. 100; Tillyard *The English Epic and its Background,* p. 340.

52. For similar passages, see IX.i.

59–64; IX.ix.34 ff.; IX. xii.54 ff. and
XII.vi.35 ff.

53. cf. 'Ane bitand brand, burly and
braid' (*Golagros and Gawane*, 934) or
'The burly blaide, was braid and
burnyst brycht' (*Wallace*, v.960).
For Shakespeare's parody of such
a style, see *Midsummer Night's Dream*,
v.i.145–6.

54. For discussion and illustration
of such phrases, see J. P. Oakden
*Alliterative Poetry in Middle English:
a Survey of the Traditions* (Manchester
1935) pp. 195 ff.; R. A. Waldron
'Oral-formulaic technique and
Middle English alliterative poetry'
Speculum 32 (1957) 792–804; also W.
Scheps 'Middle English poetic
usage and Blind Harry's Wallace'
Chaucer Review 4 (1970) 291–302.

55. Other verbs of this type are
brittyn, 'cut in pieces, kill' (II.x.183;
III.iv.26 and *passim*), and *rasch*,
'dash violently (against)' (x.vi.134).

56. All but one of *D.O.S.T.*'s citations are poetic.

57. *The Buik of the Croniclis of Scotland*,
ed. W. B. Turnbull, Rolls Series, 3
vols (1858) vol. I, p. 140. There is a
good example of this style in vol.
III, p. 177: 'Sair wes the semblie at
the first onset . . . And mony grome
la gruiflingis on the ground.'

58. See also Douglas's rendering of
IV. 135, quoted above on p. 147.

59. So too Douglas echoes but alters
the sound of Virgil's famous VIII.
596 in his 'The hornyt hovyt hors-
[is] with four feyt' (VIII.ix.123); and
see also his rendering of XII. 325–8
in XII.vi.35 ff.

60. See below, p. 182.

61. R. S. R. Fitter *The Pocket Guide
to British Birds* (1952) p. 52.

62. Such as genitives in *-ai* (IX.26),
or *olli* for *illi* (I.254).

63. cf. H. B. Lathrop *Translations from
the Classics into English from Caxton to
Chapman 1477–1620*, University of
Wisconsin Studies 35 (Madison
1933) p. 100; or Wittig *The Scottish
Tradition in Literature*, p. 78.

64. It is no less characteristic of
French; cf. 'ravir et transporter',
'confuz et frustrez', *Flodden Papers*,
pp. 128–9.

65. *Humanism and Poetry in the Early
Tudor Period* (1959) p. 251.

66. 'Gavin Douglas's *Aeneid*' in
The Scots Literary Tradition, 2nd ed.
(1962) p. 69. See also his later 'The
Scots *Aeneid* of Gavin Douglas',
pp. 165–97.

67. G. F. Nott called him 'homely,
diffuse and familiar', *The Works of
Henry Howard and sir Thomas Wyatt*,
vol. I (1815) p. ccviii; Small echoes
this (I, p. cxlv); cf. also H. J. C.
Grierson and J. C. Smith *A Critical
History of English Poetry* (1944) p. 58,
and Coldwell, I, pp. 63–5.

68. It is Douglas, not Virgil, who
uses words like 'geometry' (VI.xv.
10), 'geneology' (VI.xiii.14),
'incestuous' (VI.ix.203), 'inconsumptive' (VII.x.23), 'posterite'
(VI.xiii.5) or 'obumbrate' (VI.ii.
124).

69. See *O.E.D.* under ROVE, *sb.* 2.

70. Translating XII.379; Douglas's
text of Virgil read *quem* not *cum*.

71. Coldwell here reads *Quham*, but
Douglas is translating *postquam*, and
the correct reading is *Quhen*, i.e.
'when'.

72. See also II.vi.10–22 (= II. 304
ff.). This is praised by Mason
*Humanism and Poetry in the Early
Tudor Period*, pp. 251–2, and briefly
discussed in my 'Douglas and
Surrey: translators of Virgil'
Essays and Studies 27 (1974) 65–7.

73. For 'quytterand', see above,
p. 158; for 'grasland', see *D.O.S.T.*
under GRASSIL, *v.* Douglas uses
this verb elsewhere of the harsh,
rasping noise made by teeth (as in
III.x.17; VIII.iv.103) or ships'
ropes (I.ii.60).

CHAPTER SEVEN
The Prologues

1. See W. Geddie *A Bibliography
of Middle Scots Poets*, STS (1912)

pp. 226–7, 229–30; and C. R. Blyth 'Gavin Douglas' Prologues of natural description' *Philological Quarterly* 49 (1970) 164–77.

2. 'The Scottish Chaucerians' in *The Cambridge History of English Literature*, vol. 11, p. 262.

3. I, p. 88.

4. 'The Scottish Chaucerians' in *Chaucer and Chaucerians*, p. 191.

5. See Curtius *European Literature and the Latin Middle Ages*, pp. 128–30. The figure was not confined to poets —it was used by Quintilian (xii Prol 2), and St Jerome (Epistles, 1.2, 14.10).

6. *Boccaccio on Poetry*, trans. C. G. Osgood, p. 13.

7. Paulinus of Nola (x.21); see further, Curtius, op. cit., pp. 235 ff.

8. The phrase was traditional; cf. Boccaccio *Genealogy of the Gods*, xiv. 13: *Virgilium, Latinorum poetarum principem*; so too the title-page of Ascensius's Virgils, and the title-page of many translators, including Douglas.

9. On the symbolic interpretation of Orpheus as a figure of Christ, see Curtius, op. cit., pp. 235 and 244; and P. Dronke 'The return of Eurydice' *Classica et Medievalia* 23 (1962) 206 ff.

10. The passage in the *Troy Book* recalls Chaucer's *Knight's Tale*, 1. 886–7; for other uses, see Boccaccio *Genealogy of the Gods, Prohemium* xii; Bellenden's *Livy* (ed. cit.) p. 5; and Spenser *Faerie Queene*, v.iii.40; vi.ix.1.

11. op. cit., p. 90.

12. cf. the Epilogue to *Troilus and Criseyde*, and Lydgate's leisurely ending to the *Troy Book* (Bergen, vol. iii, pp. 868–79).

13. See *Tristia*, 1.i.1–3; *Epigrams*, 1.iii.70; *Silvae*, iv.iv.1–11. In classical poets the address to one's book usually appears at the beginning of a lyric or collection of lyrics; medieval poets tend to place it at the end of a long work; cf. J. S. P.

Tatlock 'The Epilog of Chaucer's *Troilus' Modern Philology* 18 (1921) 625–30.

14. *Verba translatoris ad librum suum*; Bergen, vol. iii, p. 879.

15. Readiness to submit to correction was a form of the modesty topos, and commonly combined with the envoi, as in the Epilogue to the *Fall of Princes*, or William Neville's 'Go humble style submytte the to correccyon' (Envoi to the *Castle of Pleasure*).

16. Osgood, op. cit., p. 141.

17. cf. also Dunbar's *Remonstrance to the King*, 28–34.

18. This passage directly follows Ovid's description of the deification of Julius Caesar. Maphaeus Vegius imitated Ovid in his own account of Aeneas's apotheosis, at the end of book xiii. It is possible that Douglas realized what Maphaeus had done, and devised his Conclusio in the same spirit.

19. op. cit., p. 307.

20. Coldwell, I, p. 87.

21. *Douglas's Aeneid*, p. 109.

22. I, p. 88.

23. The etymology is not accepted today.

24. See above, p. 76.

25. Coldwell, I, p. 88.

26. With xi Prol 62 ff. cf. ii Timothy 4.7–8; with xi Prol 73 ff. cf. Ephesians, 6.13–17.

27. Coldwell, I, p. 93; C. S. Lewis *English Literature in the Sixteenth Century*, p. 88; K. Wittig *The Scottish Tradition in Literature*, p. 85.

28. A. M. Mackenzie 'The Renaissance Poets' in *Scottish Poetry: a Critical Survey*, ed. J. Kinsley (1955) p. 38.

29. *Douglas's Aeneid*, p. 115.

30. I, p. 93.

31. John Major testifies to the absence of the vine and olive from Scotland in his *History*, 1.3 (pp. 12 and 15).

32. On the classical origins of this, see Curtius, op. cit., pp. 195–202.

The tradition was reinforced by the precepts of medieval rhetoricians, and 'focused for the later Middle Ages' by the *Roman de la Rose* (D. A. Pearsall *The Floure and the Leafe* (1962) p. 50).

33. cf. Chaucer *Parliament of Fowls*, 188–9; *Kingis Quair*, stanza 153; or Skelton *Garland of Laurel*, 656–7. In the *Complaynt of Scotlande* (ed. J. A. H. Murray, p. 37) is described a river 'cleir as berial', in which are 'pretty fische vantounly stertland vitht there rede vermeil fynnis ande there skalis lyik the brycht siluyr'.

34. *Literary Essays*, vol. IV (1893) pp. 271–2.

35. See the catalogues not of flowers but of trees in the *Parliament of Fowls*, 176–82; *Metamorphoses*, X. 90–106; *Thebaid*, VI.98 ff. and *Pharsalia*, III.440 ff. Chaucer's list-making is discussed by C. Muscatine 'The "Canterbury Tales"' in *Chaucer and Chaucerians*, pp. 94–5. On the catalogues in the *Palice of Honour*, see above, p. 66.

36. *The Feeling For Nature in Scottish Poetry*, vol. I (Edinburgh 1887) p. 264.

37. Watt *Douglas's Aeneid*, p. 115.

38. This date may have had a symbolic significance. Two other Scottish poems, the *Quare of Ielusy* (7) and the *Thrissil and the Rois* (189), are dated similarly. The feast of the translation of St Nicholas (9 May) was associated with processions and masquerades at St Andrews and elsewhere. See A. J. Mill *Mediaeval Plays in Scotland* (1927) pp. 18, 246–7, 283–4.

39. cf. *Parliament of Fowls*, 693–5; *Thrissil and the Rois*, 183; and *Palice of Honour*, 2089–90.

40. Chaucer's *Complaint of Mars* was clearly in Douglas's mind when he wrote this Prologue: see 'Gavin Douglas and Chaucer' *Review of English Studies* n.s. 21 (1970) 409–10. For echoes of Henryson and Virgil, see above, pp. 44 and 88–90.

41. A. M. Mackenzie in *Scottish Poetry*, ed. Kinsley, p. 38.

42. Coldwell, I, p. 94; Watt *Douglas's Aeneid*, p. 108; J. Speirs, 'A Survey of Medieval Verse' in *The Age of Chaucer* (Pelican) ed. B. Ford (1954) p. 60.

43. cf. J. Speirs *The Scots Literary Tradition* p. 72: 'It evidently originates in Douglas's own direct experience of the winter in Scotland'. See also F. W. Moorman *The Interpretation of Nature in English Poetry* (1905) p. 150; and W. Craigie *The Northern Element in English Literature* (Toronto 1933) p. 36.

44. Wittig *The Scottish Tradition in Literature*, p. 85.

45. cf. also the opening of the *Floure and the Leafe* (1–3). For discussion of the traditions behind Lydgate's opening, see E. P. Hammond *English Verse between Chaucer and Surrey*, p. 415.

46. See further, 'Gavin Douglas and Chaucer', pp. 407–9.

47. cf. Chaucer *Knight's Tale*, I. 2443, 2469; and *Testament of Cresseid*, 155 ff.

48. cf. the lists of birds in Alain de Lille's *De Planctu Naturae* (P.L. CCX, 431 ff.); Skelton's *Philip Sparrow*, 384 ff; Holland's *Buke of the Howlat*; and the *Complaynt of Scotlande* (ed. cit.) p. 39.

49. R. S. R. Fitter *The Pocket Guide to British Birds*, p. 72.

50. N. E. Enkvist *The Seasons of the Year* (Helsinki 1957) pp. 134–45.

51. Lowell, op. cit., p. 271; also T. F. Henderson *Scottish Vernacular Literature* (1898) p. 201.

52. So Coldwell, I, p. 204.

53. *Genealogy of the Gods*, IX.2; this interpretation was still being expounded in the seventeenth century. See the extract from Henry Reynolds's *Mythomystes* (1633) in *The Literature of Renaissance England*, ed. J. Hollander and F. Kermode (1973) p. 27.

54. Wittig, op. cit., p. 86.

55. *Dafydd ap Gwilym: Fifty Poems* trans. by H. I. Bell and D. Bell (1942) no. 44.
56. Veitch *The Feeling for Nature in Scottish Poetry*, vol. I, p. 274.
57. There is a slight resemblance here to *Aeneid* IV.522–8.
58. See *Epistolae Herberti de Losinga*, ed. R. Anstruther (1846) p. 54; and Comparetti *Vergil in the Middle Ages*, p. 92.
59. cf. IX Prol 38, and see Curtius, op. cit., p. 201.
60. Wittig, op. cit., p. 85.
61. A. M. Mackenzie *An Historical Survey of Scottish Literature to 1714* (1933) p. 102. See also D. Pearsall and E. Salter *Landscapes and Seasons of the Medieval World* (1973) p. 204.

CHAPTER EIGHT
Conclusion
1. The fullest documentation is in W. Geddie *A Bibliography of Middle Scots Poets*, pp. 231–55. This is supplemented by L. M. Watt *Douglas's Aeneid*, pp. 3–24; J. A. W. Bennett 'The early fame of Gavin Douglas's *Eneados*' *Modern Language Notes* 61 (1946) 83–8; and Coldwell, I, pp. 118–27.
2. loc. cit., p. 84. For a description of the early texts, see Coldwell, I, pp. 96–106.
3. *The Bannatyne Miscellany II* (Edinburgh 1836) p. 205.
4. See W. Beattie 'Fragments of the Palyce of Honour' *Edinburgh Bibliographical Society Transactions*, vol. III, part I (1951) 33–46. For fuller discussion of the texts of the *Palice of Honour*, see *Shorter Poems*, pp. xv–xxvii.
5. See above, p. 92.
6. R. H. MacDonald *The Library of William Drummond of Hawthornden* (Edinburgh 1971) nos. 755 and 937.
7. Durkan and Ross *Early Scottish Libraries*, pp. 87–8, 114–15.
8. *De Origine, Moribus et Rebus Gestis Scotorum* (Rome 1578) book IX, p. 396.

9. 'Adhortatioun of all Estatis', prefixed to the 1568 edition of Lindsay's *Warkis* (Hamer, vol. I, p. 404).
10. ed. W. Gregor, STS, series I, no. 3 (1884).
11. cf. *Eneados*, I Prol 4–5.
12. *ed. cit.* p. 63.
13. *The Chronicles of Scotland compiled by Hector Boece*, vol. II, ed. E. C. Batho and H. W. Husbands, STS, series 3, no. 15, p. 422. E. A. Shepperd gives an account of Bellenden's life in this appendix to the edition.
14. The text is from the *Bannatyne Manuscript*, vol. II, pp. 10–11.
15. C. S. Lewis *The Allegory of Love*, p. 292.
16. For parallels in Douglas, see *Palice of Honour*, 1134, 947, and 131.
17. Phrases like 'schouting of the larkis' and 'natures chappell clarkis' (*Cherrie and the Slae*, 101 and 104) recall *Goldin Targe*, 25 and 21; 'ay the eccho repercust' (*Cherrie and the Slae* 89) recalls *Palice of Honour*, 25. Quotations are from *Poems of Alexander Montgomerie: Supplementary Volume*, ed. G. Stevenson, STS, series I, no. 59 (1910).
18. Pierre Ronsard, Preface to *la Franciade* (1587) in B. Weinberg *Critical Prefaces of the French Renaissance* (1950) p. 255; W. Webbe, in G. Gregory Smith *Elizabethan Critical Essays*, vol. I, p. 256.
19. The six extra lines are printed by Coldwell in the textual notes to I Prol 330. For further discussion, see above, p. 84.
20. 'To the gentle and courteous Readers', *The xiii Bookes of Aeneidos* 1584.
21. *The Works of Henry Howard and sir Thomas Wyatt* vol. I (1815) pp. cciii–ccix.
22. *The Aeneid of Henry Howard, Earl of Surrey* (Berkeley 1963) particularly pp. 22 ff.; also 'Surrey's debt to Gawin Douglas' *PMLA* 76 (1961) 25–33. In both these

23. I, p. 119.

24. *Henry Howard, Earl of Surrey: Poems,* ed. E. Jones (Oxford 1964) pp. xi–xx; Surrey-quotations are from this edition. See also my 'Douglas and Surrey: translators of Virgil' *Essays and Studies* 27 (1974) 57 ff.

25. ed. cit., p. 133.

26. *Thomas Sackville: l'Homme et l'Oeuvre* (Geneva 1966) p. 179.

27. Quotations are from *The Mirror for Magistrates,* ed. L. B. Campbell (Cambridge 1938; rept. New York 1960).

28. Sackville is less close both to *Aeneid* 11.624 and Surrey (11.821–2).

29. Several other similarities of phrasing are noted by Bacquet, op. cit., pp. 183 ff.

30. *Eglogs, Epytaphes and Sonettes,* ed. E. Arber (1910) p. 72.

31. See D. Duncan *Thomas Ruddiman* (1965) pp. 48–59, 166–9.

32. He speaks of Avernus's 'fowle blacke swelth in thickned lumpes that lyes' (212). *O.E.D.* records no other user of the word apart from Douglas and Sackville.

33. For fuller details, see textual notes in Coldwell.

34. See *Shorter Poems,* p. xix.

35. 'The Authors farewell to his Booke', prefixed to *The Labyrinth of Mans Life* (1614). William L'Isle praised Douglas's translation, but found the dialect hard—'yet with helpe of the Latine I made shift to vnderstand it' (*A Saxon Treatise concerning the Old and New Testament,* 1623: To the Readers).

36. In a letter to William Dugdale, 3 February 1667/8; quoted by Bennett, loc. cit., p. 86.

37. *The History of English Poetry* (1824) vol. III, p. 119.

38. *The History of Scotish Poetry* (1861) p. 269.

39. 'The Scottish Chaucerians' *Cambridge History of English Literature,* vol. II, p. 261.

40. J. MacQueen 'Some aspects of the early Renaissance in Scotland' *Forum for Modern Language Studies* 3 (1967) 214; cf. also J. Norton-Smith, reviewing *Shorter Poems* in *Medium Aevum* 37 (1968) 356, and M. P. McDiarmid, reviewing the same work in *Scottish Historical Review* 48 (1969) 181.

41. *De Studiis et Literis,* trans. by W. H. Woodward in *Vittorino da Feltre and Other Humanist Educators* (Cambridge 1897) pp. 132–3.

42. Such as I. Robinson in *Chaucer and the English Tradition* (Cambridge 1972) p. 245.

43. *Translations from the Classics into English from Caxton to Chapman 1477–1620,* pp. 11 and 12.

44. cf. 'The Dedication of the Aeneis' in Kinsley *Poems of John Dryden,* vol. III, p. 1051.

45. 'Notes on Elizabethan Classicists' in *Literary Essays of Ezra Pound,* ed. T. S. Eliot (1954) p. 245.

46. *The English Epic and its Background* (1954) p. 340.

47. *Some English Translations of Virgil,* pp. 16–17.

48. *Translations from the Classics into English from Caxton to Chapman,* p. 82.

49. See the preface to his translation of Cicero's *De Officiis*; quoted in Lathrop, op. cit., p. 63.

50. For illustrations from Colville and Phaer, see Lathrop, op. cit., pp. 55 and 110–12. On Marlowe's use of commentaries, see R. Gill 'Marlowe, Lucan and Sulpitius' *Review of English Studies* n.s. 24 (1973) 401–13.

51. cf. J. M. Bottkol 'Dryden's Latin scholarship' *Modern Philology* 40 (1943) 242, 248–9.

Select Bibliography

1. EDITIONS

The Poetical Works of Gavin Douglas, ed. J. Small, 4 vols., Edinburgh 1874.
Virgil's Aeneid Translated into Scottish Verse by Gavin Douglas, ed. D. F. C.
    Coldwell, STS, 1957–64.
Selections from Gavin Douglas, ed. D. F. C. Coldwell, Oxford 1964.
The Shorter Poems of Gavin Douglas, ed. Priscilla Bawcutt, STS, 1967.

2. GENERAL WORKS

Fox, D. 'The Scottish Chaucerians' in *Chaucer and Chaucerians*, ed.
    D. S. Brewer, 1966, pp. 164–200.
Geddie, W. *A Bibliography of Middle Scots Poets*, STS, 1912.
Jacobsen, E. *Translation: a Traditional Craft*, Copenhagen 1958.
Kinsley, J. (ed.) *Scottish Poetry: a Critical Survey*, 1955.
Lathrop, H. B. *Translations from the Classics into English from Caxton to
    Chapman 1477–1620*, University of Wisconsin Studies, no. 35,
    Madison 1933.
Lewis, C. S. *The Allegory of Love*, Oxford 1936.
— *English Literature in the Sixteenth Century*, Oxford 1954.
Smith, Janet M. *The French Background of Middle Scots Literature*,
    Edinburgh 1934.
Wittig, K. *The Scottish Tradition in Literature*, Edinburgh 1958.

3. SPECIAL STUDIES

Bawcutt (formerly Preston), Priscilla. 'Did Gavin Douglas write *King
    Hart*?' *Medium Aevum* 28 (1959) 31–47.
— 'Gavin Douglas and Chaucer' *Review of English Studies* n.s. 21 (1970)
    401–21.
— 'Lexical notes on Gavin Douglas's *Eneados*' *Medium Aevum* 40 (1971)
    48–55.
— 'Gavin Douglas and the text of Virgil' *Edinburgh Bibliographical Society
    Transactions* IV, part 6 (1973) 213–31.
— 'Douglas and Surrey: translators of Virgil' *Essays and Studies* 27
    (1974) 52–67.
Bennett, J. A. W. 'The early fame of Gavin Douglas's *Eneados*' *Modern
    Language Notes* 61 (1946) 83–8.
Blyth, C. R. 'Gavin Douglas's Prologues of natural description'
    Philological Quarterly 49 (1970) 164–77.
Dearing, B. 'Douglas' *Eneados*: a reinterpretation' *PMLA* 67 (1952)
    845–62.
Gordon, C. D. 'Gavin Douglas's Latin vocabulary' *Phoenix* 24 (1970)
    54–73.
Hall, L. B. 'An aspect of the Renaissance in Gavin Douglas's *Eneados*'
    Studies in the Renaissance 7 (1960) 184–92.

Select Bibliography

Käsmann, H. 'Gavin Douglas' *Aeneis*-Übersetzung' in *Festschrift für Walter Hübner*, Berlin 1964, pp. 164-76.
Kinneavy, G. B. 'The poet in the *Palice of Honour*' *Chaucer Review* 3 (1969) 280–303.
Ridley, Florence H. 'Did Gawin Douglas write *King Hart*?' *Speculum* 34 (1959) 402–12.
— 'Surrey's debt to Gawin Douglas' *PMLA* 76 (1961) 25–33.
Speirs, J. 'Gavin Douglas's *Aeneid*' and 'The Scots *Aeneid* of Gavin Douglas', chapters 5 and 15 in *The Scots Literary Tradition*, 2nd edn, 1962.
Watt, L. M. *Douglas's Aeneid*, Cambridge 1920.

Index

Adamson, John, 1, 11
adjectives and epithets
  abstract nouns for substantival,
    120
  alliterative, 152-3, 154, 183
  dyslogistic, 65
  eulogistic, 64
  fixed, 140, 162
  Latinate, 119
  piling-up of, 142
Aeneas, story of, 78-80, 82-5, 87, 146
Aeneid, see Virgil
Ailly, Pierre d', 29
Alain de Lille, 35, 226 n. 48
Alamanni, Luigi, 90
Albany, duke of, 1, 2, 11, 13-15,
  17-22
Alberti, Leon Battista, 75
Aldus Manutius
  editions of Virgil: 1501, 97, 105;
    1505, 96, 105; 1514, 105
allegorical
  interpretations: astrological,
    74-6; Neoplatonist, 75-6; of
    myth, 73-6; systematic, 75, 76
allegory, courtly, 37, 40-2, 49-51,
  196
alliteration
  Douglas's: liking for, 45, 151,
    155, 200; imitation of Virgil's,
    147; response to Virgil's,
    155-8
  in: *Eneados*, 147, 150-8; *Palice of
    Honour*, 151; Prologues, 45,
    151, 154, 173, 183; Prologue
    VIII, 45, 154, 173; verse
    chronicles, 46
  paratactic syntax and, 151-2, 160
alliterative
  collocations, 153-4, 183
  epithets, 152-3, 154, 183
  pairing, 153, 158
  patterning, 151-2
  romances, 151, 155

tradition: influence on *Eneados*,
  150-8; vitality of, in Scotland,
  37, 44-5, 151, 214 n. 81
  verse, 44-5, 135
allusions
  astronomical, 184, 185, 186, 187
  Biblical, 50, 59, 60, 61
  classical, 50, 53-4, 59, 65, 67, 90,
    195
  Douglas's fondness for, 31, 50
  geographical, 108, 111-12
  historical, 46, 50, 108, 112
  in *Eneados*, 108, 111-12
  in *Palice of Honour*, 46, 50, 53-4,
    59, 60, 61, 65, 67, 195
  in Prologues, 184-5, 186, 187
  mythological, 64, 112, 184-5,
    186
allusiveness, Douglas's, 50, 181-2,
  183
anachronisms, 128-9, 130
Anderson, David, 193
Andrelini, Fausto, 26, 33
anglicisms, 144-5
Angus
  fifth earl of, 1, 2, 3, 10, 47
  sixth earl of: Douglas's relations
    with, 1, 3, 10-11, 13, 18;
    marriage to Margaret
    Hepburn, 8, 9; marriage to
    Margaret Tudor, 10-11, 17-18
  see also Douglas family
Aquinas, 29
Arbroath, abbacy of, 11-12
archaisms
  in Douglas, 64, 144-5, 148,
    154-5, 158-9, 199, 200-1
  Virgilian, 159
Aristotle, 26, 28, 33, 70, 111
Arrêts d'Amour, 55
art(s)
  in Scotland, 24, 211 n. 12
  Jerome's dream depicted in, 188
  Troy legend depicted in, 79